SECOND HOMES

Second Homes
European Perspectives and UK Policies

NICK GALLENT
The Bartlett School of Planning, University College London, UK

ALAN MACE
School of Architecture and the Built Environment, University of Westminster, UK

MARK TEWDWR-JONES
The Bartlett School of Planning, University College London, UK

ASHGATE

Published by
Ashgate Publishing Limited
Gower House
Croft Road
Aldershot
Hampshire GU11 3HR
England

Ashgate Publishing Company
Suite 420
101 Cherry Street
Burlington, VT 05401-4405
USA

Ashgate website: http://www.ashgate.com

British Library Cataloguing in Publication Data
Gallent, Nick
    Second homes : European perspectives and UK policies
    1. Second homes - Europe 2. Second homes - Great Britain
    3. Housing, Rural - Europe 4. Housing, Rural - Great Britain
    5. Housing policy - Europe 6. Housing policy - Great Britain
    I. Title II. Mace, Alan III. Tewdwr-Jones, Mark
    363.5'83

Library of Congress Cataloging-in-Publication Data
Gallent, Nick.
    Second homes : European perspectives and UK policies / by Nick Gallent, Alan Mace, and Mark Tewdwr-Jones.
        p. cm.
    Includes bibliographical references and index.
    ISBN 0-7546-4239-9
    1. Second homes--Europe. 2. Second homes--Great Britain. 3. Housing, Rural--Europe. 4. Housing, Rural--Great Britain. 5. Housing policy--Europe. 6. Housing policy--Great Britain. I. Mace, Alan, 1960- II. Tewdwr-Jones, Mark. III. Title

    HD7289.3.E85G35 2004
    333.33'8--dc22

                                                                2004017063

ISBN 0 7546 4239 9

Printed on acid-free paper

Typeset by Tradespools, Frome, Somerset
Printed and bound in Great Britain by Antony Rowe Ltd, Chippenham

Contents

List of Figures

List of Tables

Preface

Rural Second Homes in Europe (Gallent and Tewdwr-Jones, 2000) was largely concerned with reviewing the issues and debates surrounding the growth of second home ownership in Europe during the twentieth century. Some parts of the original book – prepared between 1996 and 2000 – drew on the findings of a project funded by Gwynedd County Council, which focused on the nature and scale of second home concerns across a selection of the more peripheral regions of Europe. However, it was apparent – both to the authors and the reviewers of the original text – that whilst the first book was valuable in setting out the parameters of recent and current concerns, it was not able to take the debate forward through original research findings, that might shed light on the current and future importance of second homes as a component of wider housing pressures and social change in rural areas. This new book – which updates some of the background provided in *Rural Second Homes in Europe* – deals directly with this deficiency.

The findings of three pieces of research completed since 2000 have been incorporated into *Second Homes: European Perspectives and UK Polices*. The first of these was commissioned by the Scottish Executive in 2000 and looked broadly at housing pressures across the European Union. Second homes were not the only concern of this work, though they emerged as an element of housing demand pressure in many countries, and re-affirmed the continuing importance of recreational pressures in many rural areas. This work was published as *Housing in the European Countryside* (Gallent, Shucksmith and Tewdwr-Jones, 2003) and does not form a major input of empirical material into this current text. However, some of the issues raised in the work have been woven into Chapter 5 which presents a country-by-country survey of second home issues in Europe. The second piece of research was commissioned by the National Assembly for Wales (now the Welsh Assembly Government) in 2001 and looked at *Second and Holiday Homes and the Land Use Planning System*. This research, for the devolved Welsh administration, was a response to thirty years of pressure in Wales to finally undertake serious work into the impacts of second homes and how the planning system might be able to vent pressures and lessen the perceived housing access difficulties experienced by 'local' people in those communities where second home pressures concentrate. This work enabled us to update our earlier analyses of how planning policy might respond to any specific problems that second homes create, whilst also looking more closely at the social (and more narrow housing market) impacts of second home demand. Perhaps even more importantly, it also afforded an opportunity to examine broader housing market pressures within rural areas and the importance of second homes next to retirement and general migration, commuting, and planning constraint. The final piece of research incorporated into this book was funded by the Countryside Agency in England in 2002. This work was very similar in scope and purpose to the work for the Welsh Assembly Government: it examined both the impacts of second homes in rural areas, patterns of concentration and how policy might respond to any specific housing, social or economic problems that second homes might introduce to rural communities. This final research project differed in one important respect from the work undertaken in Wales in the previous year. In 1998, Welsh local authorities were given the power to charge second home owners the full rate of Council Tax on their second homes; previously they had been eligible for a fifty per cent discount as they were judged to use fewer local services than permanent residents. However, the view in Wales had been that the discount could be scrapped to reflect the 'costs' associated with having concentrations of second homes in some rural areas. In 2001, the Department for Transport, Local Government and the Regions (DTLR, 2001a) launched a consultation on the same issue in England, with a view to either ending or reducing the discount available on second homes and long term empty properties. Therefore, when the Countryside Agency contracted a team from University College London to examine the second home issue, they were in part motivated by a desire to contribute to the Council Tax consultation and were keen for views on whether an increased levy on second homes could be justified, how much additional revenue this would generate, and how it might be ring-fenced for housing purposes. The result of the consultation is now known: local authorities in England have been handed the discretion to reduce the discount to second home owners to just ten per cent (i.e. they are liable for ninety per cent of the standard charge). This move raises two interesting questions. Firstly, is it now accepted that second homes do indeed have a negative impact on host communities? Council Tax charges connect tax paid to services' used and therefore a reduction in the discount might be viewed as punitive, in that second home owners are being charged not for the services they use but the problems they are seen to introduce. This would appear to represent a fundamental re-think of the rationale behind the Council Tax. Secondly, is government now more determined to monitor second home numbers, and perhaps at some point in the future, take more radical steps to protect sensitive communities? The thinking behind retention of a ten per cent discount (at least in England) is that authorities will be able to monitor second home numbers and be aware of where potentially damaging concentrations exist. This information might, in the years ahead, be used as part of a housing assessment that justified some form of local policy intervention or proof that the pressures and needs of one community were greater than those of another. Government clearly believes that it is important to monitor second home numbers and concentrations in England.

The new discount arrangements came into force on the 1ˢᵗ April 2004 causing a sudden (albeit probably short-lived) interest in the second home question. Media reporting focused not only on the issue of Council Tax but on the wider concerns that accompany second homes in many parts of rural Britain. The familiar questions are being asked once more: are second homes a major cause of housing affordability problems in rural areas? Do they lead to the displacement and replacement of local communities? Do they result in the closure of local services and falling school rolls? Much anecdotal evidence is again being presented to answer these and similar questions. In *Second Homes: European Perspectives and UK Policies*, it is our intention to move beyond anecdote and offer a more comprehensive analysis of the second homes question, drawing on the latest research conducted on this subject in England, Wales and in mainland Europe.

Nick Gallent
Alan Mace
Mark Tewdwr-Jones

London, July 2004

Acknowledgements

The support of a number of colleagues, friends and organizations was acknowledged in the preface to *Rural Second Homes in Europe*. We would like to express again our gratitude to the members of the 1996 EU PACTE Rural Change project team, and especially to Henry Roberts and Iwan Jones (Gwynedd County Council). More recently, Jan Dominguez, Paul Robinson and Henry Small (Welsh Assembly Government) provided guidance for the 2001 Wales study, and Jo Lavis and Paul Behrendt (Countryside Agency) played an equivalent role in the 2002 study of second homes in England. Work for the Scottish Executive was undertaken with Professor Mark Shucksmith (University of Aberdeen). Once again, we are grateful to Ashgate publishers for providing an outlet for our work, but of course any omissions or errors are entirely our responsibility.

Note on Structure

Rural Second Homes in Europe contained ten chapters divided into two broad sections, concentrating on central themes concerning second homes and past policy responses. This current book also has ten chapters, but split into three Parts. The first Part (Chapters 1 to 3) deals with broad debates and is a reworking of the first five chapters of *Rural Second Homes in Europe*. The second Part (Chapters 4 to 6) presents a mix of entirely new and substantially revised material. Chapter 4 uses research in England and Wales to provide an analysis of current trends and emergent issues in the UK; Chapter 5 is a 'survey' of second home issues in a selection of other European countries, and Chapter 6 unpicks the key differences between second home concerns in some parts of mainland Europe and in the United Kingdom. The final Part (Chapters 7 to 10) looks firstly at past policy debates (principally in the UK) before presenting a 'new policy framework' (Chapter 9) for addressing second home concerns; this draws on work undertaken for the Countryside Agency in 2002. The final chapter then draws the discussion to a close by positioning second homes in a wider array of rural housing pressures and social trends.

Chapter 1

Introduction

Locating Second Homes

Second homes are the scourge of the British countryside; they alone are responsible for the rural housing crisis, for the closure of village schools and the collapse of essential services. Second homes are choking the countryside, forcing young local people to move away, and condemning once thriving villages to progressive abandonment. This is the picture that is sometimes presented of the second home problem in rural areas. It is not a picture that would be universally recognised in all parts of Britain, let alone elsewhere in Europe. However, there is a view – sometimes powerfully articulated – that the ownership of second homes is inherently unfair and that it robs many people of their right to a home of their own. The case against second homes is a simple one and boils down to a single question: how can it possibly be fair that hundreds of thousands of people across Europe are – at best – inadequately housed or – at worst – homeless, when literally millions own purely recreational second homes? George Monbiot (1999) sees an immediate link between the purchasing of second homes in England and the displacement of local households within more picturesque villages:

> There is no greater inequality in this country than that some people should have two homes while others have none. There are 166,000 officially homeless households in England. In Britain as a whole, though the figures haven't been fully collated, there are roughly 250,000. There are also 224,000 second homes. The similarity of the numbers is no coincidence. Every time a second home is purchased, another family is shoved out of the housing market.
>
> It is not hard to see how this happens. Rich people from the cities turn up in picturesque villages and buy up the houses at prices which local people couldn't possibly afford. The locals are forced into the towns. As housing in many towns is already desperately over-stretched, the result is that someone gets displaced from the market (Monbiot, 1999).

For many people in the countryside, and for their political representatives, this fast and easy way of explaining away housing shortages has huge appeal. For local politicians, it provides an opportunity to present local problems as being externally driven, caused not by failures in the immediate economy or by misjudged policy interventions, but by the greed and carelessness of outside interests. The logical extension of this argument is that too few housing opportunities cause young people to move away, rather than any lack of diversity in the job market or educational opportunities, or indeed any desire to experience new places. Similarly, house price inflation is associated with second home pressures and not with planning constraints or low levels of house building. This suggests that second homes can be used as scapegoats, as an opportunity to divert attention from the 'local' factors that may erode the vibrancy of rural communities.

In this book, it is not our intention to offer a defence of second homes. Four years of research have demonstrated clearly that high concentrations of such properties in any community are likely to accentuate existing housing, social or economic difficulties. But the same is true of high concentrations of retirement purchasing, commuting pressure or unwarranted planning constraint. Too much of anything is likely to generate pressures that will adversely affect normal community processes; here, it is housing market processes that we are most concerned with, and particularly the link between local wage levels and the ability to compete for new and existing homes. The key difference between second homes and these other pressures lies in their propensity to provoke an emotional response; there may well be other factors affecting the operation of the housing market and limiting the supply of much-needed housing, but surely second homes represent one pressure that any society, which values the principles of fairness and equality, should be able to do away with? At the very least, we should be heavily taxing this particular luxury in a drive to minimise inequality and promote opportunity.

However, there are those who view second homes in a more favourable light and who tend to argue that growth in their numbers (to a level that has not changed a great deal over the last decade) is merely symptomatic of broader social trends (reflecting modern working patterns, preferences in leisure consumption, improvements in personal mobility and higher wages in society alongside regional economic decline in those areas that are a net importer of second homes) and, more recently, the perceived benefits of investing in property rather than in the stock market. Across Europe there are increasing concerns that demographic ageing will create future problems in terms of the costs of social welfare; fewer younger people in twenty years time will make it more difficult to support state pension schemes. People are already becoming worried that state and private pensions will be insufficient to support them in retirement; the stock market has simply not been performing well enough in recent years, and particularly since the 9/11 attacks on the United States. This realisation has fuelled investment in property, with many people believing that future equity release will make up for any shortfall in public or private pensions. Indeed, it is conceivable that pension concerns today will fuel the demand for second homes tomorrow, making them a sensible and logical investment for those who wish to retire at a reasonable age. Therefore, if second homes become a substitute for pension investment, and government is unwilling to raise income tax now to stave off a public pension crisis in the future, then the case against second homes might become increasingly eroded as acceptance of them takes hold.

This is somewhat of an aside, and one which we return to at the end of this book. Returning to the issue of 'locating' second homes within broader housing and social pressures facing the countryside, we have already noted the two opposing views: that second homes are inherently bad and are a root cause of the problems faced by some communities; or that they are merely one feature amongst many within any housing market. In between these views, there is perhaps a more sensible position: that second homes – the product of broader social and economic changes affecting different countries – have contributed in specific ways to the process of rural change, or as Chris Bollom (1978) puts it, they have become a 'complicating' factor and agent of social change in many previously less complicated rural areas:

> It is clearly difficult to isolate second home ownership as a variable because of the other agents of social change which will be operating, but if we accept the view that, rather than being the cause or the symptom, second home ownership is more an added complication of social and economic decline, then it will be an agent of social change (Bollom, 1978, p.121).

It is our intention in this book to locate second homes in their wider context, and to unravel many of the complexities of rural housing pressure in Britain and in the wider European countryside. We attempt to provide a comprehensive account of the second home issue without losing sight of the bigger picture. The more detailed aims of this book are set out briefly below.

Aims of the Book

Parts of this book draw on a study of the second home and rural housing literature undertaken for Gwynedd County Council in 1996. As noted in the Preface, this has now been supplemented with empirical evidence derived from three further studies conducted for the Scottish Executive (Shucksmith *et al*, 2000), the Welsh Assembly Government (Tewdwr-Jones *et al*, 2002) and the Countryside Agency (Gallent *et al*, 2002). The two latter studies provide the basis for Chapters 4 and 9, whilst a small amount of material from the Scottish Executive study has been fed into Chapters 5 and 6. *Second Homes: European Perspectives and UK Policies* draws on a mix of local findings (the Wales study looked at five local market situations and the study of England, a further ten), and new literature reviewed in the last four years. The aim of *Rural Second Homes in Europe* was simply to examine the origins of growth in second home numbers across Europe, to highlight European experiences and finally, to consider the need for future regulation in rather a broad sense.

The addition of new empirical work enables us to be rather more ambitious in our revised aims for *Second Homes: European Perspectives and UK Policies*. This current book still reviews the key areas of concern in relation to second homes (Part 1), but it focuses in much greater detail on local evidence and on what we consider to be the key differences between the 'endemic' second home pressures facing many parts of mainland Europe and the more 'epidemic' concerns in specific parts of Britain (Part 2). But perhaps the most important aim and contribution of this book is to consider in far greater detail (and on the back of a more robust evidence base) exactly what might be done in Britain to address not only second home 'issues' but the wider housing pressures facing rural areas. To this end, Part 3 reviews past suggestions as to how planners and policy makers might respond to these issues before presenting a possible new framework for action (Chapter 9). Again, the more general aim of this book is to locate the second home issue in a broader understanding of housing processes, and to demonstrate the folly of over-selling any one pressure as the key driver of social change in rural areas.

We use the remainder of this chapter to set out the broad historic parameters of the second home debate, and to reflect on some of the definition and data problems that have resulted in a debate often grounded more in conjecture and anecdote, than hard fact.

The Focus of Past Studies

Much of the UK literature specifically dealing with second homes emerged in the 1970s. There was a marked down-turn in academic output devoted to the issue during the early to mid 1980s but then a resurgence of interest in the 1990s which focused mainly on the 'overseas' element of second home ownership (see Buller and Hoggart, 1994a, 1994b and 1995; Barke, 1991). Abroad (particularly in Scandinavia), second home ownership was already being identified as a mature social phenomenon by the mid 1960s with the development of holiday villages to cater for that demand which could not be accommodated in the existing housing stock. In the study of second homes, the point at which the supply of 'surplus housing' (that is, vacant or dilapidated) is exhausted and second home seekers turn their attention to mainstream market housing or create a demand for new purpose-built development, may be viewed as the point of maturity. It is at this point that new demand may cause environmental concerns (because of a need to regulate the siting and standards of new development) or socio-economic concerns as seekers begin to compete directly against sections of the local population for existing housing. In Britain, this point appears to have been reached in the early 1970s (Downing and Dower, 1973, p.159) and explains much of the early concern surrounding second home growth (see local studies by Bielckus *et al*, 1972; Pyne, 1973; Jacobs, 1973; Williams, 1974) and the more academic analyses of this 'emergent problem' at the latter end of the decade (Coppock, 1977; Bollom, 1978; Davies and O'Farrell, 1981). It is perhaps also worth noting that it was not only planning authorities and a handful of academics who became concerned with the apparent maturation of the second home issue in the 1970s; in 1971, the Welsh Language Society published an analysis of the issue that attributed a range of social 'problems' – especially out-migration of younger households – to this switch in second home focus from surplus dwellings to more mainstream market housing (Cymdeithas Yr Iaith Gymraeg, 1971). Later in the same decade, nationalists in Wales began a campaign of direct action against second homes burning more than 170 properties between 1979 and 1990, and attacking English estate agents viewed as responsible for promoting second home migration. Only one arrest was made during this 'terror' campaign, though police have recently re-opened the case in the light of new forensic and DNA evidence. It was reported – in March 2004 – that further arrests are now possible.

Before undertaking a more extensive examination of the literature in the first Part of this book (Chapters 1 to 3), it is perhaps worth setting up some initial signposts to the 'traditional concerns' that have occupied the minds of many of those previously writing on the subject of second homes. In some studies, the entire range is given equal weighting whilst in others, particular issues are emphasised (such as geographical growth patterns, planning policy responses, or the impacts that second homes are thought to bring). In brief, the common issues raised include: the problems of defining 'second homes' either for statutory planning purposes or for accurate assessments of total numbers (most studies consider this issue); difficulties in collating accurate information including the types of data sources that might be used (including national population censuses, local planning studies or local government rating registers); mapping the spatial distribution of second home growth (see for instance, Crouchley, 1976; Davies and O'Farrell, 1981); explaining and modelling spatial distributions of ownership (Crouchley, 1976; Barke and France, 1988; Barke, 1991); the costs and benefits for receiving regions which include negative and positive economic impacts (for instance South West Economic Planning Council, 1975), the environmental losses and gains through the conversion of existing buildings or greenfield development and socio-cultural repercussions which are often considered through the use of attitudinal research (Thompson, 1977; Bollom, 1978). Many of the more general studies end by examining the need for a policy response (either at the local or national level) towards the expansion of second home ownership; these responses often involve the encouragement of growth (to maximise possible benefits), the curbing of growth (to minimise associated costs) or a compromise solution which involves the regulation of supply and demand and the channelling of development. Much of this cited literature is now somewhat dated, though the broad concerns established in the 1970s and 1980s remain the same today: how many second homes are there in country A or region B? What impact do they have and what do they mean for host communities? And should something be done to allay local concerns or respond to real or perceived impacts?

In *Rural Second Homes in Europe*, we noted that '[...] increasingly, it is recognised that growth in the number of second homes is not an isolated phenomenon but connects to various other elements of social change and to the macro-economy'; for this reason, any policy response should be grounded in a full understanding of wider concerns (Gallent and Tewdwr-Jones, 2000a, p. 6). We are perhaps less confident today that this is in fact true than we were five years ago, and many local politicians continue to peddle the myth of second homes as the biggest threat to rural communities (see Chapter 10). During the past few years, fieldwork in many areas apparently affected by second homes has demonstrated a desire amongst authorities to 'get to grips' with the issue by some form of direct action. Often there is a clear division between local authority officers – who are rather more circumspect on the issue of second homes and the wider range of local housing demand and supply pressures – and elected members, who frequently maintain that a ban on second home purchasing is the obvious antidote to local housing troubles. Tunnel vision remains a problem in many areas, with politicians seeking external explanations for local problems, and sometimes not seeing or not wanting to see the connections and complexities behind broader social change and local outcomes. This is an issue that we return to in Chapters 4 and 10.

Definitions and Data Gaps

Understanding what a second home is provides the obvious starting point for investigating their 'meaning' or measuring their effects on housing markets or rural communities. On the more abstract issue of meaning, it is the case that in the study of housing, key concepts include the 'household' (residing within the home), the 'dwelling' (that is, the physical structure), and the 'home' (which is more than merely a physical structure for those who dwell within; Kemeny, 1992). In the study of second homes (a subject straddling the boundaries between housing, planning and leisure), the key concept to understand is the 'second home' itself. In one sense, it is merely a physical structure, but in another, it has meaning for both those who reside within, and for those who might be excluded from the housing market because of its presence in a particular location.

Second homes can come to symbolise the inequities that exist in the housing market, and hence become a focus for concern and negative emotional reaction. In another sense, these same 'homes' may have a positive impact on the lives of their users, allowing them to position themselves within a community or in relation to other second home owners. Salletmaier (1993) has argued that 'recreation spaces' (that is, secondary dwellings) are much more than just physical places and should be seen within the context of place identity (in much the same way as a first home), having a marked influence on the user's 'action potential'. In short, Salletmaier's conception of the second home, is as a space (which is not physically limited in type) for recreation and communication that may be 'vital for the users' personal identities'. Clearly, Salletmaier's definition borrows heavily from the work of Häbermas (1987, 1991) and is more concerned with the sociological justifications for demand than the search for a practical definition. In 2001, the Department of Transport, Local Government and the Regions needed something much more basic as a way to differentiate first from second homes during their Council Tax consultation (see above): hence they arrived at the view that second homes are in fact 'furnished homes that are no-one's main residence'. In order to subtract these from the larger number of furnished but empty properties awaiting sale or awaiting a new tenant it is necessary to add that these are privately owned dwellings mainly used for vacations and, unlike holiday homes or holiday chalets, there are no planning restrictions on their occupancy. This means that second homes are identical to first homes and differentiated only by patterns of occupancy and usage. The path followed in order to arrive at this definition has been long and at times, fairly tortuous, and driven by a desire to monitor numbers, perhaps with a view to regulate these numbers at some point in the future.

In the UK at least, the story really begins in the 1970s when the debate surrounding the definition of 'second homes' (for planning and information collation purposes) was at its most intense. Terry Coppock (1977) argued that an element of stereotyping and misconception has tended to confuse the definitional issue; for planning purposes, some local authorities have historically considered static caravans as potential second homes whilst others have not. Similarly, ownership (that is, freehold tenure) has often been implied as a criterion for definition but it may also be argued that a second home, like a main residence, can be rented or leased. On top of this, second homes may be used by more than one family but at what point should these dwellings be viewed as 'rented holiday accommodation'? The issue of definition has certainly been no easier to resolve elsewhere in Europe. In Spain, for example, many owners of flats which are rented out claim that these are second homes in order to avoid tax on rental income; it is a lack of statutory guidelines which has permitted this situation to evolve (Barke & France, 1988, p.144). The first real attempts to confront the definitional problem occurred in the early 1970s and were often grounded in local experience and circumstances. Pyne (1973) arrived at a three-tier definition for vacation accommodation which might or might not be a second home:

1 *Second home*: a dwelling used by its owner and possibly other visitors for leisure or holiday purposes and which is not the usual or permanent place of residence for the owner;
2 *Holiday investment property*: a dwelling owned either locally or outside the county and not permanently occupied but let to holiday makers solely on a commercial basis;
3 *Club/institute/company holiday property*: similar to above but used only by club members or company employees and clients (Pyne, 1973, p.3).

Clearly, the principal criteria for defining a second home as such were *type* and *frequency* of use (that is, recreational and seasonal). In the following year, Pardoe narrowed the definition further, stating that a second home was:

[...] a static property which is the alternative residence of a household, the principal domicile of which is situated elsewhere and which is used primarily by members of that household for their recreation and leisure (Pardoe, 1974).

Pardoe's definition allowed the inclusion of static caravans but excluded touring caravans. Furthermore, the definition was more restrictive in terms of *who* may primarily use the dwelling for their recreation and *where* they have their first home. Second home owners were viewed as usually absent owners who resided some distance from the 'receiving' area. The notion that such owners tended to be non-local and liable to import non-local ideas and values was just one of the stereotypes pointed out by Coppock. Elsewhere in Europe, there is no necessary presumption that owners are *distant* outsiders; in the

Spanish Census of 1981 for example, a 'secondary residence' was simply a dwelling not used as the 'normal residence' but instead, used seasonally or at specific times (Instituto Nacional de Estadistica, 1983, p.9). In Sweden, a large proportion of people who own second homes tend to have properties within a reasonable distance of where they work; for instance, there is a tendency for those working in Stockholm to have second homes just beyond the urban periphery which they visit each weekend. The division between mainland European second homes (close to first homes and used regularly) and British second homes (further from first homes and used less regularly) is discussed at greater length in Chapter 6.

More recent studies of second homes in Britain – including the Survey of English Housing, undertaken periodically for the Office of National Statistics – tend to follow (and often modify) the definition employed by Bielckus, *et al* (1972):

> [...] a property which is the occasional residence of a household that usually lives elsewhere and which is primarily used for recreation purposes (p.9).

The Bielckus definition incorporates the concepts of distance (from first to second home), use type (recreational) and use frequency (occasional). In research for the Countryside Commission published in 1973, Downing and Dower followed the same definition (accepting the main criteria) but specifically excluded touring caravans, boats, whether houseboats or cruisers, properties on short tenancies and properties in major cities and industrial towns (Downing and Dower, 1973, p.1). In the same year Tuck added that the second home would be different from the normal domicile from which members of the household 'travel to work or school'. Some years later, Shucksmith (1983) chose to use the same definition but insisted that the 'occasional residence' should consist of a 'permanent building' and thereby exclude static caravans (Shucksmith, 1983, p.174). This distinction between built second homes and static caravans is now clearly defined in much of the literature and in the Survey of English Housing (DTLR, 2001b).

In defining second homes, many studies have also focused on the issue of tenure. The Dartington Amenity Research Trust's [Dart] study for the Countryside Commission for Scotland (1977) included a range of tenure types:

> [...] a property owned, long-leased or rented on a yearly or longer basis as the occasional residence of a household that usually lives elsewhere (Dart, 1977, p.12).

The Dart team (including Downing and Dower) had first raised the question of tenure in 1973 in their report to the Countryside Commission south of the border, but had failed to fully resolve the issue. In Scotland, it was decided that for statutory purposes, any workable definition would need to recognise that second homes could be occupied on the same tenure basis as main residences and that definition was fundamentally in the hands of the 'user'. They argued that irrespective of location, use type, frequency or tenure, a second home was 'a dwelling which is occupied by a household that also occupies another dwelling elsewhere, that other dwelling being regarded by the household as the primary dwelling' (Dart, 1977, p.78). The team pointed out that with such a definition, 'a head of household would be required to declare whether a dwelling was his first or second home on any occasion where the distinction mattered for statutory purposes' (Dart, 1977, p.5). This approach was also employed by Jacobs (1972) in his study of the growth of second homes in Denbighshire, Wales. Jacobs argued that the 'hidden character' of the phenomenon made it difficult and perhaps unrealistic to employ rigid definitions (Jacobs, 1972, p.4). Second homes, their type and distribution, are essentially a function of local circumstances and Jacobs argued that 'because the pattern of use might vary widely it was unwise to delineate a second home too narrowly [instead] it was left to the owner to decide whether the use of his property in Denbighshire fitted within these very broad guidelines [that is, a dwelling which was not the normal residence and was primarily used as a recreation space]'. Clearly, this type of sweeping definition allows for a broad interpretation of what constitutes a second home. However, the lack of a more robust definitional framework has caused difficulties both in Britain and elsewhere in Europe with the collation of data which is difficult to interpret and the problem of false registration.

Using the broadest definition (from Bielckus, *et al*, 1972) and a base-line figure established by Barr (1967), it was generally agreed that there were between 160,000 and 200,000 built second homes in England and Wales in 1978 alongside some 150,000 static caravans (Bollom, 1978, p.1; Bielckus, *et al*, 1972, p.39). Bielckus argued that the figure for built second homes could rise to 750,000 by 1985 (this prediction spanned 13 years of change and expected growth). However, growth was transformed into market stagnation in the mid 1970s mainly because of economic recession and the impact of the Housing Act 1974 on the eligibility of second home owners for improvement grants (see Gallent, 1997a). In fact, by 1985, it was noted in Hansard, that there were 221,000 built second homes in England and Wales (Hansard, 1985). The point to be emphasised here is that the definitional problems were far from being resolved by the time of the 1991 Census. In 1991, the total number of 'second residences' in England and Wales was calculated to be just 92,550 dwellings (OPCS, 1993, p.50). The definition employed on Census night ran as follows:

> *Second residences* were defined as company flats, holiday houses, weekend cottages, and so on, in permanent buildings which were *known* to be the second residences of people who had a more permanent address elsewhere and which were unoccupied on Census night. This classification was applied even if the premises were occasionally let to others (OPCS, 1992, p.25).

The definition used in 1991 excluded empty dwellings not *known* to be second residences and potential second homes enumerated as *occupied accommodation* on Census night. These same problems are likely to have affected second home figures derived from the 2001 Census, which suggest a total of 15,159 second homes in Wales and 135,202 in England; a fall of 19 per cent against the 1991 figure in the case of Wales, and an increase of 8 per cent in the case of

England.[1] The Survey of English Housing (DTLR, 2001b) based on a sample of 20,000 English households, suggests that of the 230,000 second homes currently owned in England, 36 percent of these are weekend cottages. Estimates made on the back of these data together with a survey of local authorities for the Countryside Agency (Gallent *et al*, 2002, p.18) showed that there are roughly 100,000 second homes in rural areas of England. This suggests that Census data does indeed present a slight underestimate in numbers. A more comprehensive analysis of second home numbers and distributions in England and Wales is presented in Chapters 2 and 4.

The scope for underestimating the total number of second homes is certainly significant and patterns of incorrect enumeration may be further confused by instances of false registration; this was found to be the case in Spain (Barke and France, 1988; Barke, 1991). The most highly publicised case of false registration occurred in Austria in 1981 (Bennett, 1985). The Austrian Census is used as a benchmark for the allocation of funds to local government (Bennett, 1985, p.298) and those local authorities with relatively large numbers of second homes receive extra sums of money whilst authorities with large numbers of second home *owners* lose money. The underlying economic logic is that second homes are seen as a consumption good and an additional household amenity in the exporting region; in the importing region, on the other hand, they are seen as being indicative of economic decline and viewed as a deprivation indicator. The state supports importing regions at the expense of exporting regions. In 1981, many of those authorities with high numbers of owners encouraged these owners to register *in* their second homes on Census night (by offering incentives such as housing grants and loans), reducing the number of owners in the first home (exporting) areas and increasing their local government allocations whilst decreasing the allocations of the importing regions. The effects on local government were dramatic and the results of the 1981 Census, not surprisingly, proved highly controversial. Bennett notes that 'false registration of people in second homes in the 1981 Austrian Census produced considerable losses of population from most of the main cities, especially Vienna' (Bennett, 1985, p.309). The gain in revenue to Vienna alone was in the region of US $2 million (1981 prices) with significant sums of money going to other large cities. The net effect on the enumeration of second homes (and their observed distribution) is not noted by Bennett, who is primarily concerned with the macro-economic effect of false registration. However, it is clear that a lack of clear statutory guidance on what constitutes a second home leaves the system open to inaccuracy either because of abuse or honest misinterpretation. Common to many national censuses is the problem of grouping together all occupied dwellings, even if they are not used as the main residence.

This experience in Austria more than twenty years ago has its parallels in Britain today. We noted in the preface that Council Tax discounts on second homes in Wales were scrapped in 1998 (though authorities retain the discretion to grant a 50 per cent discount); the discount on second homes in England was reduced to 10 per cent in April 2004 though authorities may still charge just 50 of the full levy if they so wish. It is unlikely that false registration of homes will be a problem as the motivations which led to authorities 'cooking the books' in Austria do not exist in the UK. However, it is interesting to note that whilst a decision was made in Wales to end the discount completely, in England, a nominal reduction of 10 per cent is being retained. The reason for this is a simple one: by giving owners some incentive to register their properties as second homes, it is possible to keep track of second home numbers and their distribution. Therefore, if house prices were to rise in a particular area, the local authority might be better placed to link such rises to a concentration of second homes. It could also mean that additional revenue derived from all second homes in an area could be re-invested in affordable housing programmes in those areas most affected by this type of property purchasing. Arguably, Council Tax registrations offer the most effective means of monitoring second home numbers and changing distributions by area, though this is no longer possible in Wales.

Indeed, the situation in terms of data on second homes in England seems to have improved over the last ten years (from 2000). Figures have been available from the Survey of English Housing since 1993; these suggest a fall from 230,000 second homes in England in 1993, to 185,000 in 1995/96 and a subsequent climb back to 229,000 by 1999/2000 (DTLR, 2001b, p.19). This trend follows the recent pattern of peaks and troughs in England's wider housing market. These data can be compared to Census figures and to local survey data; again the most recent attempt to generate a national picture from local sources was made by the Countryside Agency (Gallent *et al*, 2002) based on its listings of rural authorities in England: this put the total number of rural second homes in England at 100,000 units. Comparable work in Wales suggests a further 16,000 spread across all twenty-two Welsh unitary authorities We believe that these studies have provided an evidence base on which to develop a much clearer understanding of second homes in Britain; previously, a lack of comprehensive or reliable data frequently resulted in a 'plethora of ill-founded opinion and conjecture' (Rogers, 1977, p.85). There are a variety of reasons why data on second homes has been historically sparse including:

- An unwillingness amongst second home owners to be interviewed by those trying to profile the issue because of perceived local hostility, especially in the 1970s (Downing and Dower, 1973, p.1);
- The 1971 Census recorded instances of vacancy but did not specifically look for second homes;
- Rating registers in the 1970s offered one source of information on second home, but some owners tried to make their second homes look empty to avoid rate levies; this is not a problem today as second homes and long term empty properties are subject to the same Council Tax rules (DTLR, 2001a);
- Many surveys (pre-dating the Survey of English Housing) in the 1970s and 1980s were irregular and patchy, including the British Home Tourism Survey (BHTS) and the British National Travel Survey (BNTS);
- Issues of definition have also plagued past data collection exercises: for example the Office for Official Publications of the European Commu-

nities classifies non-hotel, hostel, guest-house, camp-site, and so on. accommodation as 'private tourist accommodation' sub-divided into 'rented rooms in houses', 'homes rented from private individuals', 'accommodation provided without charge by friends or relatives', 'own dwellings which comprise visitors' second homes' and 'other' (including tents on unofficial camp-sites or boats at unofficial moorings). Normally, only 'own dwellings' are treated as second homes but this label could perhaps apply equally to the middle three categories. In 1993, eight of the twelve member states failed to provide accommodation data which fit into these categories and the data which were provided appeared to underestimate the phenomenon; for instance, there appeared to be just 1,691 'second homes' in the whole of the Republic of Ireland (European Union, 1993, p.33). This problem with tourist information regarding second or 'holiday' homes is recognised in Europe. In 1995, the Official Journal of the European Communities carried an article admitting that the problem of classifying different types of holiday accommodation was preventing accurate and up-to-date data collection (Official Journal, 1995, c236, p.20).

• Also, throughout the 1970s, many local studies were used to present what was viewed by many as a national picture of the second homes issue. Perhaps the most cited studies were undertaken by Tuck (1973) in Merionethshire, Pyne (1972) in Caernarvonshire and Jacobs (1972) in Denbighshire as well as other English-focused studies in the Lake District and Norfolk. These studies were usually sponsored, if not fully implemented, by the local planning departments and illustrated a growing concern for second homes as a complicating factor in local planning and housing issues. In Scotland, a number of local and regional studies were undertaken by the Highlands and Islands Development Board, the Crofters Commission and the Forestry Commission (Dart, 1977, p.18).

The key problem in the 1970s and into the 1980s was that local anecdote was often presented as hard fact, galvanising opinion against second homes in many rural areas. It is only very recently that data on second homes, at least in the UK, has improved. The Survey of English Housing now gives much more comprehensive treatment to the issue, and for the first time in thirty years, national studies have been undertaken in England and Wales, and for the whole of Europe as part of a wider analysis of the housing marker (Gilbert, 2001). This makes it far easier to 'locate' the second homes issue within a broader picture of changes in rural housing markets, especially as data on commuting within Travel to Work Areas is available from the Office for National Statistics and on retirement to more rural regions from the government's population and household projections. A widening of data sources and a number of very robust analyses of rural housing concerns (including work by Bevan *et al* in 2001) has created an opportunity to understand second home pressures within the broader context of housing supply and demand pressures, shifts in rural economies, and within the context of a changing planning framework.

Conclusions

In this chapter, we have set out the parameters of the second home debate, firstly by offering a general statement of the second home issue in Britain, and secondly by reflecting on the major concerns that found their way into the more academic literature on the subject during the 1970s. We have noted also that until very recently, gaps in available data and a lack of agreement over the definition of a 'second home' – two very closely related issues – perhaps acted as a barrier to serious analysis. Given that these gaps are now being filled and that some consensus has been reached over the broad definition of a second home, there is now greater scope for a more constructive debate on the impact of second homes within rural areas and on what action might be taken to restore the social balance that has been lost in some rural communities as a result of a combination of different migration pressures, economic failure, and, perhaps, planning constraint. It is certainly too early to enter into a wider discussion of these issues, but in the remainder of this book, we extend the analysis sketched out in this introduction, looking more closely at:

1   The impacts of second homes in Britain and in mainland Europe, first in very general terms (Part 1), and then using more specific case studies and closer analysis (Part 2);
2   What might be done to deal with market pressures (Part 3), bearing in mind that second homes need to be located in a broader suite of rural pressures and processes.

Note

1   The 1991 figures were 125,587 (England) and 18,714 (Wales); these are 'second residences' plus 'holiday accommodation' and are taken from Table LBS 61. The 2001 figures are taken from Table KS016 in which data on second residences and holiday accommodation is aggregated.

PART 1
THE SECOND HOME DEBATE

Chapter 2

Second Home Ownership and Demand

Introduction

The purpose of this chapter is to provide a broader historical context for the various issues examined in later parts of this book: our focus here is on changing patterns of second home ownership – that is, the profile and motivations of second home purchasers – and on the nature of demand (the types of properties that are sought and in which types of locations). In order to provide a broad base for later analysis, we briefly examine:

- The early origins of second home ownership and use;
- The factors and reasons behind second home ownership;
- The types of property that are frequently used as second homes in rural areas;
- The distribution of ownership and demand, illustrated using an overview of the current market in England; and finally
- The factors which shape demand distribution, and that might be used to predict the future geographical spread of this market.

During the twentieth century, second home ownership spread from the upper classes to be embraced by a much wider cross section of society. Differences in the economic performance of regions, combined with mass car ownership and improved road systems have helped make owning a second home in the country an option for an increasingly broad spectrum of people, and especially those with stored equity in urban property. However, the ability to afford a second home need not be translated into ownership. One key argument posited in this chapter is that the decision to purchase what is essentially a luxury-leisure good is based on a combination of cultural factors – including an idealised view of the countryside as a place of tradition and retreat – and on more utilitarian considerations such as the investment potential of owning a home in the country. These idealised and utilitarian drivers combine to influence both the locations and the types of properties favoured by potential second home buyers. They result in a specific geography of demand and ownership, and lead to concentrated impacts of the type discussed in Chapter 3.

The Origins and Spread of Second Home Ownership

Briefly setting aside the more functional and modern definition of second homes arrived at in the first chapter allows us to take a wider historical view.

This exercise serves not just to add some background, but also sets the scene for issues that run through much of the book, including the issue of class (and conflict) that underlies the more obvious urban – rural divide. The basic desire to seek retreat from 'urban living' has deep roots: in pre-conquest Mexico, for example, Cuernavaca served as a retreat for the Aztec nobility from what is now Mexico City. Cortez later established his own personal residence in Cuernavaca and to this day the town serves as a weekend retreat for the wealthier members of Mexican society seeking respite from the modern day capital. Worldwide, numerous other historic examples could be cited. In Europe, the use of second residences has a similarly long history, which Coppock (1977) traces from the multiple villas owned by wealthy Romans through to the shooting box, or lodge, of Victorian Britain. Clearly, these examples relate to the activities of a very privileged stratum of society: the cultural and social impact of these periodic movements on local society would have been limited by extreme differences in power and wealth that would have served to physically separate the two groups. Further, as these incomers were representatives of the ruling class neither the values they imported, nor the legitimacy of their part-time residency, was likely to be challenged.

The growth of the 'modern' second home is a twentieth century phenomenon. In Scandinavia and North America, the 'tradition' of owning a second home goes back to the 1930s. Britain was slower than its European neighbours to develop a second home market in the twentieth century because of early urbanisation and the loss through decay of much rural stock; economic depression also suppressed demand until more recently (Downing and Dower 1973). In England and Wales the significant increases in second home ownership came after the mid 1950s, growing from an approximate base of 40,000 units (Coppock, 1977). Across society as a whole, in economically developed nations, increases in personal mobility (through higher rates of private car ownership and the increased accessibility of many rural backwaters; Rogers, 1977, p.99), more disposable income and reductions in working hours (giving more leisure time) have produced the conditions for increases in second home ownership, particularly in the post-war period.

These economic and social trends that facilitate second home ownership have been most apparent in the more affluent regions with economies increasingly based around new industries and financial services. They have been of lesser importance in those regions dependent on a traditional and declining economic base such as agriculture or extractive industry. Socio-economic change, therefore, has been expressed in the form of improving standards of living and population growth in the *exporting* regions and economic decline and depopulation in the *importing* regions. Variations in regional economic vitality obviously has an impact on house prices; in general terms, the affluent regions experience house price rises (which remain affordable) whilst the relatively poor regions experience falling house prices but with locals still spending a far greater proportion of their disposable incomes on housing costs than their regional neighbours. Economic decline also brings diminishing employment opportunities and therefore generates pressure for depopulation. In Britain and elsewhere in Europe, this pattern of regional advantage and disadvantage often follows rural and urban cleavages (although not exclusively). Urban economic advantage makes second homes attainable whilst rural disadvantage (manifest in falling house prices, depopulation and a growing number of vacant or empty dwellings) provides an ideal focus for demand.[1] But what factors have resulted in 'attainability' being translated into a real desire to own second homes?

Reasons for Ownership

While socio-economic processes make growth in second home ownership possible they do not necessarily explain why growth has become a reality. The potential British demand for second homes in rural France in the late 1980s was outwardly the result of house price differentials, widened by the property boom (Hoggart and Buller, 1995). But this factor does not explain why *potential* demand was transformed into *effective* demand. Low rural house prices, rises in urban income and mobility have combined with a growing cult of nostalgia for the countryside (Newby, 1980b) and the desire to escape the pressures of city life (Coppock, 1977, p.9). This tendency is, arguably, linked to one of the fundamental tensions of modernity; individuals are increasingly 'free' to construct their own self identity, unconstrained by convention, yet must inevitably be exposed to the insecurities that flow from this separation with tradition (Savage *et al*, 2003). This tension finds a crude metaphor in the supposed contrast between the urban and the rural, where the (pathological) urban represents change, instability and shifting values as against the (ordered) rural which represents tradition and security. This idealisation of rural life and the associated simplicity represented by the peasant cottage is traced both by Williams (1973) and Gilliatt (1973) through reference to the literature of – among others – Jane Austen. Here the rural cottage is no longer simply the hovel where a rural worker's family finds basic shelter and amenities. In the novel *Persuasion*, following Charles Musgrove's marriage, Uppercross Cottage is to be '[...] elevated into a cottage for his residence making it more eye catching than the great house up the road' (cited in Gilliatt, 1973).

Arguably then, the growth in the rural second home market in Britain is predicated on a romanticised view of the rural as being a place of tradition and stability, a place that is other to the chaotic urban. As Doreen Massey (1993) observes, in an increasingly frenetic modern world, '[...] one desperately needs a bit of peace and quiet; and "place" is posed as a source of stability and an unproblematic identity' (Massey, 1993, p.63). For Crouch (1999) the idealised rural leisure space is enhanced by a sense of knowing familiarity; or in modern parlance, by becoming a stakeholder, '[...] abstract notions and senses of sites being – corners, enclosures, "home" – may be inflected by an actual knowing of spaces in material, everyday encounter. This space is important in metaphorically "shaping" the enjoyment of leisure' (Crouch, 1999, p.2). The second home owner is literally buying in to the rural experience. A more empirical approach leads Coppock (1977) to argue that personal motivations might include a desire to participate in some activity which requires access to rural resources, a wish to maintain links with a rural area where the owner or relatives originated, providing a place for holidays, securing an investment, conferring status or providing a place for retirement (Coppock, 1977, p.10); these 'practical' reasons are evidenced in the research findings that are reported in Chapter 4 (case studies examining local experiences in England and Wales). Finally, in considering why the second market has developed, it is important to note that, unlike other recreational consumption goods, second homes may serve both short-term and long-term objectives; in the short-term, they provide an occasional recreational space and in the long-term, they may be transformed into a first home or a place to retire (Clout, 1977, p.57). This gives them greater potential utility value and so will certainly influence the decision to purchase a second home.

However, once the opportunity to own a second home has been taken, it does not follow that it will necessarily live up to expectations. Robertson (1977) argues that purchase decisions are based primarily around 'anticipated utility' (relating to the functional value of the acquisition as a recreational space or an investment). Once acquisition occurs, Robertson argues that further decisions centre around 'actual utility' (the realisation or non-realisation of expectations) and may involve the disposal of a dwelling which does not produce the expected gains (consequently, the tide of second home growth may expand further, stabilise or retreat). The third segment of 'utility evaluation' according to Robertson is 'projected utility' (Robertson, 1977, p.135). Following on from initial acquisition and the experience of ownership, the owner's knowledge is more complete and if the projected utility value of the second home is held to be high enough, some owners may anticipate retiring to their second home in future years (Robertson, 1977, p.136).

This 'utility evaluation' model for explaining the motivating factors influencing changing patterns of ownership seemed to have some clear plausibility in Hoggart and Buller's study of British property owners in rural France. In that particular study, the authors noted that potential demand was generated by widening house price differential (between southern England and certain parts of rural France) in the late 1980s and that the motivation (or the 'anticipated utility') for acquiring French property was the perceived status attached to rural living and the 'rural dream' (Hoggart and Buller, 1995, p.180). However, on arrival in France, some owners found that the 'actual utility' of ownership was diminished by language barriers and a failure to integrate in rural communities despite the friendliness of the local population (Buller and Hoggart, 1994b, p. 208). Some of these owners subsequently decided to sell their French second home. This transition from anticipated to actual utility has been marked by a marginal decline in the number of British second home owners in France since 1991. Nevertheless, other owners with perhaps greater tenacity have managed to overcome linguistic and administrative barriers (these are the 'most fluent and established francophiles') and with greater 'projected utility', some expect to, or already have, made France their first home.

Owners may find their ability to fit in constrained by resistance from the existing local population. Where controversy is apparent it is often expressed in terms of class/culture differences between incomers and this is fuelled by modern day differentials between the average income of second home owners and the general population. Structural economic differences between the importing and exporting regions can further lead to resentment and feelings of domination and submission (notably in Wales where it linked to invasion and oppression). However, any differences of culture or class would be minimal in the absence of obvious competing interests (as in the earlier times of the hunting lodge). The increase in second home ownership has led to direct competition as the market has reached maturity and the stock of available underused housing has been exhausted, leading to direct competition – and accompanying tensions – in some housing local markets. Therefore, we now look at the type of properties and the locations that are the focus of interest for second homes owners.

Property Types

The first part of this discussion focuses attention on the types of dwellings used to accommodate second home demand. It has already been argued that shifting emphasis from surplus rural stock to existing mainstream housing and purpose-built second homes is indicative of a 'maturing' of the second home phenomenon and has been characterised by increasing concern over the impact of second homes. These particular concerns are examined in later chapters.

One of the underlying causes of second home growth in importing regions is economic decline. With this decline, some dwellings cease being first homes and fall empty (Bollom, 1978, p.2); in the early 1970s, the Ministry of Agriculture estimated that the number of farm-holdings in England and Wales had been declining at a rate of 10,000 units annually (Downing and Dower, 1973, p.23). These 'surplus' rural dwellings are the *initial* supply source for second home seekers, a phenomenon reported by Hoggart and Buller in rural France (Hoggart and Buller, 1994a, 1995) and by the Dart team in Scotland (Dart, 1977, p.61). Pyne (1973) notes that the early development of chalets was brought under control by the Town and Country Planning Act 1947 and the consequent demand for static caravans was curbed by the Caravan Sites and Control of Development Act. At this point, demand was transferred to inexpensive, empty and often derelict cottages (Pyne, 1973, p.1) left in the wake of rural depopulation. This demand was given added impetus by greater economic prosperity in exporting regions in the 1960s. In Wales, *vacant* farmhouses in agricultural areas, and dilapidated terraced quarrier's cottages in slate-quarrying areas were the first types of dwellings to accommodate the demand for second homes at a time when the growth in ownership was seen as being purely symptomatic of social decline in the importing region. Coppock (1977) argued that second homes are normally of two types, either adaptations of pre-existing structures (that is, conversions) or new purpose-built dwellings (Coppock, 1977, p.8). Whilst this is broadly the case, the 'adaptations' can be further divided between those homes which were surplus to local housing need (often derelict) and other dwellings which may have been required by local families, but which (arguably) became second homes when locals were outbid in the property market. The latter dwelling may well represent a 'transitional type' between vacant properties and purpose-built second homes, which are likely to be converted to second home use in a period of non-market saturation before local government takes steps to divert demand from existing housing (by building new second homes), or seeks to control change of use (by acquiring and then letting, existing properties which come onto the market). Arguably then, the 'evolutionary' transition in dwelling types sought as second homes is from vacant dwellings, through existing mainstream housing, to purpose built units. However, this pattern is neither universally accepted nor applicable. Wolfe (1977) in his study of summer cottages in Ontario argued that profound changes had occurred in the types of dwellings used as second homes between the 1940s and the mid-1970s; in particular, he noted that 'the greatest change of all has been the growth in the number of second homes that are *not* purpose built. It is astonishing how many working farms have been abandoned throughout Ontario [...] and are now serving the inessential purpose of being a second home' (Wolfe, 1977, p.29). The development of second homes world-wide exhibits both 'contrasts and parallels' according to Bielckus (1977). In North America, for instance, the market has been commercially motivated (with the holiday homes for commercial letting / sale) whilst in Europe 'rural properties left vacant by migrants from agricultural areas have been taken over as second homes' (Bielckus, 1977, p.35). The dominance of early commercialism in North America accounts for large numbers of purpose-built second homes. In Britain and in Europe generally, developers have not, in the past, tended to become involved in second home developments, and the more recent arrival of holiday villages and individual purpose built second homes is indicative of both growing commercial interest and a concern amongst planners to encourage tourist growth whilst diverting second home pressure from the existing mainstream housing stock. In 1972, Dower noted that:

> [...] until now, built second homes were mostly converted from existing buildings, without the planning authority having much say. From now on, they may be mainly new-built second homes, or newly sited static caravans or chalets, and the planning authorities may have a significant influence on what is built where, and how many are built (Dower, 1977, p.159).

In Scotland, the emergence of holiday villages (comprising chalets) in the 1960s was in part a result of commercial pressure and in part a response to planning concerns. Crofts (1977) noted that rising numbers of static caravans in rural Scotland was increasingly regarded as a planning problem in the 1960s (Crofts, 1977, p.103) and loopholes in the Caravan Act made their growth difficult to control. However, the regulation of built second homes and chalets was far more straightforward with a specified legal framework contained in the Town and Country Planning (Scotland) Acts and the Building Standards Regulations (Scotland) Act 1963 (amended 1967). In certain regions, and particularly in Argyll, it was decided that the 'blight' of caravans was such that the best way forward was to 'substitute' them with more permanent structures (which could be better regulated) and as a consequence of the 'substitution' process, holiday villages were created with the advantages of controlled design specifications and improved siting (Crofts, 1977, p.111).

The transition in second home types and the move towards mainstream housing and purpose-built dwellings (as sources of surplus housing have diminished) has generated much of the concern over the last 20 years for regulating second home growth through the use of planning control. By 1976, for example, the supply of vacant dwellings appeared to have all but evaporated in Scotland (Dart, 1977, p.6) and so revived demand (after the economic recession of the mid-1970s) would mean direct competition for existing dwellings or would involve new building and a structured response from local planning authorities. Despite these trends, the conversion of derelict or vacant housing into second homes may still be seen as beneficial, particularly if buildings are *preserved* by their change of use (Dower, 1973); studies by Hoggart and Buller in rural France have shown that second home owners have been the driving force behind significant improvements in the rural housing stock (Hoggart and Buller, 1995, p.196). In reviewing prior studies, it is often impossible to distinguish between the conversion of surplus and mainstream housing. In the South West Economic Planning Council's study of second homes in the South West of England (1975), it was found that a sixth of the region's second homes were purchased as new (many being purpose built) while the remainder were acquisitions of existing dwellings. Significantly, 68 per cent of these acquisitions had full amenities when purchased, clearly suggesting that they were not derelict properties; 30 per cent of owners made improvements and 11 per cent with the use of grants (although the rules governing improvement grants for second homes were amended in the Housing Act 1974 (Part VII, s60) (SWEPC, 1975, p.10)). Pyne's study of second homes in Caernarvonshire (1973) showed that 74 per cent of second homes were unimproved or modernised existing dwellings (Pyne, 1973, p.10), and in Wales as a whole, most of the stock of built second homes had been created by change of use (Downing and Dower, 1973, p.8), although by the early 1970s, Wales had the highest concentration of static caravans across Britain, a fact that provided the focus of much disquiet (Llywelyn, 1976). The early studies demonstrated that by the early 1970s, the demand for second homes was increasingly focusing on the mainstream property market and the acquisition of derelict properties may have been declining whilst new-build remained marginal. For this reason, the 1970s onwards may be seen as a transitional phase in the types of properties being used as second homes, reflecting a fall-off in the supply of empty or derelict properties (Pyne, 1973, p.10) and the lesser importance of new build in accommodating demand at that time (although Williams points to a 'small number' of purpose built developments emerging across Wales at the beginning of the 1970s (Williams, 1974, p.12; see also Cymdeithas Yr Iaith Gymraeg, 1971)). In response to this trend, Downing and Dower argued that:

> While second homes consist merely of properties no longer wanted as first homes, they cause relatively few problems, but when they grow beyond this, political, social, economic and environmental problems arise (Downing and Dower, 1973, p.32).

This phase in the second home phenomenon saw a growing concern that locals were having to compete directly with outsiders for mainstream housing (particularly for small dwellings with low rateable values which may have been suitable for first time buyers; Jacobs, 1972, p.9), the result being that inflationary pressure was being exerted on house prices and locals were being left without homes. These particular concerns are detailed in later Chapters. Another concern emerged from the Housing Act 1980. Because new purchase rights were awarded to local authority secure tenants (through the right-to-buy), it was believed that former council houses in the most attractive rural areas would become the next target for second home seekers, accentuating the rural housing shortage. As a result of this fear, the Government placed restrictions on the resale of council houses in certain designated rural areas in England and Wales (under Section 19 of the 1980 Act) and certain local authority pre-emption rights on re-sales in Scotland (Williams and Twine, 1994, p.193). In a study of the resale process in Scotland by Williams and Twine (1994), it was shown that of 8,249 dwellings sold to sitting tenants by 1991, 723 (or 9 per cent) had been sold-on. The study considered the extent to which re-sales became second homes; only four properties were confirmed as second homes whilst another seventeen may have been converted to this use. Clearly, most of these former council houses became the sole residences of their occupants with three-quarters of purchasers being local. The general conclusion was that affluent outsiders do not compete for these properties and:

> [...] despite the fears raised concerning second homes when the right-to-buy legislation was drafted, the evidence from the case study areas clearly indicates that resold council houses are not being used as second homes to any significant extent (Williams and Twine, 1994, p.207).

This study had particular resonance later in the 1990s with the introduction of purchase grants (in the Housing Act 1996) for the tenants of registered housing associations in England and Wales. Despite the exemption of dwelling in certain sizes of rural community, there was some fear that housing association dwellings, lacking the regimented design standards of 1950s and 1960s council housing, would be an attractive proposition for second home seekers. An article in *The Independent* newspaper (17 August 1995) described how 12 cottages built in the Lake District Village of Rothwaite by Home Housing Association in 1953 had been sold to tenants in the 1980s under the right-to-buy (which originally affected association secure lettings). By 1995, 11 of the 12 cottages had been sold-on by their original tenants (with significant profit) and most are now second homes. Clearly, such anecdotes fuelled fears that houses which should be serving the needs of local communities are falling prey to the expansion of the rural leisure industry.

At the other end of the market there is a reported growth in demand for second homes centred on high value properties, with prices sometimes exceeding those paid for first homes. One national estate agent in 2000 reported average second home prices of £415,000 for high end rural properties as against an overall market average of £380,000 (Gilbert, 2001). Of course, these averages do not represent direct comparisons between properties forming the portfolio of individual buyers, but they do indicate an emerging market for high-end property that is probably closely connected to retirement plans. While this market will not impact directly (in housing terms) on the most disadvantaged locals – such as first time buyers – any increased demand at the high end of the market is likely to result in a cascading of house price inflation. More immediately, this may make it more difficult for current local owners to trade up (a situation often aggravated by a restrictive planning framework in rural areas) before it eventually impacts on entry level prices. A range of impact concerns is examined more closely in Chapter 3.

Distribution of Second Home Demand

Clearly, where demand is focussed on types of property that bring second home owners into direct competition with local people, tensions may arise. These are made worse when demand in concentrated on particular settlements. The partial 'democratisation' of ownership which has led to overall increases in demand for second homes may not have resulted in any great controversy had it been evenly spread geographically, so reducing the impact on any one local housing market. But in reality, demand tends to focus on particular regions and, even more, on particular settlements within those regions. The distribution of second home demand, and its concentration in particular places, is driven by a range of factors. In France, for example, inheritance is often a key factor in determining the acquisition and distribution of second homes; it is not rare for a city-dweller to inherit a rural home from grandparents (Clout, 1977, p.58) and this is likely to be true elsewhere in Europe where rapid urbanisation has occurred in the twentieth century. However, more contemporary studies in France (Buller and Hoggart, 1994a; 1994b) argue that recent French generations have been increasingly cut off from rural origins and the process of inheritance is becoming less important. In the Balearic Islands, patterns of inheritance are still important but attitudes towards the land have changed and local people who retain ownership of their parent's or grandparent's land often move to main residences in the urban centres, turning their land into 'hobby farms' or weekend homes (Barke and France, 1988, p.144). In the Balearics and in Spain generally, a peculiarity in the second home phenomenon is the 'duality' in the distribution of ownership; foreigners tend to purchase properties on the coast in key tourist resorts (such as Palma and Manacor); that is, in areas with maximum leisure utility potential. Spanish nationals on the other hand are more likely to acquire smallholdings in the interior which provide weekend retreats. These distributions represent cultural objectives and preferences which often complicate patterns of second home ownership.

In the UK, and especially in England, it has already been noted that there has been a longer period of separation between town and country. General family ties with a region may encourage ownership, but this factor is often less important than in other countries. Tourism is an economic fact of life for many rural areas and is returned to in subsequent chapters. While it may be an economic necessity, anecdotal evidence suggests that it impacts strongly on decisions to buy a second home in a particular settlement and so may be viewed as mixed blessing. The influence of tourism is closely related to the cost and ease of travel which opens up holiday destinations and can make importing areas sufficiently close, in terms of travel time and cost to allow for second home use. This now has international dimensions with an increase in cheap flights (and favourable exchange rates) apparently opening up a strong market for the UK buyer in Europe (Gilbert, 2001). Holiday choices will typically also relate to areas with natural advantages, such as lakes, rivers and exceptional scenery and the relative importance of these elements has been the subject of a number of studies.

Coppock (1977), for example, has argued that the spatial distribution of second homes in importing regions is controlled by a number of factors including the distance from major centres of population, the quality and character of the landscape in importing regions, and the presence of specific physical features such as the sea, rivers, lakes or mountains. Davies and O'Farrell (1981), for example, found that proximity to a beach was an important factor in determining the location of second homes in West Wales while Barke's study of Malaga Province in Spain (1991, p.16) also noted this tendency for second homes to concentrate on the coastal fringe. Other factors include the presence of other recreational resources, the availability of land (or property), the different climates of the importing and exporting regions (Coppock, 1977, p.6), and the availability of services (Barke, 1991, p.17). Because of the issue of accessibility, determined by transport infrastructure and car ownership, Coppock notes that second homes in England and Wales tend to be within 100 to 150 miles of major population centres although Gardavský (1977) notes that the building of highways in Czechoslovakia meant a greater and more varied spatial dispersal of second homes in the 1970s. The earlier interpretations of growth patterns tended to rely heavily on these factors to explain the pressures on particular regions. In addition, where the growth of rural second homes was observed, it was often noted that demand reflected patterns of economic decline and rural depopulation. In North Wales, for example, Bollom (1978) noted that the distribution of second homes (around Blaenau Ffestiniog and the Machno valley) was due to properties ceasing as first homes with the decline in slate quarrying. Areas of economic decline (as was explained in the previous discussion) attract an influx of second home buyers (Bollom, 1978, p.2) and if this in-migration and replacement of the existing population results in the inflation of house prices, further depopulation may occur (Bollom, 1978, p.2). For this reason, patterns of demand often reflect current patterns of second home ownership. This was true in France in the early 1990s, but not because of pressures on rural house prices. If properties, because of their type and location, are more suitable for recreation purposes than first home use, those second home owners selling on may sell to incoming second home seekers, generating an autonomous sub-market, superimposing new patterns of ownership on old (Hoggart and Buller, 1995, p.194). In addition to this particular process, 'colonisation' of second home owners may occur in some areas where existing owners inform friends of new properties coming on to the market (40 per cent of second homes were acquired in this way in Denbighshire in Wales; Jacobs, 1972, p.15). More generally, those factors affecting distribution highlighted by Coppock are seen to have particular relevance. Clout (1977) noted that in the early 1970s, many French second home owners were attracted to the Mediterranean coastline (Clout, 1977, p.53) whilst Cribier (1969) noted that 'second home hinterlands have been identified around French cities, with diameters increasing in relation to city size and consequent volume of demand, and chronologically in response to improvements in transport technology' (Cribier, 1969, p.55). Psychogios (1980) argued that geographically, 'concentric ring patterns' (of the type used in classical models of urban analysis) may describe the evolution of second homes acquired for leisure purposes (in terms of distance) but this simple pattern is complicated by a multitude of factors as tangible as resources or as unquantifiable as individual idiosyncrasies or tastes (Psychogios, 1980, p.38; Crouchley, 1976, p.3). The presence of 'water surfaces', both natural and man-made may also provide a focus for second home growth. In general Clout argued that the distribution of second homes must be seen in the context of:

[...] existing patterns of settlement, the volume of rural out-migration, availability of vacant housing, existence of social or cultural attractions for particular groups to particular areas, and the role of inheritance in the acquisition of second homes (Clout, 1977, p.55).

The factors outlined by Coppock and others can be used to explain the various rural or coastal regional biases of second home ownership. However, Rogers (1977) argues that national or broader regional trends should not obscure the fact that the distribution of second homes is also important at the local level 'for it is here that the contrasts and conflicts are particularly evident from the viewpoint of both landscape and social contact' (Rogers, 1977, p.89). At the local level in Wales, reports from Caernarvonshire (Pyne, 1973), Merioneth-shire (Tuck, 1973), Carmarthenshire (Hughes, 1973) and Denbighshire (Jacobs, 1972) suggested little evidence of any regular pattern in the location and distribution of second homes; they did, however, appear to show a preference among second home seekers for smaller settlements in these rural areas. However, in a study of Cemaes in West Wales, Davies and O'Farrell (1981) found no evidence of any reduction in the number of second homes with increasing settlement density although they did find that smaller settlements do tend to have a higher proportion of second homes. This could point to a lack of particular preference for small settlements on the part of second home seekers; however, it also highlights the potential for a greater second home impact in smaller communities (Davies and O'Farrell, 1981, pp.103–104). In second home use and ownership, local studies have tended to emphasise the importance of the motor car and its association with the types of holidays and recreational use that goes with second home ownership. Car ownership may have two impacts on the distribution of second homes. Locally, second home ownership is certainly linked to recreational opportunities and therefore the distribution of homes should be related to facilities; however, the possession of private transport militates against the need for close proximity to particular attractions or facilities (Pyne, 1973, p.20). Nationally, access to private transport should define the distance relationship between importing and exporting regions (and therefore between second and first homes). However, in the early 1970s at least, despite relatively high levels of car ownership, movement patterns from first to second home still tended to be highly local, even when observed at the national level (Rogers, 1977, p.90). In Denbighshire, for example, 62 per cent of second home owners lived within 40 miles of Ruthin (Jacobs, 1972, p.13). Downing and Dower noted that 'most owners have their main residence either in the same region as their second home or the adjoining region' (Downing and Dower, 1973, iv). Rogers noted that:

> Even with the limited amount of evidence available at present, it is clear that there are very definite and individual patterns of movement within the country, related to the dispersion of the urban population on the one hand and suitable areas for second homes on the other (Rogers, 1977, p.93).

The distribution of second home growth areas needs to be understood in the context of the interaction of the importing and exporting regions. In the first instance, a diversity in social processes create the conditions for supply and demand in each region. More visible perhaps is the fact that a population interchange (and the growth in second home ownership) may be encouraged by increased accessibility with the development of motorways tending to open up rural backwaters. The extension of the M5 and M4 motorways in South West England and Wales respectively, for instance, has meant increasing accessibility to the National Parks and Areas of Outstanding Natural Beauty in those areas (the same is true of the extension of the A55 Expressway in North Wales). Second home regions are not geographically isolated and the expansion of second home ownership is dependent on the importing region's social, economic and physical relationship with neighbouring 'feed' or exporting regions. Rogers argues that 'as with many other elements of the rural economy the mistake of viewing problems of second homes as though they were isolated from the rest of the region [or other regions] has meant that only part of the problem has been appreciated' (Rogers, 1977, p.99). However, whilst it is true that broader perspectives add much to the analysis of a particular phenomenon and help avoid disjointed and partially relevant conclusions, it may be worth noting the point made by Cloke (1985) that 'rural studies as a framework of study may be threatened if social science continues to espouse structuralist epistemologies with their aspatial connotations' (Cloke, 1985, p.2). The local view must be balanced against the national perspective. Clearly, the issues surrounding second homes demand this balance. Rogers notes that someone from Liverpool with a second home in Ruthin is in fact underusing resources in Liverpool during time spent in Wales (Rogers, 1977, p.100). Rogers adds that, 'in short, second homes should not be regarded as isolated rural phenomena with isolated rural problems, but as elements in the economy of the city-region which have substantial spatial and temporal variations' (Rogers, 1977, p.100).

The distribution of second homes therefore may be determined by a variety of social and physical factors which increase the attraction of the various importing regions. The location of exporting regions is also important and local second home areas must be seen in the context of the city-region framework; this accounts for the fact that many of the second home owners in rural North Wales originate from urban North West England (Crouchley, 1976, p.3). More generally, in 1972, between 20 and 30 per cent of all second homes in the UK were located in Wales with another core concentration in the Lake District with both areas drawing a large proportion of owners from Merseyside and the surrounding region (Bielckus, *et al*, 1972, p.101). In examining the distribution of second homes, it is also essential to bear in mind those personal motivations, already touched upon, which encourage demand in the first instance. Patterns of distribution are increasingly grounded in personal motivations rather than in wider structures of socio-economic change; their prediction and interpretation is becoming ever more complex. The distribution of second homes in England is examined briefly in the next part of this chapter, and provides a backdrop to later analysis of the English market (Chapter 4).

The Current Second Home Market in England

The most recent data on second home numbers in England comes from the Survey of English Housing (SEH): this was first carried out in 1993 and therefore provides time-series market data for just under a decade. The Survey is designed to provide '...a wide range of information on the housing circumstances of households in England, for use in the development and monitoring of housing and related policies'. Prior to 1993, these data were collected via the Housing Trailers to the Labour Force Survey. The SEH looks at a nationally representative sample of 20,000 private households, taking a random selection of households within a sample of post-code sectors.

Data on second homes have been collected since 1994/5 and since that time, analysis has shown that a little over 200,000 households in England have a second home. Yearly variations are normally attributed to sampling error (DTLR, 2001b). The most recent data on second homes estimates that in 1999/00, '...230,000 households whose main residence was in England had a second home also in England'. Figures for the years 1994 to 1999/00 suggest that second home numbers are stable: despite the yearly fluctuations, there were roughly the same number of second homes at the end of the period as at the beginning.[2]

The Survey of English Housing also provides basic information on the location of second homes, as well as the reasons why households have such properties. A breakdown of the 1999/00 figure across the English regions is presented in Table 2.1: this breakdown is rather crude, though it reveals that many English second homes are located in built-up as opposed to rural areas: London and the South East, for example, has 32 per cent of the English total

Table 2.1   Location of Second Homes in England

Region	Number of second homes (average 1997/98 to 1999/00)	
	Number	Percentages
North East and North West	32,000	14.0
Yorkshire and the Humber	23,000	10.0
Midlands	30,000	13.0
East	34,000	15.0
London	34,000	15.0
South East	39,000	17.0
South West	41,000	18.0
England	**234,000**	**100.0**

Source: DTLR, 2001b, Table A1.37, p.147. Note: Not all Government Office regions can be shown separately due to small sample sizes.

and it is not unreasonable to assume that a significant proportion of these are located in London. The same may be true in the other regions, though it is impossible to tell from these data.

However, the figures in Table 2.1 contain second homes held for reasons other than leisure (such as working away from home and intending to sell), if these are stripped out, only 36 per cent remain in the category 'Holiday home/ retirement home/weekend cottage'. Holiday homes are let out on a commercial basis; retirement homes only constitute second homes if their owner has not yet retired and retains a main residence elsewhere. 'Weekend cottages' equate with the general definition of second homes, recently set out in the DTLR's 2001 consultation on council tax – as 'furnished dwellings that are no-one's main residence' – and also with Shucksmith's view that a second home is 'an occasional residence of a household that usually lives elsewhere and which is primarily used for recreation purposes' (Shucksmith, 1983, p.174). If we accept that only 36 per cent of the 229,000 total are traditional 'recreational' second homes, then there are only 82,440 such properties in England. But there is a likelihood that many of these are located in rural areas.

In 1991, Census data suggested there were just over 92,000 second homes distributed across 366 English boroughs and districts. Using Audits of Great Britain Ltd data, Shucksmith was able to show a sustained growth in the second home market between 1968 and 1982. These more recent data for the 1990s suggest that the second home market has leveled out. Today, less than 1 per cent of households have a second home in a rural area and fewer than 1.5 per cent own any form of second home either in the countryside or in urban England. However, the central issue with English second homes is not their overall number – or proportion relative to the national housing stock – but their tendency to concentrate in the most attractive areas and to combine with retirement purchasing to create a range of highly localised difficulties.

Most of the prior studies concerned with second homes agree that the growth in ownership experienced since the World War II is set to continue, particularly given the greater scope for development in Britain compared to other European countries, which are still experiencing growth but where the second home phenomenon is certainly more advanced. After all, second home ownership is not just a passing phase in outdoor recreation (Williams, 1974, p.37). The endemic nature of the problem in the UK has led to periodic calls for intervention to deal with the second home growth phenomenon. This has created a need to analyse growth patterns in such a way as to provide a platform for effective and relevant policy decisions.

Modelling and Prediction (of Future Demand)

Robertson notes that a 'better understanding of the [purchaser's] decision-making process will increase the likelihood of developing successful models of patterns of second home development' (Robertson, 1977, p.136). Whilst the motivations driving the market are becoming ever more complex, a number of attempts have been made to model and predict market change; these are now reviewed.

Crouchley (1976) attempted to formulate a seventeen-variable model which could assist in such decision-making. He related the distribution of second homes in Denbighshire against agricultural intensity, the provision of public services, recreation facilities, the motivations of second home seekers, land ownership patterns, existing patterns of second home ownership, the decline in employment opportunities and rural depopulation and a number of other variables which he identified, from other studies, as potentially affecting distribution (Crouchley, 1976, p.12). Crouchley argued that the 'aggregated motives and factors which explain the spatial distribution of second homes can be grouped and transformed into a set of indices' (Crouchley, 1976, p.14) which can then be examined using multiple regression techniques and principal components analysis. From this type of data exploration, Crouchley hoped to arrive at a predictive model (Crouchley, 1976, p.60). In terms of the most significant indices, he concluded that patterns of future growth were likely to occur in areas with lower dwelling and population densities, lower accessibility indices and lower agricultural grades. That is, in parts of existing importing regions which are more isolated (although generally accessible) and where land is less likely to be in agricultural use. In Denbighshire, Jacobs noted that there were more second homes in areas of lower soil quality, rural depopulation and closer proximity to Merseyside (Jacobs, 1972, p.7). However, Crouchley's predictive model was limited by the percentage of variation in distribution patterns which were left *unexplained* (Crouchley, 1976, p.76) mainly because of the high level of data aggregation, the scale of the analysis, poor operational use of indices, errors in measurement, random variations and the failure to make the model temporally specific. In fact, the model was able to explain fewer variations than earlier models developed by Aldskogius (1967) and Burby, Donelly and Wiess (1972). Crouchley concedes that models of all types tend to be better at predicting the behaviour of parts rather than wholes. The second home phenomenon, in contrast, is the product of socio-economic changes occurring at the national level, and not simply in the importing region. Clearly, this fact in itself has implications for the way in which policy to deal with growth should be developed. Should, for example, policy seek to sever the flow of second home seekers from exporting regions, adopting a prohibitive stance? Or should, on the other hand, a more holistic approach be developed which recognises the legitimacy of urban leisure demand and also the need to protect rural communities from the potentially negative impacts of growth?

The locational analysis attempted by Davies and O'Farrell (1981) was slightly more effective in producing particular policy recommendations. Their analysis of second homes was based upon cross-classification and regression analysis and found that growth patterns (around Cemaes in West Wales) had been determined by proximity to the nearest beach and a tendency to locate in smaller villages (Davies and O'Farrell, 1981, p.103). However, they also found that increasing distance from open land and higher settlement densities did not seem to deter potential second home owners from purchasing properties. Two key policy implications sprang from this analysis; firstly, second home seekers might be attracted to developments built at a comparatively high residential density (that is, in the form of holiday villages) and secondly, the location of demand suggested that housing policy could not deal separately with 'the housing needs of the local community and the pressure for second homes arising from outside the local area' (Davies and O'Farrell, 1981, p.107).

These types of studies suggest that under certain conditions, and where growth has developed in a particular way, second homes are likely to have social, economic and environmental impacts. It is easy, in this context, to point to the need to control growth, particularly through the use of the planning system which has proved relatively effective in controlling other types of development in the countryside since 1947. However, planning is not simply about control and restricting the expansion of particular activities. The encroachment of town into remoter rural areas means that 'a stage has been reached when there is virtually no use of the countryside to which someone will not object' (Williams, 1974, p.6). But these objections should not obscure the fact that planning has two legitimate objectives. Certainly, the first of these is to minimise the potentially negative impacts of new development. However, the second objective, which demands equal emphasis, is to ensure that possible benefits inherent in new development are maximised. For this reason, the costs and benefits of all development types (including second homes) need to be considered before policy responses are formulated; this weighing of costs and benefits is the subject of the next Chapter.

Conclusions

Second homes have always brought different cultures into geographic proximity. However, traditional social divides and demand for widely different housing separated the incomers and the host communities. In developed economies increasing numbers of people are able to afford a second home. As markets mature, 'the demand for built second homes exceeds the supply of housing which is genuinely surplus to local needs [it is then] that strains appear' (Dart, 1977, p.62). This, combined with a focus on particular settlements can lead to particular problems in those places. Under these circumstances tensions arise that are easily suffused by a number of broader social issues, but that are rooted in the very nature of the demand for second homes. These are usually expressed as simple opposing forces: rich versus poor; upper versus lower class; incomer versus local; rural versus urban and so on and so forth. This has the unfortunate effect of removing the subtlety from our understanding of the drivers of this market which in turn deprives us of the ability to make considered policy responses.

Notes

1   At this stage it should be noted that while second home ownership may have filtered down the social strata, the mean income of United Kingdom second home owners, at £45,000, is well above average national incomes Gilbert (2001). Over half of second home owners have an income in excess of £36,400. Of course, these findings are hardly surprising, but they do serve to highlight that in a broadening market, second home ownership still represents a considerable privilege.
2   The estimates of households owning second homes do not include '[...] those whose second home is the main residence of someone else, nor those whose only reason given for having a second home is that they are in the process of moving or they have inherited a property which they are intending to sell. Nor does it include those who have a second home outside England, but it does include those who rent rather than own a second home' (DTLR, 2001b, p.18).

Chapter 3

The Impacts of Second Homes

Introduction

The sustainability of any activity is today judged in terms of its social, economic and environmental consequences: second home purchasing and subsequent use is no exception. One useful metaphor is to view these 'components' of sustainability as the legs of a 'stool', liable to collapse if any one is damaged or broken. In environmental terms, second homes may be seen as inherently unsustainable: they add to housing pressure in the countryside, contribute to land-take, and serve no particular accommodation need. However, some second homes may be drawn from unneeded housing stock, and development cannot be judged environmentally harmful merely because it does not fulfil a particular or 'acceptable' social role. Indeed, the role played by second homes might be viewed as beneficial, meeting the leisure and recreation aspirations of owners and users. Indeed, the 'stool' metaphor suggests the need to strike a balance between the social, economic and environmental costs of any activity. This means that a 'balance sheet' approach allows environmental costs to be offset by social gains, or an economic price to be balanced by environmental benefits. Although this approach to understanding and achieving sustainability is not without its critics (see for example Dawe & Ryan, 2003) it is a useful way of reviewing the impacts of second homes, recognising as it does the inherent need to make judgements based on relative social, economic and environmental gains and losses.

It is extremely difficult to quantify the impacts of second homes; their social benefits (fulfilling legitimate leisure demand) and social costs (displacing permanent residents) are hard to pin down. Similarly, even their economic consequences are disputed: do owners being money and investment to rural communities? Do they spend in local shops and support local services? Or is there no net economic benefit, because those using second homes acquire their property through urban estate agents, and, when using their second home, bring food and other supplies from home? The reality is that it is certainly impossible to accurately 'model' the positive and negative impacts of second homes on any 'balance sheet' or for any of the 'three legs' of sustainability. Indeed, as Pyne (1973, p.21) has argued, any scientific cost-benefit analysis of the second home phenomenon is 'rendered meaningless' by the great number of necessary arbitrary assumption that feed into any model. Hoggart *et al* (1995, p. 178) adds that '[...] whether or not the outcome [of second home growth] is regarded as positive or negative by communities can depend heavily upon local circumstances'.

With these difficulties in mind, we attempt in this chapter to provide at least an overview of the potential positive and adverse consequences of second homes in rural areas. The issue of local context determining the exact impact of second homes in any particular area is of course critical. The environmental impact of second homes will be far greater where purpose-built and poorly designed properties are used by weekend visitors; the social costs may be higher where concentrations of second homes are significant and where they combine with other economic factors to 'weaken' local communities; and the economic advantages may be most visible where they provide an additional source of investment in local housing, where local services and shops benefit from visitor trade, and when cross-competition for housing – that is between local buyers and incomers – is not a significant problem. The discussion presented in the remainder of this chapter is structured around the three legs of sustainability; in each section, we present a general analysis using past studies and where possible, refer to work undertaken for the Welsh Assembly Government (Tewdwr-Jones *et al*, 2002) and the Countryside Agency in England (Gallent *et al*, 2002). Inevitably, most of the illustrations are taken from England or Wales.

Part 1: Social Impacts

Perhaps the most controversial issue surrounding the expansion in second home ownership in recent years has been the social effect that this growth has had on those regions and particular rural communities where second home demand has been concentrated. Any 'harmful' social impacts are closely allied to the negative economic effects that second homes may produce in some circumstances, notably, inflationary pressure on house prices, the displacement of existing permanent residents and the cessation of village services. These more specific concerns are dealt with later in this chapter, under the heading of economic impact.

On a more general level, the social impact of second homes – and broader migration pressure – is often expressed as opposition to second home purchasing. This opposition may become part of a socio-cultural analysis in which the complexity of the housing market is lost, and portrayed as a 'conflict' between working class 'locals' and middle class 'newcomers'; or indeed, between town and country. Implicit in this analysis is the view that the traditional rural community comprises a homogenous group of vulnerable poorer people, whilst any threat the community faces comes from an equally homogenous but wealthier urban 'elite'. In Wales, this analysis is given further weight by a legacy of perceived domination: in one anthropological analysis of the residents of Blaenau Ffestiniog (North Wales) it was observed that:

> [...] all their resentments as working class people against the ruling class; as country people against the towns, as ordinary people against the powerful officials, are poured into the Welsh-versus-English mould and given strength to the battle that it would not otherwise possess (Emmett, 1964).

It is clearly important to acknowledge the potential role played by class tensions in re-enforcing resentment between local groups and newcomers (Cloke & Thrift, 1987). However, the promotion of this division as the key influence on modern communities tends to obscure the complexity of rural life (Emmett, 1982). More generally, Edwards *et al* (2003) have argued that government's tendency to view rural communities as single, homogenous entities – and a failure to understand the inner dynamics of these communities – reduces the likely success of initiatives aimed at encouraging greater engagement with policy development and delivery. In recognising that rural communities are diverse, it follows that second homes will not have a 'standard' or quantifiable social impact in any given area. Again, any measurable benefits or problems will be as much a product of broader context as the specific issue of second home buying.

Generalisations have a special place in the second home debate in the UK. They are commonly painted as the wreckers of rural communities, displacing the 'traditional' populace and creating 'ghost towns' (Simms *et al*, 2002). Some of these broad negative generalisations were noted in Chapter 1 and whilst they may have some truth in certain instances, elsewhere, more positive impacts may be felt. For example, in some instances, second home purchasing may help secure the future viability of a community which has thinned out as a result of economic out-migration. The arrival of second home buyers may help support services (for example village shops) that would otherwise cease to be provided. Müller (1999) has pointed out that in some parts of Sweden and Finland, second home investment has been welcomed and encouraged for this reason, though the logic of supporting this investment depends on there being spare capacity in the local housing market to absorb demand without adversely affecting the housing access opportunities available to local buyers. A similar argument – drawing on research undertaken in Ireland – is that given favourable conditions:

> [...] tourists bring numbers, money and reassurance to those who live in isolated rural communities, with an enhancement to self-esteem perhaps having the most profound effect (Hoggart, *et al*, 1995, p.179).

The injection of tourist investment may increase confidence in the local economy and generate new opportunities in the rural labour market. The argument that we are leading up to is that second home investment may, in some instances, be welcomed. But because communities are not homogenous – residents will have a range of different backgrounds, needs and aspirations – reactions to second homes, or to anything that happen or changes in that community, are unlikely to be uniform. Some people may welcome the vibrancy that comes from having a tourist economy or the diversity that may stem from inward migration. Similarly, those with a vested interest in the local property market – as home owners – may welcome the investment that second home buyers inject into this market and the effect this has on the potential value of their own property. The view that rural communities are united in their opposition to second homes or migration is as fallacious as the view that these same communities are united in their poverty. This is not an argument in favour of second homes, but merely a reminder that social impact can often be gauged through local reaction and that this reaction is hardly ever uniform: impacts are subjectively and personally experienced and defined.

Finally in terms of broad social consequences, there is the argument that second homes represent a softer and a less socially harmful or 'colonial' form of tourism: indeed '[...] the term *home* implies becoming native to the place, setting down roots, and investing oneself in a place' (Crouch, 1999, p. 214). However, in the same way that communities lack homogeneity, second home owners may display very different preferences in terms of how they wish to use their second homes. Certainly, some will embed themselves in their adopted community, spending money in local shops, drinking in local pubs and perhaps even involving themselves in local institutions. But others are perhaps more likely to use the second home more as a dormitory, and as a base to engage in recreational activities that set them apart from permanent residents. It is also the case that the community will welcome and encourage their active participation in some instances, but elsewhere this engagement may be resented, particularly when obvious cultural or linguistic barriers are present, or where incomers are seen to bring values or modes of behaviour that are viewed as somehow alien. This has certainly been the case in some parts of Wales where second home purchasing may be viewed as simply another pressure weighing down on Welsh speaking communities.

Community Tensions in Wales

Between 1979 and 1990, the extremist group, *Meibion Glyndwr* (or the 'Sons of Glyndwr', arsonists claiming to be carrying on the work of a fifteenth century crusader against English rule) carried out 171 arson attacks in North Wales on isolated dwellings (Pilkington, 1990, p.18), returning them to the derelict state that many were in prior to renovation by second homeowners. It has been claimed that the threat of being 'burned out' resulted in an 'English retreat' from North Wales; across the county of Gwynedd, the total number of second homes fell by 2,500 to 8,000 by 1994 (*The Observer*, 17 April 1994), although it is difficult to isolate the effect of the arson campaign from other factors such as the collapse in the property market in the early 1990s or the re-focusing of some demand on properties abroad. These attacks were motivated by fundamental misconceptions, the ease with which such isolated dwellings could be targeted, and a desire to focus publicity on the entire second home issue. In Wales, second homes (*per se*) have come to symbolise a threat to Wales' distinctive culture and language making it particularly difficult to disentangle the various strands of the second home debate (that is, the underlying causes of social decline and the differing social and economic impacts of different second home types). Whilst it is clear that in some circumstances, '[...] the strength of the chapel and the vitality of the language may be threatened' (Shucksmith, 1983, p.181) directly by second homes, Newby (1980a) has argued that 'loss of community' is the result of more general socio-economic change and cannot be attributed to newcomers

(Newby, 1980a, pp.164–178). On the whole, second homes are visible and perhaps convenient scapegoats whilst the less tangible underlying causes of 'community decline' – a failing economic base and the changing nature of family life – are less visible and are far more difficult to address. Arguably, rural communities, by becoming less 'traditional', are becoming less recognisable and a fear of change is generating a hostility towards those features of the rural landscape which have come to symbolise that change. However, these more holistic perspectives cannot disguise the fact that an influx of '[...] wealthy town-dwellers with cultivated accents and liberal or agnostic views' is often accompanied by a degree of cultural shock (Downing and Dower, 1973, p.30) in the summer months, followed by a loss of social vitality in the winter and the creation of 'ghost' communities. This shock may be emphasised by the '[...] physical configuration of housing, which often segregates the local working classes in social housing estates, while incomers colonise the old core of the village' (Hoggart, *et al*, 1995, p.216).

The concentration of second homes in some parts of Wales (see Figure 3.1) is central to the perception of a general 'problem'. Local reactions to newly built *holiday home* developments are well documented – but although they may be viewed as a blot on the landscape, their social impact is less obvious. Holiday villages remain 'ghost' communities for much of the year, occupied only during vacation periods. On the other hand, second homes *within* village cores 'rob' locals of the dwellings which should 'rightfully' have been theirs (see Meacher, 1999): it is external sources of core housing demand which is perceived to represent the greater threat. Philip O'Connor's seminal work on second homes in 1962 highlighted local despondency over the plight of the language in Croesor in the light of new English monoglot arrivals; the erosion of Welsh usage was seen to herald a loss of community (O'Connor, 1962). In the 1970s and into the 1980s, a proportional decline in the number of Welsh language speakers in the traditional language 'strongholds' was attributed to counter-urbanisation alongside the broader impacts of tourism (Bowen and Carter, 1975), retirement related in-migration and the growth in second home ownership (Aitchison and Carter, 1985; 1986). However, explanations of language change and stability have, to date, only defined a loose association between declining Welsh usage and second homes. This association stems from the fact that incomers from a dominant culture are apparently helping shift the linguistic balance in the traditional strongholds of the Welsh language (James and Williams, 1997) – and contributing to an eroded sense of community.

The 2001 Census confirms that the linguistic map of Wales is shifting, with the proportion of Welsh speakers in the former 'strongholds' – in the rural north and north-west of Wales – falling whilst the more urban south-east has experienced a percentage gain. But this shift is being driven not by housing pressures (predominantly), but by economic factors: firstly the draw of higher paid jobs in South Wales, and secondly the greater 'economic value' placed on Welsh language skills by a growing media and civil service sector in the south. The decision to locate the Welsh Assembly Government in Cardiff is a major factor driving this language shift in Wales, with Welsh today becoming as much the language of government as the language of the rural community.

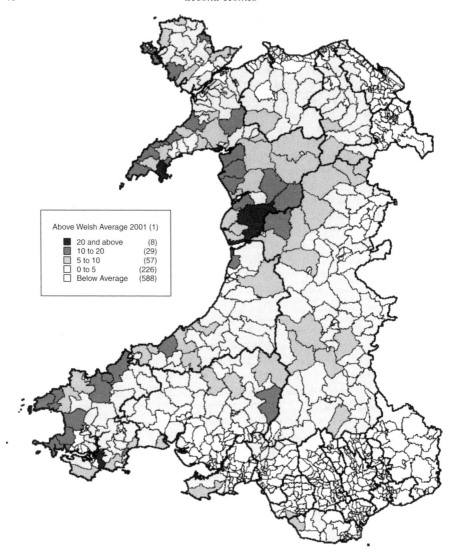

Above Welsh Average 2001 (1)

■	20 and above	(8)
▨	10 to 20	(29)
▨	5 to 10	(57)
□	0 to 5	(226)
□	Below Average	(588)

**Figure 3.1   Estimate of Second and Holiday Homes in Wales 2001 – Percentage
Points Above the Welsh Average (Average = 1.31)**

But recognition of these broader trends has not led to any easing of the
tensions that now accompany second home purchasing in Wales. Indeed, this
bigger picture is frequently obscured by local concerns and by pressure to act
locally to defend rural communities: see Chapter 9. Local politicians need to
explain to the electorate why not enough affordable housing is available

locally, why younger people are moving away, and why fewer people seem to be speaking 'Welsh in village shops. There are clear challenges threatening the former 'stability' of some rural communities; real explanations – including the lack of investment in housing, planning constraint, a focussing of economic opportunities in towns and cities, and demographic aging – are often complex, whilst the carelessness of a rich minority moving in and buying up housing is an easy way to explain certain undesirable consequences of social change. The view adopted is an introverted one: all problems and solutions are local, and broader linkages are denied or presented as inherently negative. This may lead communities to define themselves '[. . .] though simple counter-position to the outside' whilst perhaps a more positive sense of community '[. . .] can come, in part, precisely through the particular linkages *to* that "outside" ' (Massey, 1993, p. 67). In the absence of finding and understanding such linkages, those who seek local explanations for the broader social shifts occurring in rural areas may ultimately come to be seen – and dismissed – as reactionary.

Part 2: Economic Impacts

It was noted at the beginning of this chapter that economic impacts often form the flip-side of social impacts: the two are closely related. This often means that social effects are the symptom of an economic consequence. For example, housing market pressures drive up house prices; these changes can be quantified, but the social repercussions can be more subtle than people simply 'moving away because of a lack of housing'. In theory, younger people may spend longer living with parents, or larger families may be forced to live in smaller homes. The social effect tends to have an economic cause. But the cause-effect relationship is not always clear-cut, hence the complexity of the debate surrounding second homes and the suggestion that causes are more complex and greater in number. For example, the view that second home purchasing drives up house prices, which in turn leads to out-migration (particularly of the young), and to a reconfiguration of communities, places too much attention on 'push' factors, and too little emphasis on the 'positive' decisions made by young people in the light of external 'pull' factors. For example, second home purchasing is often judged significant when it appears to be accompanied by an exodus of younger households; a link is often drawn between these two processes – that is, cause and effect. However, in many instances these outwards flows are to positive attractions such as greater social, educational and career opportunities – local rural economies often fail to retain younger people.

In this section, the potential economic impacts of second homes have been divided into two groups: firstly, those that relate directly to housing, such as house price inflation and improvements to the housing stock by second home owners. And secondly, the more general economic impacts such as potential sources of new employment created by second home investment, or the costs associated with supporting services in an area where many residents are absent for much of the year.

Housing – (a) Competition

In 1981, Mark Shucksmith noted that:

> The essence of the housing problem in rural areas is that those who work there tend
> to receive low incomes, and are thus unable to compete with more affluent
> 'adventitious' purchasers from elsewhere in a market where supply is restricted
> (Shucksmith, 1981, p.11).

Shucksmith argued that a free market in rural areas allocates housing to the most affluent whilst local populations are frequently left with the poorest and cheapest accommodation (if any). The crux of the problem is that insufficient houses are built and these go to affluent outsiders (for first or second home use). The real problem, according to Shucksmith, was that whilst rigid planning restrictions on land supply 'reinforce the inequitable consequences of a free-market allocation and lead to socially regressive distributional consequences', non-intervention has an equally negative impact and it has long been established that intervention is required to deal with efficiency and inequity problems (Shucksmith, 1981, p.13). Clearly, outside competition has a potential impact on property prices which may or may not be realised; outside competition however, may be viewed as only part of the problem with low rural wages largely contributing to the inability of locals to compete in a property market differentiated by more than just two consumption groups.

The nature of the market and particular tenure divisions mean that – as with culture – there are no simple dichotomies between rich and poor or locals and newcomers. Peter Saunders (1984), for example, argues that owner occupiers form a middle 'domestic property class', advantaged by the cumulative potential of their tenure whilst those in rented accommodation have no similar advantage. Clearly then, the level of local owner occupation is important; it will influence the effect that outside competition has on a rural market and offers the potential for cumulative wealth (determined by local property values) within the local population. Similar 'housing class' classifications have been developed by Ambrose (1974), Pahl (1966) and Dunn, Rawson and Rogers (1981). Domestic property classes are characterised by 'consumption cleavages' which define access chances and the ability of different households to compete in the housing market.

While Shucksmith (1990b) contends that access chances broadly differ between households with 'low income and low wealth' and 'more prosperous groups' (Shucksmith, 1990b, p.225) he notes that there are numerous sub-divisions within these broad categories. The first group will include young couples and single persons barred from entry to waiting lists (this group is often perceived as experiencing the greatest difficulties in gaining entry to the housing market; Cloke, *et al*, 1994, p.4), other tenants of rented or tied accommodation, pensioners retired from local employment, or former in-migrants now facing financial difficulties and local authority tenants who are more fortunate and who may be eligible to buy their home with a discount. The latter – more prosperous group – might include indigenous owner occupiers, retirement migrants with capital available from a previous home, holiday home buyers and commuters. Clearly, this typology demonstrates that certain groups will face disadvantage in the rural housing market, not only in competition with newcomers but also with local owner-occupiers who have the advantage of an established equity base. Rural housing markets are more than just local interest versus second home demands. However, simple logic would suggest that were there is strong demand for second homes there is at least the possibility for this demand to cause local house price inflation. This possibility is investigated further below.

Housing – (b) House Price Inflation

Perhaps the main concern of those opposed to, or concerned about the growth in second home ownership is the supposed impact on local house prices where locals and 'newcomers' compete directly for mainstream housing stock. Bollom (1978) notes that in North Wales, 'younger people who wish to purchase properties may be frustrated in their attempts because of the greater purchasing power of potential second homers in the local housing market' (Bollom, 1978, p.112). However, the notion that second home seekers and locals compete for the same housing has not received universal endorsement and many observers contend that 'aspiring second home owners and local people compete for different forms of property' (Rogers, 1977, p.99). Whilst this is certainly the case in many areas (with demand concentrated in the surplus housing stock), there are case studies which reveal evidence of direct competition and upward pressure on house prices and these studies were becoming more prolific throughout the 1970s as the supply of surplus dwellings dwindled (Dart, 1977).

Pyne (1973) and Tuck (1973) have also acknowledged that rising house prices have been associated with the growth in second homes in some areas. Downing and Dower (1973) are more cautious, explaining that it is the combination of direct competition, economic depression and low rural wages that creates a housing affordability problem for rural households; they concede, however, that competition for housing in small towns and villages (as opposed to more isolated dwellings) can act to bid up prices (Downing and Dower, 1973, p.31). One of the more comprehensive studies of this relationship was carried out by Clark (1982) in a study, of the Lake District, which compared different communities, house prices and patterns of second home ownership. Clark claimed to have uncovered robust evidence to support the argument that second homes do exert inflationary pressure on property values. The work of de Vane (1975), on the other hand, failed to reveal any *regional* empirical evidence to attribute local rises directly to second home ownership and it is clear that only local anecdotal studies have been able to demonstrate a potential relationship (noticeably Jacobs, 1972). Jacobs tackled the issue directly in Denbighshire in Wales; he identified areas where the sale prices of second homes (and surrounding housing) had soared in recent years (quoting from studies in the Peak District and the Lakes) and claimed that the same trend was discernible in North Wales. In Denbighshire, prices had risen by 9.3

per cent between 1962 and 1972 compared to a national rise of 6.7 per cent for existing properties over the same period. There was certainly local evidence that second home owners were competing against first time buyers for smaller properties, accounting, in part, for the differential between local and national house prices (Jacobs, 1972, p.42). On Anglesey, a study by Jenkin (1985) of fifteen parishes with the highest proportions of second home ownership revealed that the 'chances of first time buyers securing a home in these parishes was bleak' (Jenkin, 1985, p.41) with only 1 in 25 houses valued at below £16,000 compared to 1 in 10 in the remaining parishes on the island. He concluded from this that claims put forward by The Welsh Language Society (Cymdeithas Yr Iaith Gymraeg, 1971) – that houses go to the rich with a subsequent inflation of surrounding property prices – were well-founded. What Jenkin failed to take into account, however, was that those factors attracting second home owners to particular parishes may also have drawn more affluent locals, and people retiring to the area.

It is wrong to suggest that all local house price variations can be attributed to second home ownership in the same way as is wrong to assume that all 'locals' survive on low incomes (see discussion above). Shucksmith (1990) has acknowledged that competition for housing occurs between a range of income and social groups and that crude 'local-newcomer' dichotomies should give way to the more nuanced typologies of competitive consumption groups developed by Saunders (1984), Ambrose (1974), Pahl (1966) or Dunn, Rawson and Rogers (1981). Jacobs (1972) is more sensitive to the fact that different groups compete for different housing. He notes, for instance, that the increase in the cost of an isolated cottage has little impact on local families seeking housing as these dwellings are often not ideal places in which to bring up a young family. Similarly, it may be the case that when properties are on the market, altruistic locals may give first choice to friends and relatives. However, these offers are often not taken up by young people who gravitate to larger key settlements due to the greater availability of services and employment. A profile, undertaken by Jacobs, of the Llanrwst (North Wales) employment exchange between 1952 and 1969 revealed that scattered employment (that is, jobs on isolated farms and in small villages) had declined far more than absolute employment, a trend that is likely to be repeated in numerous rural areas. For this reason, 'workers follow the jobs and migrate to the new centres of employment' (Jacobs, 1972, p.44) which may mean that they do not always compete with second home seekers for isolated properties or properties in small villages. Examples of direct competition between local households and newcomers seeking second homes certainly occur but may only be identified by fieldwork in particular locations. More recent research by Cloke *et al* (1994) in twelve case-study areas in rural England concluded that:

> There did seem to be widespread occurrences of affluent in-migrants outbidding local people for the limited available housing stock (Cloke, *et al*, 1994, p.161).

Although this phenomenon is not universal, it might be argued that it is becoming more commonplace as the supply of isolated surplus dwellings is depleted. But, again, this pattern will not be repeated everywhere as different localities are characterised by contrasting housing stock mixes and different patterns of population change (Cloke, *et al*, 1994, p.161). Cloke *et al* add that an 'established culture of uneven competition' is often the hallmark of rural areas subject to restrictive planning; housing supply rather than outside competition is the principal component in house-price inflation. This same argument is forwarded by Hoggart (2003, p.153) who points to the inherent 'scarcity' of housing in many parts of the British countryside.

It is also the case that local price rises in rural areas need to be placed within the wider setting of national house price inflation and inadequate supply. Although second homes may contribute to price pressures in particular communities, general high levels of house price inflation tend to spread out from the South East of England across the rest of Britain. At the beginning of the new millennium a number of factors are contributing to higher levels of house price inflation: historically low interest rates, poor stock market performance (that has resulted in greater investment in the property market), and extremely low rates of new house building. In 2001, the total for new housing completions – both private and social – in *Britain* stood at 162,000: the lowest for 54 years. The current house building shortfall is concentrated in England. During the second half of the 1990s, household growth in England exceeded expansion of the housing stock by around 59,000 units per year: 'Put another way, 41 per cent more dwellings should have been built in the last five years than were actually completed merely to keep pace with household growth' (Stewart, 2002, web reference). The upward pressure on prices has spread across Britain, affecting both urban and rural markets. It has been driven by scarcity and by the falling cost of mortgage borrowing; it has resulted, however, in severe difficulties for those trying to enter the housing market for the first time.

In Wales there have been similarly steep increases in house prices despite a relatively higher rate of house building – around 8,500 annually – which '[...]should ensure that demand and supply issues are almost in equilibrium' (Halifax, 2003). However, this apparent equilibrium in Wales hides two important points. First, that the average income of *home buyers* stands at 165 per cent above the *general average* income in Wales, supporting the contention that the position for some housing groups – such as the young – is bleak, and the supply in Wales appears to be sufficient because incomes are simply too low to turn aspirations into effective demand. And second, much of this increase in supply is centred on urban areas such as Cardiff, emphasising once again that it is necessary to consider the local picture when considering the impacts of the housing market on communities. As elsewhere, these increases in house prices can be seen as beneficial to local homeowners who are experiencing a considerable increase in their stored equity as a result. However, the increase disadvantages those aspiring to buy for the first time as well as those who cannot afford to buy at all, as both these groups are excluded from the gains that house holders are making as the market rises steeply. Under these broader circumstances it is possible for problems of housing affordability to become conflated with cultural – and even nationalistic – concerns where it is believed that processes are not merely generic (that is a result of scarcity affecting the national market), but are being driven by external pressures: 'our home, *ein gwlad* (our countryside), is rapidly turning into a massive Hilton where the Welsh are 'in service' to an elite, foreign, rogue regime' (Welsh Republican Comment, 2003, web reference).

But what specific evidence is there to show that house prices are being driven up by second home purchasing? During work for the Welsh Assembly Government in 2001, the Council of Mortgage Lenders (CML) Cymru argued that even broad supply concerns do not account for affordability problems in many parts of Wales: these are more properly attributed to 'ineffective' local demand and weaknesses in many rural economies:

> NAW (the National Assembly for Wales) and others have tended to see the affordability problem as one of supply. This has led to proposals to restrict the sale of former Right to Buy (RTB) properties in rural areas and to the proposals by Plaid Cymru and others to limit the number of second homes. In the view of CML Cymru, this analysis needs further examination. A glance at the land registry figures (see Figure 3.2), shows that the three out of the four areas (Gwynedd, Anglesey, Ceredigion and Carmarthenshire) most usually identified with problems of rural affordability, actually have average house prices below the Welsh average. It should not be forgotten that the Welsh average is only around 66 per cent of the average for England. These figures raise the question as to whether the problem of affordability stems not primarily from problems of supply, but from problems of ineffective demand caused by the poor performance of local economies and low or unstable personal incomes. If this analysis were to prove to be correct, this would suggest that what is needed in those areas are not restrictions in the supply of certain types of housing for certain purposes, but stimulus to and investment in local economies to help bring incomes up to an acceptable level. Such an analysis would suggest that far from being negative phenomena, the provision of second homes and holiday homes and indeed in-migration, could be important factors in rejuvenating local economies and in addressing problems of affordability (CML, quoted in Tewdwr-Jones *et al*, 2002, p. 89).

The figures referred to by the CML were taken from the Land Registry and compared April-June 2000 with April-June 2001 (see Table 3.1). Analysis for the Welsh Assembly Government revealed a -0.21 correlation between house price change (2000–2001) and point differences in second/holiday homes (1991–2001) suggesting that, on an all Wales level, house price rises are slower today in those areas that have experienced second home growth over the last 10 years. This is difficult to interpret. Firstly, the correlation is very weak. But it could simply suggest that second and holiday homes are of minor importance in the national market: house prices, in general, remain lower in rural counties which may, or may not, have more second and holiday homes (relative to urban price hot-spots). This seems to confirm that affordability issues, where they arise, are the product of ineffective local demand as suggested by the Council of Mortgage Lenders.

However, the analysis provided by the CML and the data in Table 3.1 refer to the national and the unitary authority level. It is concentrations of second

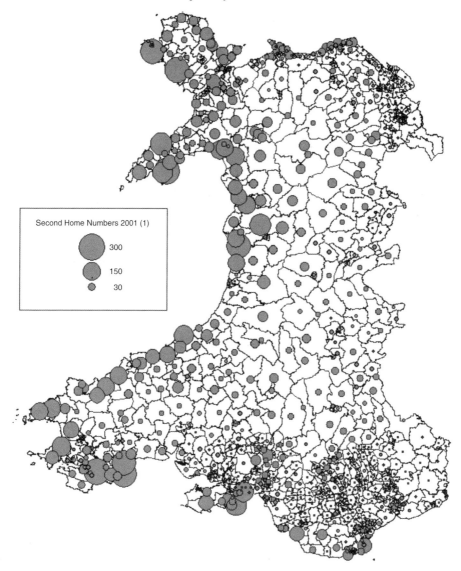

Figure 3.2   Estimate of Absolute Numbers of Second and Holiday Homes in Wales 2001

homes in particular communities that are thought to have most influence on housing prices and on housing affordability. For this reason, *local* patterns of external demand and impacts on house prices – together with related impacts – were examined in separate surveys of Welsh and English planning and housing departments, and of National Park authorities in 2001 and 2002 respectively.

Table 3.1   Average Price of Residential Property Sales Completed (Wales: 2000–2001)

	April-June 2000	April-June 2001	% Change 2000–2001
Anglesey	59471	66842	+12.39
Blaenau Gwent	39572	34865	− 11.89
Bridgend			
Caerphilly	52172	55253	+5.91
Cardiff	83154	88907	+6.92
Carmarthenshire	54273	59215	+9.11
Ceredigion	68778	76480	+11.20
Conwy	64405	72217	+12.13
Denbighshire	58530	64639	+10.44
Flintshire			
Gwynedd	59942	63929	+6.65
Merthyr Tydfil	37676	41052	+8.96
Monmouthshire	92157	106875	+15.97
Neath and Port Talbot	49029	54986	+12.15
Newport	67248	71304	+6.03
Pembrokeshire	63367	69394	+9.51
Powys	72998	77128	+5.66
Rhondda Cynon Taff	47706	47165	− 1.13
Swansea	63987	69250	+8.23
Torfaen	58456	56458	− 3.42
Vale of Glamorgan	85788	86823	+1.21
Wrexham	60433	70165	+16.10
(England and Wales)	105924	117398	+10.83
ALL WALES	**64767**	**68963**	**+6.48**

Source: Land Registry.

Two thirds of respondents believed that within their local areas, external housing demand pressures – as opposed to *just* second homes – have a significant or very significant bearing on house prices (see Table 3.2). However, respondents noted that it is difficult if not impossible to separate the effects of second home purchasing from retirement or commuting pressures, which may dominate in some areas.

Table 3.2   Significance of External Housing Demand – Wales (2001) and England (2002)

Officer Rating	Wales (n) %	England (n) %
Very significant	(6) 24.0	(44) 37.6
Significant	(10) 40.0	(60) 51.3
Minor	(5) 20.0	(13) 11.1
Not at all significant	(4) 16.0	(0) 0.0
Total	(25) 100.0	(117) 100.0

Source: Tewdwr Jones *et al* (2002), p. 31 and Gallent *et al* (2002), p. 31.

Table 3.3 The Effects of Strong External Demand Pressure – Wales (2001) and England (2002)

Impact	Wales (n) %	England (n) %
House prices have risen in particular places	(18) 75.0	(68) 57.6
New housing is no longer affordable for local people	(14) 56.0	(85) 72.0
House prices have risen across the authority area	(12) 48.0	(86) 72.9
Old/existing housing is no longer affordable for local people	(12) 48.0	(71) 61.2
Local people find it difficult to rent property	(5) 20.0	(51) 43.2
Local people are leaving the area	(5) 20.0	(46) 39.0
Other effects	(3) 12.0	n/a
Local people are unable to return to the area	(1) 4.0	(49) 41.5

Source: Tewdwr Jones *et al* (2002), p. 32 and Gallent *et al* (2002), p. 32.

In the light of this 'significant' and 'very significant' reported demand, officers were asked about the effects of pressure on the housing market, including impacts on house prices generally and the affordability of new and existing homes. Responses are presented in Table 3.3. In the Wales study, the key findings emerging from the survey of local authorities (planning departments) and National Park Authorities were that:

- House prices have risen in particular 'hot spots' within the unitary authorities;
- Fewer, but still almost half of the respondents (48 per cent), suggest that house prices have risen across their authority as a direct result of external housing demand pressure;
- 56 per cent and 48 per cent suggest that *new housing* and *existing housing* respectively is no longer affordable, in some instances, for purchase by local people.

The responses from England suggest a more generalised pressure on house prices as a result of external demand (72.9 per cent as against 48 per cent in Wales) and that house prices in England act as more of a barrier to people returning to their home village (41.5 per cent as against 4 per cent in Wales – although note small sample size). This final difference may be at least partly explained by the fact that housing in Wales is, on average, only 66 per cent of the cost of housing in England and that many rural areas in England (including the Lake District, Cornwall, and the Home Counties) have experienced unprecedented house price rises in recent years.

The data presented in Table 3.3 are of course averages: they conceal the range of responses from individual authorities. Whilst only '4 per cent' of Welsh authorities (1) reported that local people find it difficult to return to the area in later life – having left when they were younger – this was a critical concern for one Welsh authority which was keen to draw attention to the 'barrier erected by external housing demand pressure'. Market concerns – including concerns over second homes – are frequently highly localised. Some authorities may report 'second home pressure' when what they really mean is that one or two local villages have high concentrations of second homes whilst the remainder of the authority has extremely few second homes. These local patterns are bound to be hidden in any national analysis. For this reason, Chapter 4 turns to look at local situations examined through a series of case studies that accompanied this survey analysis.

But once again, it is extremely difficult to make general statements about the effects of second homes – from either a purely economic or a socio-economic perspective – without reference to local economic and market conditions. In some instances, second homes and other forms of housing pressure can easily be accommodated; elsewhere, their impact on housing affordability and access may be more immediate. One generalisation that can be made, however, is that external pressures tend to concentrate in particular types of settlement. This point is made in Table 3.4 (survey responses) and again in Figure 3.2, which depicts the pattern of second home ownership in Wales in 2001.

In both England and Wales, external housing pressures tend to concentrate in smaller and more 'attractive' villages, and in coastal locations. The coastal phenomena is perhaps even more important in Wales (Figure 3.2) than it is in England, and nowhere was the localised nature of the pressure more evident than on the Lleyn peninsular in North Wales. Here housing and planning officers reported that while housing was not affordable for local people in some coastal villages, inland there was the additional pressure from local people and politicians not to build any more social housing. Local councillors believed that in the absence of local demand any increase in supply (of low-cost homes) would draw in non-locals and further erode the number of Welsh speakers in the area. However, the local nature of the phenomenon, and the presence of other pressures on housing – including the national market and other forms of in-migration – does not deter some observers from claiming that all increases in rural house prices (particularly in Wales) and the number of homelessness cases accepted by local authorities are directly attributable to second home purchases and the influx of permanent English residents (Pilkington, 1990, p.19). This is one of the 'myths' that we return to in Chapter 10.

Table 3.4   Patterns of Demand Concentration – Wales (2001) and England (2002)

Pattern	Wales (n) %	England (n) %
Small villages	(14) 58.3	(96) 80.1
Coastal settlements	(11) 45.8	(30) 25.2
Open countryside	(6) 25.0	(60) 50.4
Larger towns/settlements	(5) 20.8	(74) 62.2
Specific communities	(4) 16.7	n/a
Small towns	(3) 12.5	n/a

Source: Tewdwr Jones *et al* (2002), p. 32 and Gallent *et al* (2002), p. 31.

Housing – (c) Initial Acquisition

Compared to the issue of house price inflation and direct competition between locals and second home seekers, other economic impacts may appear far less controversial. However, the balance of costs and benefits associated with a range of other housing-economy factors have also been examined and debated. Firstly, many of the studies undertaken in the 1970s and 1980s have considered the local effect of the initial acquisition of second homes (Dart, 1977; SWEPC, 1975; Pyne, 1973; Shucksmith, 1983; Jenkin, 1985). Jenkin (1985), for example, notes that the acquisition of properties by outsiders may inject investment into the local economy by:

- Generating work for local solicitors, estate agents and surveyors. Indeed, recent State of the Countryside Reports from the Countryside Agency in England (2001; 2002; 2003) have drawn attention to the growth in such 'service sector activities' in some rural areas, associated with a buoyant property market;
- Generating a direct profit for the vendor which may then be re-invested in the local area through further home purchasing; or
- Causing inflation in potential local property values, allowing home-owners to borrow against equity and invest in home improvements, resulting in additional work for local contractors and a growth in DIY trade, creating new job opportunities locally.

However, Jenkin (1985, p.14) adds that these economic benefits are dependent on money accrued being reinvested locally (producing the multiplier effect noted above). On this issue, an earlier study by the South West Economic Planning Council (SWEPC, 1975) argued that in terms of local income, 'expenditure on the purchase of second homes will usually be insignificant' (SWEPC, 1975, p.18) as profits will tend to accrue to just one person or household. On the one hand, this may mean that profits are generated only for the vendor and a question mark will inevitably remain over exactly how this money may be re-invested. On the other hand, a more serious problem may be the tendency amongst some second home buyers to use their own solicitors for the transaction, which will mean that money is retained in their home area. Similarly, many properties are advertised through urban estate agents, especially when vendors are trying to tap into the second home or retirement market. This means that agents' fees are not retained locally and that local buyers may not even know that a local property is up for sale. In the worst case scenario, it is possible that the property being sold is already a second home, that the vendor lives outside the area, and that the property will be sold to another second home buyer; in this scenario, an autonomous sub-market is created with conveyance and agents' fees changing hands outside the local area (Pyne, 1973, p.21). In 1972, the SWEPC estimated that £1.6 million (1972 prices) was spent each year on purchasing second homes in the South West of England and half of this regional total was spent in Cornwall (SWEPC, 1975, p.18).

The costs and fees associated with initial acquisition may bring some economic benefits to particular localities, especially if second home purchasers generate fresh demand in hitherto stagnant parts of the property market or stimulate new construction or contracting activity (Pyne, 1973, p.21). In contrast, acquisition may have an adverse effect on the property market, reducing the availability of rented housing, as local owners decide that selling rather than renting out property is a sounder financial proposition. The reduction in rented rural accommodation, however, certainly owes more to the effect of successive Rent Act legislation since the 1920s and the loss of council homes through the right-to-buy since 1980 (Hetherington, 2000) than the arrival of second homes (Shucksmith, 1983, p.179). In France, Hoggart and Buller (1995) have noted that many vendors were unable to sell their properties before the British buyers arrived; acquisition on the part of Britons and subsequent profits for the French vendors meant that local people could afford to move into new homes or make improvements in their existing dwellings (Hoggart and Buller, 1995, p.189). The net effect of initial acquisition is difficult to judge and quantify but it is clear that benefits or costs in different regions will depend on the types of dwellings purchased as second homes. If mainstream housing is acquired, the benefits for the local vendor may not be shared by other members of the local community.

Housing – (d) Property Speculation

The issue of second home property speculation has received far less attention than other economic aspects of second home growth. Property speculation in the second home market was a growing problem in the early 1970s and was linked to the availability of improvement grants. Business-minded people were able to buy derelict properties which they could renovate using the improvement grants administered by local government. These properties could then be sold-on with substantial profits and the cycle could then be repeated. Clearly, in this situation, there is no benefit for local people unless they are directly involved in the speculation process. However, this practice was brought to an abrupt end in 1974 when the Housing Act of that year introduced measures to make second homes ineligible for improvement grants (Pyne, 1973, p.23; see also Gallent, 1997a). Although second home speculation has not been cited as a particular problem in Britain, it has caused a certain amount of disquiet abroad. In Greece, for example, a Royal Decree in 1967 allowed *Lyomeno* vacation houses to be erected anywhere on land where no 'Master' plan existed. This move was supposed to open up the chance of owning a second home to middle and low income families, accelerating the process of 'social democratisation' in second home use and ownership. What it achieved instead was a huge rush in land speculation led by large firms which subsequently erected more expensive vacation accommodation for households in the upper income brackets (Psychogios, 1980, p.95).

Nevertheless, back in the UK, during periods of strong house price inflation, it is likely that the 'bonus' of owning a leisure asset that is appreciating in value is only likely to increase the attractiveness of owning a second property. This is

Table 3.5   Main Reason for Owning a Second Home in England by Tenure of Main Residence 1998/9

Reason for Second Home	Tenure of Main Residence	
	Owned outright %	Buying with a mortgage %
Holiday home, weekend cottage, pre-retirement home	49	40
It is an investment	39	49
Other	32	48
Working/living away from home	22	46
All households	37	48

Source: DETR survey of English housing 1998/9.

reflected in findings from the Survey of English Housing. Although the majority of respondents reported they owned a second home for holiday or pre-retirement purposes, a substantial proportion (39 per cent) also viewed the second home as an investment. The data presented in Table 3.5 relate to second homes located in both urban and rural areas; arguably there are more speculators in the urban second home market (for example buying properties in London) than in the rural market.

Housing – (e) General Housing Stock Improvements

The general improvement of properties purchased as second homes supposedly has both a general economic impact and leads to the improvement of the overall quality of the rural housing stock (Hoggart and Buller, 1994a; 1995). Buyers of second homes have tended to be far less concerned with the condition of properties than those looking for main residences; this has made the issue of improvement particularly important. Obviously this has much to do with the initial purchase price and the availability of surplus properties. However, both Jacobs (1972) and Hoggart and Buller (1995) have shown that many second home buyers have a market preference for older properties which they can improve and apply their own tastes and ideas to (Jacobs, 1972, p.10). This point is demonstrated by Jacobs. In 1970, the Forestry Commission put 14 surplus properties on the market in Denbighshire, Wales. They received 4,000 replies (using a closed bid system) and 13 of the properties were bought immediately; the only one not selling straight away was *not* in need of repair. Before 1974, the benefits accruing from the improvement of properties was confused by the use (often considerable) of local authority improvement grants on the part of second home owners. Jacobs (1972) showed that second home owners represented 6 per cent of the property owners in Denbighshire but claimed 10 per cent of the grant expenditure. He conceded that this direct comparison was not necessarily fair as many of these second homes had some of the lowest rateable values in the county and were in serious need of repair.

However, Jacobs pointed out that 'second home owners are 1.7 times more likely to apply for improvement grants than people who are permanently resident in the county' (Jacobs, 1972, p.23). Pyne (1973) showed that 70 per cent of second homes purchased in Caernarvonshire were old and in need of repair; when grants were available, the cost of these repairs was partially incurred by local government, but it was estimated that these costs were recouped within four years by increases in rateable values (Pyne, 1973, p.24). Once grant availability was restricted, more studies tended to point at the 'economic and environmental benefit for local economies' generated by improvement (Jenkin, 1985, p.16). Shucksmith (1983) argued that home improvements result in greater rateable values and therefore extra revenue for local authorities (Shucksmith, 1983, p.180), a finding supported by the earlier work of Pyne. The SWEPC estimated that £325,000 (at 1972 prices) was being spent annually on the improvement of second homes in the south-west region (above improvement grant expenditure) (SWEPC, 1975, p.18).

Home improvements often generate employment for local builders (Shucksmith, 1983, p.179), but on the down side, it might be argued that local builders are in fact being diverted from the task of building new housing for local people. However, this argument is a fairly weak one; it is unlikely that builders would be prevented from undertaking major construction contracts because they were being kept busy re-tiling roofs or laying patios. On the other hand, concern over the use of building resources on second homes could grow if the number of purpose-built dwellings increases substantially (Downing and Dower, 1973, p.28). There has been very little empirical work on the extent of second home improvements undertaken by owners; one notable exception however, is the work of Jacobs (1972). Jacobs' study of second homes in Denbighshire showed that owners go to a 'great deal of time and effort to improve their property' and only 13 per cent had carried out no repairs at all (Jacobs, 1972, p.21). The sums of money spent on repairs were considerable, with half of the owners studied by Jacobs having spent in excess of £200 (at 1972 prices). Eleven per cent had spent more that £1,500 (Jacobs, 1972, p.22) and in aggregate, it was estimated that £314,096 had been spent on repairs across Denbighshire between 1965 and 1972, with many local builders benefiting from improvement work. These prior studies show that there is clear potential for the rural economy to benefit from improvement expenditure with the creation of employment in the construction industry. However, these studies are now somewhat dated and refer to a phase in second home growth when the supply of surplus rural dwellings (in need of substantial repair) in many areas was able to accommodate second home demand. This situation has now changed in many areas and the types of properties used as second homes are now either unlikely to require substantial improvement work (because they are drawn from mainstream housing) or are new-built. For example, a study of the occupancy of new housing in the Pembrokeshire Coast National Park in 2002 revealed that more than a quarter of new houses were being used as second homes. Depending on the mainstream housing circumstances in the local area, new-built second homes may represent either an unwarranted drain on local construction resources or a welcome source of additional building contracts. In the case of Pembrokeshire, the use of new homes by weekend visitors is viewed as extremely problematic given a general shortage of new housing to meet local requirements (see Chapters 7 and 8).

Broader Rural Economies

The dramatic shift in the economic base of many rural areas over the last fifty years was clearly and dramatically illustrated by the British 'Foot and Mouth' crisis of 2000 and 2001. The initial government response was to focus on cushioning the impact of the crisis on farming, primarily by compensating beef producers. However, the closure of large tracts of countryside to visitors quickly revealed that it was not only agriculture that was being critically affected, but also other businesses and the tourist trade (Lowe and Ward, 2002). Although tourism is often dismissed as a low-wage, poor job security industry (see for example, Hansard, 1997), it provides a significant source of income in many rural areas. Second homes are part of the wider tourism industry in the countryside and therefore it is necessary to consider how they may contribute to general tourist expenditure, and how they may contribute other forms of revenue to local economies.

Rural Economies – (a) General Expenditure

General expenditure by second home users (on local goods and services) is a subject of much speculation and some empirical analysis. That owners bring additional revenue into the local economy during the tourist season (and at other specific times throughout the year) is a key argument in the case for the defence of second homes. Clearly, the growth in second home ownership provides an opportunity for keeping domestic holiday expenditure within the UK. At the local level, second homes provide a flow of money into the importing region, supporting the rural economy. Once an owner has acquired a second home, he/she (or friends and relatives) will visit the same area year after year without the need for any words of encouragement from a tourist office (Dower, 1977, p.157). Indeed, Downing and Dower have argued that the annual influx of second home owners into importing regions represents a flow of permanence which is not characteristic of any other form of tourism (Downing and Dower, 1973, p.29). Opponents, however, contend that the general revenue contribution is slight. The most comprehensive – but now very dated – study of this particular economic impact was undertaken by the South West Economic Planning Council in 1975. The general expenditure contribution in the importing region is a function of second home use (that is, the average annual length of time that a second home is occupied) and whether visits are of a long or short duration (that is, short being for a weekend, whilst longer visits might be in excess of a week). During short visits, consumables might well be purchased in the exporting region; however, with longer stays in the second home, it will become increasingly likely that consumable goods will be purchased locally. Jacobs (1972) found that on shorter breaks in Denbighshire, there was some evidence of self-sufficiency, but local expenditure on consumables (for example, milk, bread, groceries, meat and vegetables) increased on longer stays (Jacobs, 1972, p.26). The SWEPC study found that 32 per cent of owners only used their homes during the summer months (SWEPC, 1975, p.14) and that on average, 'the majority of second homes in the south-west are occupied for between a quarter and a third of the year'. The total amount of usage comprised visits by the owner and his immediate family, occasional loans to friends and relatives and in some areas, informal lettings on short tenancies to holiday makers during the height of the tourist season (SWEPC, 1975, p.16). In Denbighshire, Jacobs was able to demonstrate that the typical owner spends sixteen weekends a year in his second home and that many second homes were occupied during nearly every weekend during the summer months. In addition, 57 per cent of owners in Denbighshire lent their cottages to other people, giving an average of 17.6 weekends of use per annum; longer visits accounted for 7.5 weeks a year and therefore the use of second homes appeared to be intensive (Jacobs, 1972, p.19–20). It is likely that similar patterns of usage occur today, with second homes being used for a mix of shorter and longer stays. Logic suggests that longer stays will involve greater local spending, whereas shorter stays will involve less, with visitors bringing their own provisions for an overnight or weekend visit to their second home.

Recurring general expenditure includes the cost of 'food' items, 'non-food' items (such as petrol or gas) and 'annual costs' (electricity and gas). The SWEPC in the 1970s found that £7 million was spent in the region annually on these recurring items (£3 million of which was spent in Cornwall alone). However, some owners already lived in the region whilst some consumables may have been purchased elsewhere. Allowing for a multiplier effect (using a 1.2 figure suggested by Lewes (1970)), the SWEPC estimated that second homes generated approximately £5.1 million of additional revenue for the south-west's economy each year (this figure included expenditure on improvements and initial purchase and represented less than 0.25 per cent of the region's income). The inevitable conclusion from this analysis was that the contribution of second homes to the *regional* economy was negligible. However, it was recognised that Cornwall took a disproportionately large slice of this additional income and that the *local* economic effect of second homes could be significant and should not, therefore, be discounted (SWEPC, 1975, p.21). In a study of Denbighshire a planning officer calculated that 6 second homes produced the equivalent of one full time job in the locality (Clout, 1972). Meanwhile, in Caernarvonshire, Pyne showed that second home owners spent, on average, 83 days in the county each year and during this period, spent £1.2 million on food and non-food items (Pyne, 1973, p.25). The total expenditure in the county each year totalled some £2.8 million (including initial purchases and rates payments) and a study by the University College of North Wales in Bangor (Archer, 1973) showed that this level of recurring expenditure was sustaining as many as 990 jobs and providing a reliable contribution to the local economy. In this particular analysis, Pyne argued that financial (and perhaps environmental) benefits from the second home phenomenon were visibly outweighing the costs although the economic up-side must be seen in the context of a significant socio-cultural down-side (Pyne,

1973, p.31). The prior studies tend to concede that the growth in second home ownership does have an economic benefit in importing regions and a significant element of this benefit relates to use and recurring general expenditure. However, it is also clear that the local impact is often far more important proportionally than the part owners play in the regional or national economy. Again, although these studies are now somewhat dated – and have not been updated through more recent analysis (work for the Welsh National Assembly (2001) and the Countryside Agency (2002) did not look at second home expenditure) – they demonstrate that second home use does generate income for many rural economies, and given the concentration of second homes in some areas, this may be significant in particular places.

On balance however, even at the local level, the economic contribution of temporary residents must be set against the potential loss of contribution from full-time residents. If a dwelling changes use (from first to second home) and a local person is displaced, as might be the case in some areas where the demand for second homes is focused on mainstream housing, will the contribution of the second home owner be greater than the potential contribution of the displaced local? This point is raised by Shucksmith (1983) who argues that calculations of economic contribution 'fail to consider the alternative use of the housing and any associated expenditure thus foregone' (Shucksmith, 1983, p.180). He adds that in the Lake District, for instance, 'it may be that a second home owner has displaced a potential permanent resident who would surely have spent more than £480 (1972 prices) in the year' (Shucksmith, 1983, p.180). Again, the type of housing used as second homes in a specific area is a crucial issue; where surplus housing is brought into second home use, no displacement of the local population occurs and therefore, economic contribution need only be set against economic loss (of the type described by Shucksmith) where there is evidence of cross-competition for housing and subsequent displacement. At the regional level, different areas and communities will vary in their experience of the second home phenomenon in this respect, as the balance of effective and non-effective housing stock is dependent on an array of factors, including the past history of economic decline and dwelling abandonment, private and public sector new-build and public sector sales policies.

In terms of economic impact, the potential adverse effect that second homes have on some rural communities means that it is extremely difficult to incorporate second homes into classical models of domestic tourism expenditure. Numerous commentators have pointed out that recurrent expenditure by second home owners in the importing regions is extremely difficult to quantify; the effect of differing use patterns, self-sufficiency, potential loss of hotel revenue and the displacement of permanent residents (with the loss of their economic contribution) all vary between second home regions and between different local communities. However, analysis by the University College of North Wales in Bangor (Jacobs, 1972, p.50) appeared to offer strong evidence that localised economic impacts across rural Wales was generating £4.2 million annually for the Welsh economy as a whole and sustaining 1500 jobs. Similar analyses across Wales (see Pyne, 1973) led Jacobs to conclude that 'second home ownership brings large financial benefits to the rural areas' (Jacobs, 1972, p.50). The economic benefits in Denbighshire were largely welcomed because of an observed lack of direct competition for mainstream housing between local and newcomers. Jacobs noted that 'fact and local opinion combine to suggest that local families and second home owners do not compete in the same housing market. They seek different qualities from their housing to match their different purposes' (Jacobs, 1972, p.50). It is clear from these older studies that second home growth brings economic gains in some areas which are normally characterised by the presence of second homes outside the effective housing stock. Measures to maximise the economic contribution from second homes might seek to divert attention from mainstream housing; a move which would bring positive economic and socio-cultural benefits. The separation of first and second home markets (if possible) would also allow for the accurate modelling and quantification of their economic impact.

Rural Economies – (b) Council Tax Contribution

In most of the prior second home studies, the economic contribution from rates (or council tax today) is often studied as a separate economic component and not aggregated with general recurrent expenditure. This is because rateable income and Council Tax is more directly linked to the sustainability of local services and the viability of rural communities. In the past, it was generally recognised that rates formed a significant part of the overall economic contribution of second home owners and two views on the importance of rates emerged. First, rateable income for the local authority helps sustain local services particularly as absent ratepayers (that is, the second home owners) place little strain on these services for much of the year. Second, the opposing view is that although these ratepayers contribute to the running costs of certain services (especially education), their displacement of the permanent population results in only residual service demand for much of the year and a subsequent decrease in supply. If services are not used, then the local authority will not provide them because regular *use* rather than rates provides by far the greater part of service support income. The argument that the payment of rates (and increases in rateable values through the improvement of poor-quality dwellings) on the part of second home owners benefits the full-time local population has been used by Shucksmith (1983), Tuck (1973) and Bollom (1978). Shucksmith argues that because second home owners make little use of services compared to their rates contribution, they are in fact 'subsidising' local use of services such as schools (Shucksmith, 1983, p.180), but he concedes that the irony is that these same services may be withdrawn because of the same under-use which is in fact partially funding them. Other observers (Jenkin, 1985; Dart, 1977) also noted that these rates must be used to cover the costs of new infrastructure (particularly where new-built second homes are concerned) and it may be some time before the local population experiences the benefits of increased local authority revenue. It is also clear that whilst the payment of rates (or Council Tax) may outweigh the *current* use of services, the second home owner:

[...] may, of course, make greater claims on those services if he later uses the property as a retirement home: some local authorities have expressed concern about the isolated nature of many second homes for this reason (Downing and Dower, 1973, p.31).

There is the potential in some areas for past rates contributions to seem meagre in the context of over-use of social services on the part of retirement migrants. However, it must be remembered that the second home phenomenon has not been exclusively responsible for the increasing numbers of elderly people living in the countryside. In fact, Davies and O'Farrell (1981) have pointed out that a greater appreciation of the difficulties associated with rural living (on the part of second home owners) may in fact discourage this group from retiring to the countryside. It could be argued that those people without this same experience and who are 'taken in' by the myths of the rural idyll as retirement approaches are more likely to settle in distant rural areas (perhaps in areas where they have spent one or two summer vacations in the past) and subsequently put pressure on already stretched rural services. Anecdotal evidence from estate agents and housing officers in rural areas suggests that, in fact, rural retirement sometimes moves through two phases. Early retirees may move to more remote rural locations but in a later, second phase, will move to market towns where there is easier access to services, especially primary health care (Tewdwr-Jones *et al*, 2002).

Again, the economic impacts associated with rates or Council Tax will differ between local areas. Where second homes are predominantly new-built or conversions from surplus housing stock then there is a strong case for suggesting that second home owners contribute a 'hidden subsidy' to permanent residents through local authority rates or Council Tax (if the argument is up-dated). In Denbighshire for example, Jacobs was able to argue that 'the increased demand for public services is slight and the county and the district benefit substantially from the presence of the second home owners' (Jacobs, 1972, p.49). In contrast, where demand for second homes is accommodated in the mainstream housing stock, it can be argued that there is no revenue advantage; Council Tax payments are simply replacing those that would have been paid by permanent residents and this displacement will mean that underused services are no longer offered.

Debates over Council Tax discounts to second home owners have captured the attention of the media in recent years. Until April 2004,[1] the owners of second homes in England were eligible for a 50 per cent discount on their Council Tax bills; after April 2004, local authorities were given the discretion to charge up to 90 per cent of the full rate; the logic for keeping the 10 per cent differential being that it offers a means of identifying numbers of second homes (an otherwise difficult piece of data to source in the UK). The debate surrounding Council Tax since the government's consultation on the issue in 2001 (DETR, 2001) has focused not on the contribution that second home buyers make by paying Council Tax, but on the loss in terms of local revenue that the discount represents. It is assumed that second homes are replacing or displacing full time residents and that the discount constitutes a clear reduction in the money that local authorities have to spend on village services. Various calculations of this loss in rural areas have been made, the most recent for the Countryside Agency in 2002 (Gallent *et al* 2002, pp. 42–44). This analysis suggested that the typical rural authority in England has between 501 and 1000 second homes (with a mean of just over 800 units; ibid. p. 43). The average loss of Council Tax revenue because of the 50 per cent discount (estimated by housing department) was a little over £375,000. These averages were extrapolated to give a crude global figure for England's 143 rural authorities. The overall loss of revenue to these authorities is in the region of £53 million per annum. In terms of 'economic impact', this has today become the headline message. Broader debates over second home spending and revenue from purchasing have been relegated behind the Council Tax issue; there is certainly no new analysis of what types of properties are used as second homes, and whether such properties would have in fact have been bought, renovated and used by permanent residents. In fact, the debate today has become one of simple fairness, with a prevailing belief that the discount on second homes is inequitable. However, because Council Tax is designed to reflect service usage, it might be argued that scrapping the discount (as happened in Wales in 1998 and England in 2004, albeit with a small discount being retained) means that the link between services used and tax paid has been severed. The counter-argument is that second homes put a strain on services through under-use, and should be costed – or penalised – accordingly. However, a survey of planning and housing officers in England – undertaken as part of the Countryside Agency study (2002) – revealed that very few authorities (7.4 per cent) believed that additional revenue from Council Tax on second homes would be sufficient to support failing local services, suggesting that it is not the concentration of second homes that places significant pressure on rural services. That said, half of respondents supported the 'ring-fencing' of additional revenue for rural housing provision (ibid, p.42), though government has shied away from such a caveat in new legislation.

Overall Economic Impact

It is extremely difficult to provide an overall statement on the economic impact of rural second homes. The economic contribution of the rural tourist industry generally is difficult to assess given the lack of empirical evidence (Hoggart, *et al*, 1995, p.179). In the past, much of the work undertaken by local authorities has tended to conclude that second homes offer significant local economic benefits. One of the most positive contributions to this debate was offered by Jacobs (1972) more than thirty years ago, who argued that 'all these [economic] benefits accrue without imposing any extra burden upon the local housing market' (Jacobs, 1972, p.50). However, this view was based on a number of highly subjective judgements regarding the economic costs and benefits of second homes which appear to defy rigid econometric analysis (Thompson, 1977, p.10). It appears that a key element in the local economic impact of second homes is the degree of separation between the first and second home property markets. Where second home demand is accommodated outside the effective local housing stock, the adverse impact of house price inflation will be largely avoided whilst money spent on general improvement may inject life into the local construction industry (the same may be true of purpose-built second homes). Likewise, the benefits of recurrent general expenditure or increases in Council Tax revenue will not be off-set by a reduction in demand, and the subsequent closure, of local services. In contrast, where there is no separation between the first and second home markets, competition between locals and outsiders for mainstream housing (the 'effective' stock) can generate inflationary pressure on property values. The subsequent displacement of former local residents will mean decreased demand for services despite the fact that local Council Tax revenue is now (after April 2004) sustained. On top of this, fewer of these properties will be in need of renovation work and therefore there may be little additional work for local builders. Clearly, the economic impact of second homes needs to be seen in the local context and is heavily dependant on the types of dwellings converted into second home use. The transitional phase in second home growth mentioned Chapter 1 (following the saturation of the non-effective housing stock and preceding policies to divert pressure from mainstream housing) is perhaps the most problematic in terms of economic and social impact. The identification of those areas at most risk requires careful analysis of local housing markets; without such analysis, it is impossible to draw any objective conclusions concerning the relative economic benefits of second homes.

Part 3: Environmental Impacts

Very little research has been undertaken on the environmental impacts of second homes, though past concern has focused on the siting of holiday home villages or static caravan parks. There is also a longstanding and more generic concern for the quality of house building in rural areas and development in the open countryside. Recent versions of Planning Policy Guidance on Housing (PPG3; 1992 and 2000) have emphasised the need for higher design standards in house building, and for a greater concern for the sustainability of new development, by encouraging reductions in car dependency and siting developments closer to essential services. But these generic concerns may have little direct bearing on the 'environmental impacts' of second homes drawn from existing housing stock. That said, two key concerns can be highlighted:

- The resource implications of second home usage, including travel patterns and the broader environmental pressures endured by second home 'hot spot' areas;
- The pressure for new build housing in second home areas, driven (a) directly by external demand for new homes and (b) indirectly, by the pressure for new housing to meet local needs that is created when existing dwellings are used as second homes.

Resource Usage Implications

The first of these includes the impact of growth in the leisure industry generally, involving increasing pressure on environmentally sensitive areas (particularly National Parks and Areas of Outstanding Natural Beauty) and traffic congestion associated with an increasing numbers of people travelling into established second home areas annually. Thirty years ago, Downing and Dower (1973) observed that two-home households use more building resources, more road space and are generally higher level consumers; this means that 'the prospect of widespread ownership of second homes does raise issues of resource consumption and environmental impact which are currently growing in the world's mind' (Downing and Dower, 1973, p.28). As we noted at the beginning of this chapter, second homes are a luxury good and might be viewed as inherently unsustainable in environmental terms. However, if we take a practical view, that people with surplus income will spend that income in one way or another, then it could be argued that discouraging second home ownership *in Britain* could lead to alternatives that are even more detrimental to the environment. Travel by air has become progressively cheaper and this has led to an increase in the popularity of buying homes abroad, where better weather and an alternative culture can heighten the appeal of second home ownership. Television programme makers are exploiting the attraction of owning property abroad with programmes such as 'A Place in the Sun' offering viewers a '[...] show that helps buyers find their dream home in an exotic overseas location' (Channel 4, see web reference). Anecdotal evidence currently suggests that the overseas market is strong (FDP Savills, 2004), and that in some cases buyers use the UK market to 'test out' second home ownership before buying abroad (Tewdwr-Jones *et al*, 2002). Under these circumstances and from a European or global perspective, comparatively local travel to second homes within the UK may be considered to be more sustainable than making regular short-haul trips to the south of France or Spain.

New Development and Building Conversion – (a) Direct Pressure

In the past studies of second homes, the main concerns have been the impact of new development and conversion. Conversion may offer positive environmental benefits as restoration and change of use can lead to the preservation of derelict properties on the verge of being demolished (Dower, 1977, p.156; Hoggart and Buller, 1995). Pyne (1973) argued that renovation contributes to the visual character of the surrounding area and noted that second home owners are often willing to accept advice on how renovations should be undertaken (Pyne, 1973, p.28). Downing and Dower (1973) have noted that preservation justifies renovation particularly where buildings have an historic value (Downing and Dower, 1973, p.32) and have argued that for this reason, public bodies might steer second home seekers to derelict or neglected buildings (perhaps by providing renovation grants) as '[...] such action could well have great value in relation to buildings of recognised historic and architectural interest both in town and countryside, and also to many humbler buildings of vernacular character' (Downing and Dower, 1973, p.37). Newly-built second homes are a different matter, having the same impact on the environment as other forms of new development. In this case, it is the responsibility of local planning departments to minimise environmental impacts. This applies equally to static caravans which require careful siting and stringent regulation, particularly where caravans are to be substituted by permanent chalet development. On the Lleyn peninsular in North Wales, however, Pyne (1973) argued that some new second home development was taking on a 'suburban' rather than a rural character and was having a detrimental effect on the rural landscape (Pyne, 1973, p.28).

It appears from the prior studies that there is a clear divide between that second home development which has the potential to bring environmental benefits and that which may, if not carefully regulated, cause serious and probably irreversible damage. Even carefully regulated new developments (whether as second homes or to house locals 'displaced' by second home ownership within the existing stock – see below) will have considerable resource implications. In simple environmental terms this must be seen as a negative, but again there are other considerations. Second homes can more readily be seen as part of the leisure market and so provide, or substitute for, holiday lets and hotel accommodation which may need to be developed in the absence of second homes. Taking a less austere view of the environmental arguments, the Dart study (1977) claimed that second home development could be either 'neutral or beneficial'; again the benefits accrue from the restoration of derelict properties, but the effect of new-build can invariably be neutral where good planning practices are applied; rich tree cover in Scotland meant that 'there was no need for development [of new built second homes] to be either obtrusive or alien to local character' (Dart, 1977, p.62).

New Development – (b) Indirect Pressure

However, pressure to develop new second homes is less important in many areas than the indirect pressure to provide more low-cost housing as a result of homes – bought by incomers – being 'lost' to the local market. This is certainly the case in Pembrokeshire Coast National Park where there is considerable pressure to reduce building rates but still accommodate local housing needs; the Park Authority argues that this can only be achieved by retaining all new housing for local use, though it also recognises that it will be extremely difficult to keep house building rates low whilst the area remains popular for second home buyers. A recent consultant's report on housing in the Park noted that 'continuing past rates of housing completion would be detrimental to the character of the Park if the houses built are not appropriately designed and sensitively sited'; it was also noted that 'damage to the landscape of the Park would have economic repercussions through a loss of revenue from tourism' (Tewdwr-Jones & Gallent, 2002, p. 6). It is perhaps ironic that second home buyers gravitate to 'unspoilt' areas but by doing so add to the pressure to build more homes, thus changing the character of the area. The new homes that are often proposed in local plans are needed – in some instances – because of second home and retirement pressure, but it is frequently second home owners and retired households who oppose new developments. Indeed, it is often recognised in Regional Planning Guidance that second home demand will increase the need for higher rates of local house building: hence the additional environmental pressures caused indirectly by second homes are often reflected in larger new housing allocations. In Pembrokeshire, the level of demand projected in the local area (that is, in the Park *and* in the County) was seen as a serious environmental threat, and one that was being accentuated by external housing pressures:

> Building for the demand projected by the housing need assessment will cause serious environmental degradation during the life of the Joint Unitary Development Plan. This may lead to substantial depreciation in the value of [the Park's] environmental asset. At a more local level, substantial new house building will impact upon the character of villages and especially those Sustainable Communities [identified as pressure points] where current demand pressure is already high and likely to remain concentrated over the next 15 years (Tewdwr-Jones & Gallent, 2002, p.13)

The role that second home purchasing plays in pushing up demand and the pressure for new build is perhaps the key environmental impact in many areas, and especially those with more 'sensitive' landscapes.

Overall Environmental Impact

Like the economic concerns, the environmental aspect of second home growth is closely linked to the types of dwellings used for this purpose. The trend in recent years has been away from derelict and empty surplus dwellings towards new-build and the use of mainstream housing stock. In the latter case, the direct environmental impact is likely to be neutral, though the indirect impact may be significant as in the case of the Pembrokeshire Coast National Park. In the case of new-build, the impact will range between being neutral and being negative depending on the effectiveness of local planning control and the application of design and siting standards. In France, Hoggart and Buller (1995) have argued that second home acquisitions are having a positive environmental benefit with British buyers 'making significant additions to the rural housing stock of France through the acquisition and renovation of buildings that are unsuitable for human habitation' (Hoggart and Buller, 1995, p.188). However, the rural housing market in France can still accommodate this type of demand in surplus stock; the same is not true in Britain where the outside demand for *effective* housing in some importing areas has generated economic, environmental and social tension. Environmental tensions and impacts have perhaps received less attention in the past, though this is certainly changing today as the second home debate becomes subsumed in wider concerns over house building in the countryside.

Conclusions

Arguably, the strength and persistence of the opposition to UK second homes over the last thirty years is sustained partly by the fact that it is not possible to clearly quantify the extent of the benefits and disadvantages referred to throughout this chapter. In other words, the debate about second homes is one centred on estimating the balance of benefit and detriment, and so it will always be possible to mobilise opposition to second homes by associating them with a range of social and economic consequences, safe in the knowledge that even if the case against them cannot be definitively proven, at least it cannot be entirely repudiated. Given this, and when social divisions are drawn, it appears that a complex housing market – that may include an element of second home purchasing – is often reduced to just two competing groups: working-class, low-income locals and middle-class, high-salaried incomers. In this simplified framework, it is easy to attribute blame for various socio-economic tensions or housing market 'distortions' either on incomers generally, or on second home owners specifically. However, rural housing markets – together with rural communities – are complex entities, often comprising unique configurations and defined by many different interactions. The idea that rural markets comprise a mix of 'housing classes' – each with its own characteristics, demands and aspirations – provides a more helpful framework in which to understanding, and perhaps respond to, socio-economic impacts. Indeed, one of the key myths of second home ownership is that people investing in homes to meet a leisure demand are invariably non-local. Research in both England (Gallent *et al*, 2002) and Wales (Tewdwr-Jones *et al*, 2001) explodes this myth, revealing that many rural people increase their personal wealth and income by investing in and renting out holiday homes. Sections of the rural populace directly benefit from second home ownership.

However, to contend that second homes are not the sole – or even the main – driver of housing difficulties in rural areas is not to entirely dismiss their potential to bring negative impacts. Indeed, economic common sense suggests that there is a potential for second home purchasing to drive an inflation of house prices that may then affect the housing opportunities open to some local people. This 'common sense' perspective has shaped perceptions of a broad second home 'problem' in the UK. However, given that there is a real shortfall in absolute housing supply in parts of the countryside, and that this may undermine the stability of local communities, there is a pressing need to look for ways of enhancing the housing opportunities of local buyers both through further house building and by strengthening rural economies. We look more closely at responding to second home pressures in the third part of this book, and in Chapter 9.

Finally, it was noted above that the environmental consequences of second home demand have perhaps received insufficient attention in recent years. Two key questions may need further attention in future research: firstly, what is the exact environmental cost to rural communities accruing from tourist pressure? And secondly, to what extent does second home demand increase the level of new house building locally as opposed to pushing local people out of villages to adjacent towns (if this does indeed happen in some instances)? Answers to the first question will invariably reference the pressure on rural roads during the summer months and consequent air and water pollution: basic environmental concerns. The second question is in some ways easier to answer: surely for every second home purchased a new home will need to be built? The complicating factor here is that second home demand concentrates in the most attractive villages when great weight is placed in landscape protection: further house-building here will have a far greater environmental cost than say in London, where migration may indeed result in a need for more homes, but where many of these homes can be accommodated on brown field sites (perhaps in the Thames Gateway). In rural areas, a paucity of land recycling opportunities mean that either the environmental cost of new house building may be judged greater, or restrictions on building may lead to a physical displacement of local buyers who are forced to look elsewhere for housing. The social and environmental costs of second homes relate to the fact that the housing stock in small villages is incapable of accommodating local need whilst also absorbing new demand. Something has to give: this means opening up green field land to development (an environmental cost that can be mitigated through high quality development) or displacement (a social cost that only occurs where there is direct cross-competition for homes).

Impacts are invariably locally-specific and are determined by the state of the local economy, by the existence of other pressures affecting services or housing opportunities, by environmental priorities, and by the operation of the planning system. Given this local specificity of potential impacts, generalisations regarding social or economic consequences may be politically expedient, but often not robust. Second homes need to be positioned in the wider context of socio-economic change in the countryside; the effects they might have on communities need to be viewed in an objective and rational framework; and any future debate or policy response needs to be grounded in a robust analysis of local circumstances.

Note

1   Part 6 (Council Tax Provisions) of the Local Government Bill came into force on the 18th November 2003; changes to Council Tax on second homes took effect from the billing year commencing 1st April 2004.

PART 2
SECOND HOMES IN CONTEXT

Chapter 4

England and Wales: Case Studies

Second Homes in Context

The focus of Part 2 of this book is 'second homes in context'; that is located and discussed in the context of the United Kingdom (Chapters 4 and 6) and mainland Europe (Chapters 5 and 6). The material presented in these chapters draws on three main sources: firstly case study work undertaken for the Welsh Assembly Government and Countryside Agency in 2001 and 2002 respectively; secondly a review of past European studies carried out in 1996; and thirdly a review of housing pressure in rural parts of Europe for the Scottish Executive in 2000. We have brought these sources together here in order to offer a more localised analysis of second home 'pressures' and concerns in rural areas. This current chapter looks at local authority and National Park areas in England and Wales; the next chapter presents national overviews for various European countries with some local insights, and Chapter 6 compares British second home pressures to those experienced elsewhere in Europe. The overarching aim is to provide a body of evidence to illustrate some of the points made in Part 1, and also to provide a context in which to discuss policy options for the United Kingdom in Part 3.

England and Wales

This chapter reports on findings emerging from two sets of case studies, the first from Wales (undertaken in 2001) and the second from England (undertaken in 2002). The material presented builds on the literature reviewed in the last chapter, providing examples of housing market change within particular local authorities and specific communities across England and Wales. These two case studies formed part of wider research projects looking at the extent of second home demand in Wales and England, and at the potential role of the planning system in addressing 'second home concerns' in Britain, which has itself been a subject of considerable debate and speculation for several decades (see Chapters 7, 8 and 9). Indeed, several indirect and direct forms of intervention have been suggested including the use of occupancy conditions designed specifically to stop new housing being used as second homes; it is also possible to prevent change of use from primary to secondary residence by making a legal distinction between first and second home use. These options are reviewed at length later in this Book. For the moment, our concern is with the importance of second homes in rural areas, and with the specific case that exists to formulate a policy response. The research findings provide an opportunity to examine the possible impacts of second homes – introduced in the previous chapter – more thoroughly, drawing on the experience of housing and planning professionals working in rural areas; and on the basis of local experience, to formulate appropriate responses (or at least answer the basic question as to whether intervention is in fact justified).

Research Approach

To understand the present role and future possibilities for land use planning in managing second homes it was first necessary to gain a more detailed appreciation of the part that second homes play in local housing markets in particular areas; when and where are second homes a problem in need of particular management? Furthermore, it was considered prudent to draw on professional experience in order to better understand how policy might operate and be implemented by local authorities. The *necessity* and *capacity* to act were key concerns in this research

Again, the case studies referred to throughout this Chapter formed part of two separate research projects, one based in Wales and carried out for the National Assembly Government's Planning Division (Tewdwr-Jones *et al*, 2002) and the other in rural English authorities completed for the Countryside Agency (Gallent *et al*, 2002). Some of the material presented below forms part of the reports produced for the two commissioning bodies. In Wales, data were initially collected through forty-seven telephone interviews: twenty-two with planning officers within the unitary authorities; the same number with housing officers; and three with officers of the National Park Authorities (Snowdonia, the Brecon Beacons and the Pembrokeshire Coast). The next phase comprised a series of face-to-face interviews (twenty-eight in all) in five case study areas: the Brecon Beacons National Park; Ceredigion; Gwynedd (focused on the Lleyn Peninsula); Pembrokeshire Coast National Park; and Powys (focused in the pre-1996 district of Radnorshire). For these 'case studies' local estate agents were also interviewed as a means to better understand market pressures and the sources of external housing demand. The given justifications for each of the five Welsh case studies are set out in Figure 4.1.

The choice of case studies was made at the beginning of the project, in consultation with the Welsh Assembly Government and its appointed Project Steering Group. A number of assumptions were made regarding the characteristics of the five areas. These assumptions drew heavily on past studies and literature and led to a view that this particular choice of areas would adequately reflect the full range of housing pressures affecting rural Wales.

Lleyn Peninsula, Gwynedd
An area with a strong and established second and holiday home base, stretching from the Lleyn Peninsula and into the Snowdonia National Park. Second and holiday homes have become a highly politicised issue in recent years, with the local

authority chastised for over-charging council tax (under the former discount regime), and the Welsh Language Society taking up the case of a proposed 800 unit chalet development at Morfa Bychan. Gwynedd is seen to represent the classic Welsh situation, forming part of the Welsh language heartland, and with communities particularly sensitized to migration and housing demand pressures.

Ceredigion
Here, second homes are mixed in with a wider range of housing concerns, particularly loical people owning a number of properties (as an income-supplement, and as a diversification strategy for some farmers). The local planning authority has been pro-active in piloting different solutions, and has run into its fair share of controversy. Here, we are dealing with another stronghold of the Welsh language (as in Gwynedd), but a weaker tourism base. Ceredigion is used to represent more sporadic second/holiday home concerns away from a National Park honey pot, but where the economy is being diversified and where language issues remain critical.

Pembrokeshire Coast National Park
This is the first of two National Park studies, more remote than the Brecon Beacons, but accessible as a result of the M4 extension. Of particular concern here is the relationship between the coastal fringe (the horse-shoe of the Park itself) and inner Pembrokeshire (the County). The focus is on the tension between Park and Unitary Authority in the face of external housing demand. The demand for properties in this area is expected to derive from urban South East Wales as well as England. Hence, there may be a more domestic second home market in this part of Wales.

Brecon Beacons
The Brecon Beacons (and also Radnorshire) is believed to have a less developed second home market, but is affected by external demand pressures in the form of retirement and commuting. The aim here was to consider the relative importance of different pressures and to explore these in a context which is arguably less culturally and linguistically sensitive.

Radnorshire
This is a borders study: far removed from North Wales, but a more accessible area for midland and south east house purchasers. This is considered a compromise area, containing high areas of landscape amenity but not as pressurised as Snowdonia. The declining use of Welsh is less of an issue in Radnorshire, but that does not mean second and holiday homes are any less important. This is a borders study, with perhaps a more complex market situation, mingling with larger border towns in England, and also attracting in-migrants for economic reasons.

Figure 4.1   Case Study Selection: Wales

The English case study phase comprised thirty-five telephone interviews; fifteen with planning officers within the unitary authorities; sixteen with housing officers; and four with officers of the National Park Authorities. Face to face interviews (thirty-eight in all) were then carried out (again, including estate agents) in ten case study areas; the Cotswolds, Exmoor National Park, the Lake District National Park, the New Forest, Ribble Valley, Restormel, Scilly (Isles of), South Shropshire, Suffolk Coast and the Yorkshire Dales National Park. The selection of English case studies followed a similar line of logic to that followed in Wales, with some areas (for example the Lakes and Exmoor) seen as 'classic' second home destinations, but with other areas (for example Suffolk Coastal) perhaps experiencing a greater mix of pressures. Interviews in both England and Wales were structured around a 'pro forma'. These detailed 'interview schedules' focused on '(i) how the local housing market has changed in recent years, and how particularly communities have fared under changing conditions, (ii) the impacts of these changes on local communities, (iii) the management of these changes through presently available tools and (iv) the need for new approaches and how these might operate locally. This pro forma was used in face-to-face interviews and made available to respondents in advance of arranged interviews' (Gallent *et al*, 2002, p. 96). Schedules were adapted for different types (housing officer, planning officer or estate agent) of interviewees.

Again, the findings presented and reviewed in this chapter are derived largely from the case study material. This is qualitative data drawing on the experience and perceptions of individual professionals. A number of themes were examined in the interviews and these are used here to structure the analysis:

- The nature and mix of local housing demand and pressure, including the importance of second homes within local markets;
- The impact of second home purchasing – relative to other housing pressures on the affordability of local housing;
- Second homes as a component of the tourist industry;
- Additional concerns emerging from the case studies.

However, it is the local differences and variety that is of key concern in this chapter, and which emerge in the presentation of case study material.

Theme 1: The Nature of Housing Demand and Pressure

In 2001/02, the general reported view of the second home market was of a 'steady turnover' in the sale of *existing second homes* to new buyers, but no discernible increase in the proportion of primary residences 'changing use'. This was a general market picture, created through an aggregation of local views. In some villages, however, where there was already a high proportion of second homes – especially in Devon and Cornwall and the English Lake District, and in Pembrokeshire and Gwynedd in Wales – the strength of external demand for local housing was considered problematic, though this was not confined to second home purchasing and instead related to the general increase in the number of households looking to move into these areas.

Estate agents reported that an increasing proportion of interest in rural property came from people 'surfing the web', and who were either targeting specific parts of the country or looking for a bargain outside of London.

However, the use of the internet to seek out potential second homes did not appear to be affecting the overall size of the market; but rather, it was resulting in a more even spread of demand. Those buyers looking for rural property 'by foot' tended to concentrate on specific areas and villages; those using the internet tended to cast their nets more widely. Estate agents in England and Wales were not able to quantify the effect of the internet on the second home market; they simply pointed to the opening up of new – hitherto unexplored – markets in the UK and abroad. Of course, the internet is not the only factor broadening demand; certain areas have over-heated and buyers are attracted to places where property prices remain lower. Similarly, movement abroad may be aided by internet-based search and purchasing services, but it is cheap flights to a greater number of European destinations that actually opens up these markets. Estate agents drew attention to three key characteristics of second home purchasing in the UK:

- Some buyers 'try out' second home ownership by purchasing property in the UK before subsequently buying abroad;
- A considerable proportion of movement in the second home market comprises the buying and selling of existing second homes;
- There is a tendency for many second home buyers to comprise families with children who use these properties as bases for family holidays; younger people without children are less likely to buy second homes, as are older people who are more likely to retire to a rural area than buy a second home.

It is also the case that as the European market opens up and becomes more popular – and available to a wider range of socio-economic groups – the second home market in England and Wales may become more concentrated in particular areas and characterised by higher income groups. This could mean that the domestic second home market becomes more 'elite' with higher earning UK buyers preferring to buy in the Lake District, Wales and the Cotswolds rather than heading for the Spanish 'Costas'. It is already the case that there is a perceived division in tastes and incomes between groups buying on the Spanish and Portuguese coasts and those preferring inland rural property in Spain, the Dordogne and Provence, and in Tuscany. The second home market across Europe is becoming more socially divided. The same division may become a feature of the UK market in the years ahead: if the typical domestic buyer becomes more affluent, then this could reinforce the general class schism in rural areas, between locals and incomers, noted by Emmett (1964; 1968), Pahl (1970) and Cloke and Thrift (1987).

But although many second home buyers are relatively wealthy, their resources are not endless. The strength of the local market (determined by the buying power of local people, together with retiring households and commuters) will affect where people purchase second homes. This point has recently been emphasised by FDP Savill (2004): where there is stiff competition in the local market, second home owners are likely to look elsewhere. This same point was raised by a Brecon-based estate agent:

I've got to say that I don't come across a lot of people who have second homes. Obviously there is a certain percentage. [...] There obviously have been the odd few, but I don't think it is an increasing percentage, because I think we are relatively expensive, because the housing stock is limited because we are a National Park. I think there are cheaper areas: probably West Wales and North Wales; there are cheaper areas there for people to buy second homes there and still have the same benefits of a wonderful coastline, lovely walking country and views and amenities (Estate Agent, Brecon).

Whilst this often means that second home demand is deflected to other cheaper areas, it is sometimes the case that incoming buyers 'work hard' to find bargain properties: often homes that are not sought after by permanent residents. In the case of Brecon (and the surrounding area), examples were given of small properties in need of renovation (and in one case, in a location liable to flooding) that appealed exclusively to the second home market.

But not all demand is concentrated on bargain properties: some second home buyers have the means to compete in rural markets irrespective of the strength of the local market and local house prices. Many buyers are looking specifically for top-end properties, which are often more expensive than their first homes. When this is the case, the purchase of a second home may represent the first step in a lifestyle change. Buyers may be intending to spend almost as much time in their second home as in their first: the purchase might also be a precursor to permanent retirement to the new community.

I'd have thought they are looking for something individual in location, in type, [and] in character. There are a number who would look for something of character, rural, semi-rural location perhaps, maybe with a large garden, a couple of acres, so a small holding type of thing. [...] something a bit special so if it's not a country property it's a town property but it's nearly at the top end of the market that they're looking for (Estate Agent, Brecon).

Purchasers of these top-end properties would not be in direct competition with first time buyers, but would contribute to a cascading down of house price inflation through the market. This process was described in the Cotswolds as a 'stretching of the market': growing families might find it difficult to 'trade up' because bigger properties have been purchased by second home buyers. This means that they stay put, but spend money extending their current home. In the Cotswolds, a rising number of planning applications for home extensions was viewed as evidence of the increasing difficulty people experience in trying to move within the market. This 'bottleneck' has wider implications: local homeowners find it increasingly difficult to trade up and therefore fewer properties are freed up at the bottom end for first-time buyers. However, the real implications of this 'stretching' are difficult to quantify and evidence is anecdotal.

It is also the case that even where there is apparently direct competition – for properties in the same price bracket – between those seeking a second home and first time buyers, there is not necessarily direct competition in terms of location. First time buyers – who are generally younger, newly forming households – are more likely to be driven by the need to secure employment and so tend to favour living in towns:

> You find locals wouldn't want to live in isolated rural places – they want the 'convenient lifestyle' as opposed to the 'retirement-tranquillity lifestyle' (Estate Agent, Ceredigion).

But this is not always the case. There were examples of direct competition between 'local' and second home buyers, with both looking for 'bargain' bottom-end of the market, small, starter properties. The burgeoning buy-to-let market was a significant competitor in this respect, and was referred to in nearly all of the Welsh and English case studies. This market frequently comprised *local* people looking for an investment. It provides rented accommodation for the local market but makes access to owner occupation – often the preferred tenure – harder for younger local people. And where there is a strong holiday market, the returns achievable from holiday letting are likely to be far higher that the returns from renting to young local people. This sometimes means that local renters were only able to occupy properties on a seasonal – that is winter – basis. As noted above, this point was made by officers and estate agents in many of the local case studies, though it appeared to be a particular feature of Ceredigion (West Wales). In this authority area, it was suggested that the 'holiday let' market is more important than the second home market, and is controlled by older, more affluent local people. This is a key barrier to local housing access, and not the purchasing of second homes by more distant buyers.

A strong retirement market was also common feature of the vast majority of the case study areas. In Gwynedd, (North West Wales) one housing officer drew attention to a 'huge increase' in the number of retirees moving into the Meirionnydd coastal belt (that is around communities such as Porthmadoc, Llanbedr, Harlech and Barmouth). There was a clear concern for the way in which retirement migration can skew a community, change its needs, and undermine its vibrancy and long term viability. Retirement and the 'flight' from towns and cities has been viewed as a key driver of social change in rural areas, and is underpinned by a belief that the countryside is relatively safe, clean, healthy and crime-free compared to many larger towns and cities. The tendency for sections of the urban population to move progressively away from urban areas (that is, through the process of counter-urbanisation) has been charted by Champion *et al* (1988). More recently, Champion (2000) has argued that the movement of people from urban to more rural areas is driven by a 'trilogy' of factors, categorised under the headings 'flight', 'quest' and 'overflow'. 'Flight' suggests a one-way movement away from cities by people – including those retiring – pushed by negative urban drivers. 'Quest' is the process that leads some people to move away from urban areas in search of alternative lifestyles (for example those retiring or 'down shifters') with people seeking a different lifestyle or particular residential qualities on which they place a personal premium (especially later in life). The final process in Champion's trilogy is that of 'overflow': here, a lack of room in cities results in a natural drift away from urban areas. This third process also sits squarely with the concept of a 'cascade', with population gravitating firstly to satellite towns (in mid-life) and eventually to locations further afield (on retirement). This process is depicted in Figure 4.2.

Despite a promotion of urban living since the late 1990s – marked by a call for an 'urban renaissance' (Urban Task Force, 1999) – there is little evidence to suggest that the English (or indeed the Welsh) have turned their backs on the desire for a home in the country. Access to good schools – for those with cars – together with the perception of greater safety and a higher quality of life continue to draw people away from cities. But the weakness of many rural economies means that those moving to the countryside – and not for retirement – have to retain their economic ties with urban areas. In recent years the opportunity to 'telework' has allowed some sections of the population to base themselves in rural areas during much of the working week, commuting to a city office perhaps only a few times each month. This process sometimes obscures the division between first and second homes with an increasing number of people having first homes in the country and retaining smaller *pied-à-terre* in the city. The Survey of English Housing (DTLR, 2001b), the 2001 UK Census and FDP Savill (2004) confirm a current concentration of second homes in London, and especially in the Boroughs of Kensington and Chelsea, Westminster, and the City of London.

Clarke (2000) notes that 'teleworking' is not strictly defined but often involves the use of ICT, allowing people to work from home for at least part of the week. Within the case studies, commuters and teleworkers were often viewed as a single group, though Clarke has suggested that teleworkers are sometimes regarded as being similar to second home owners, and represent another component of gentrification in the countryside. Few respondents in the case studies believed that teleworking was a positive force in the local economy: ICT provides a connection to urban areas, and ties villages into a wider urban economy, but it does not create local jobs or promote local economic vibrancy.

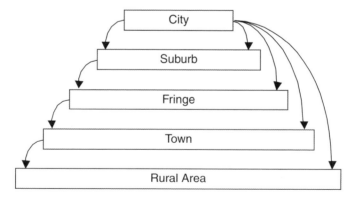

Figure 4.2   The Counter-Urbanisation Cascade
Source: Champion, 2000, p. 14.

This is largely because it is newcomers who have the skills to telework; local people tend to be locked out of this activity – teleworking is imported and is hardly ever 'indigenous'.

Finally, the traditional daily commuter was also seen as important in many of the local housing markets examined, especially where there was good road and rail links to major centres of employment. This was particularly the case in some of the English studies, including the Cotswolds and the Ribble Valley. In Wales, slower road networks tended to act as a barrier to longer distance commuting, though many smaller villages and hamlets were affected by 'local commuting' with people moving out of nearby towns and setting up home in more picturesque rural settings. This process had a clear impact on these local markets. But elsewhere, better transport links had led to increased market activity. For example, the recent upgrading of parts of the A470 between Brecon and Cardiff had resulted in an increase in commuting pressure; with this feature of the market seen as being at least as important as retirement and second home buying. House price fluctuations in many parts of Wales are a reflection of internal commuting patterns as people spread out from market hot-spots in search of rural bargains. In many parts of England, a more extensive motorway and rail network (Wales has no direct rail or motorway connections between the North and the South and has only one major motorway – the M4 – running along the south coast), can bring commuting pressure to geographically more remote rural areas. This is certainly the case in the Cotswolds:

> A two bedroom cottage in need of modernisation in the village of Bleddington – half a mile from Kingham railway station (80 minutes to Paddington) – fetched £225,000 – this was for a wreck (Housing Officer, Cotswold District).

The discussion above reveals that in all case study areas, market activity comprised a mix of local movement, second home purchasing, buy-to-let investment, retirement, teleworking and commuting. Second homes are just one component of housing pressure. Respondents in a wider survey of unitary authorities in Wales and rural districts in England were asked to rate the relative importance of different 'external pressures' in their local area; findings are presented in Table 4.1. This analysis yielded some fairly surprising results, though it is important to note – given the likely differences between local situations – that the responses have been aggregated to provide general overviews for Wales and England. In both of the countries, retirement (48.0 per cent and 66.3 per cent respectively) and commuting (58.3 per cent and 76.9 per cent) were perceived – by housing and planning professionals – to be the most important components of external housing demand pressure (the figures above have been calculated by adding together 'very significant' and 'significant' ratings). The greater importance of commuting in England can perhaps be explained in terms of the accessibility issues referred to above: more rural areas are accessible to a greater number of economic centres (for example Exmoor linked to Bristol via the M5; the Lake District linked to Manchester via the M6; and the Cotswolds linked to London via rail).

Table 4.1   The Components of External Housing Pressure in Wales (2001) and England (2002)

	% Very Significant		% Significant		% Minor		% Not at all significant	
	Wales	England	Wales	England	Wales	England	Wales	England
Retirement	24.0	31.0	24.0	35.3	36.0	25.0	16.0	8.6
Commuting	20.8	25.6	37.5	51.3	25.0	20.5	16.7	2.6
Teleworking	Nil	1.0	Nil	3.9	20.8	51.5	79.2	43.7
In-migration for economic reasons (to take up employment)	8.3	4.5	37.5	33.0	33.3	43.8	20.8	18.8
Purchasing for private holiday use	4.0	12.5	20.0	32.1	32.0	30.4	44.0	25.0
Purchasing for rental investment	Nil	6.1	20.8	28.1	54.2	48.2	25.0	17.5
Purchasing for holiday letting	Nil	8.8	4.2	26.3	58.3	33.3	37.5	31.6

Source: Tewdwr-Jones *et al*, 2002, p. 33 and Gallent *et al*, 2002, p. 32.

Perhaps even more surprising is the perception that market activity has increased as buyers have moved into the different rural areas to take up employment (45.8 per cent in Wales and 37.5 per cent in England), though this economic in-migration may involve people gravitating to market towns rather than smaller villages. The final two points emerging from this statistical overview are particularly significant. Firstly, 76.0 per cent and 55.4 per cent of surveyed authorities in Wales and England (respectively) judged 'purchase for private holiday use' to be of either minor significance or no significance whatsoever. Secondly, 96.0 per cent and 65.0 per cent of authorities made the same judgement in reference to 'purchasing for holiday' letting. The fact that second homes are of minor concern in many rural areas, relative to retirement and broader migration pressures is an issue that we return to in Chapter 10. It needs to be emphasised, however, that these general figures hide the much greater importance of second home purchasing in particular areas and specific villages.

There is clearly a wide range of housing pressures bearing down on many rural areas, and it should not be assumed that all of these pressures come from external sources. In Ceredigion, local investment in property for holiday lettings has increased market activity and inevitably impacted on house prices, particularly in the most attractive villages. House prices in the UK have risen consistently since the mid 1990s, with recent inflation fuelled by historically low mortgage interest rates and greater confidence in the housing market over stock market investment. It is certainly incorrect to assume that it is only external buyers who have aggressively exploited this situation. Often, local people with local knowledge and connections have ploughed money into rental investments and holiday lets. As one housing officer noted:

> We have some villages where one [extended] family probably owns between six and twelve properties [and] are renting them out as seasonal holiday lets (Housing Officer, Eden District).

Hence, general interest in rural housing – and its inherent scarcity – is perhaps the biggest pressure in many areas, rather than specific forms of investment. These patterns, however, differ between more accessible rural areas (perhaps with more market towns and better links to bigger urban centres) and less accessible, remoter, rural areas. Before turning to the issue of housing affordability and the effectiveness of local housing demand, it is perhaps worth reflecting on how broadly different types of rural area may be affected by housing market pressures.

Accessible and Deeper Rural

According to some case study participants, there is a clear tendency for younger people to move away from less accessible rural areas where there are fewer services and jobs, to larger towns where social and economic opportunities tend to concentrate and where there is a greater choice of rented accommodation.

> We are not necessarily talking of people moving out of Gwynedd, but from the most rural settings. Our experience in terms of providing rented accommodation is that we find that people are being attracted more to the towns – predominantly Pwllheli and Porthmadoc for Penlleyn [Lleyn Peninsular] – and finding that there are certain areas, such as Trefor, where housing associations now have a number of vacant properties (Housing Officer, Gwynedd).

Respondents in Gwynedd and Brecon suggested that this movement occurs early on in the life-cycle and it is often the case that these short-distance migrants wish to return to their home villages later in life, perhaps when they have young families. It is at this point that problems become apparent: firstly, the scarcity of rural housing combines with external demands on the stock to create issues of market housing affordability; and secondly, these smaller and remoter settlements offer few social housing opportunities. The first point then with regards to types of rural area is that the problems faced in more peripheral areas are not uniform; there is an internal patterning to the issues experienced.

This is also true in relation to retirement. Estate agents reported that 'early retirees' often choose to live in more isolated properties, sometimes in remoter rural areas. This might be seen as a reaction to urban living, with people wanting a complete lifestyle change which involves the privacy and perceived 'romance' of relative isolation and putting significant distance between themselves and the 'rat race'. However, during a second phase of retirement, this lifestyle becomes more difficult to sustain and loses its appeal, as retirees become less mobile and more reliant on the support of others. At this point, they may move to larger market towns where primary health care, better services and public transport are more accessible. In some instances, they may even return to cities where they can draw on the support of family in later life.

Clearly then, as well as there being multiple demands on the supply of housing in the countryside, there is also a cycle of movement between more accessible and more remote rural areas. In some instances, there is a propensity for stiff competition between newly forming households moving back to remoter areas and those moving in either to buy second homes or as first-phase retiring households. Rural markets are internally dynamic and this dynamism creates opportunities and, at times, heightens market pressure. But in order to gain a more complete picture of why local buyers cannot always compete effectively for housing – or gain access to low-cost homes – it is necessary to look more closely at local incomes, social housing provision, and market supply. In many instances, the balance of supply and the ineffectiveness of demand is the prime barrier to housing access in the countryside. All of these issues were touched upon in the case studies.

Theme 2: Affordability and Effective Local Demand

Another recurrent theme running through the case studies was that local people in housing need were typically on low-incomes, and in insecure employment frequently linked with tourism. In North Norfolk – an area that sustained a clear concentration of second homes between 1991 and 2001 – one planning officer lamented the current lack of full-time secure skilled employment and questioned the ability of local communities to sustain themselves on a 'cream tea' tourist economy:

> The balance has changed in that locals are no longer able to compete; in Blakeney, a two-bedroom property there is around £100,000. A local employed in tourism or agriculture cannot afford these [prices] (Planner, North Norfolk).

Although a low-pay tourist economy is unlikely to be the aspiration of any area, the fact remains that it is a significant contributor to economies overall, not just in rural areas, and officers were quick to note that policies that undermined this section of the economy – including assaults on holiday letting and even second home purchasing – would not generally be welcomed. The reality in many rural areas is that tourism is a key component of economic activity, and it simply does not need skilled labour, and hence does not pay skilled labour salaries. In contrast, teleworkers, commuters, and second home buyers, tend to derive incomes and wealth from skilled urban jobs. The inevitable lack of parity in incomes results in 'ineffective' local demand for housing, which is perhaps unavoidable in any open market.

Because of ineffective local demand, general market housing is unlikely to satisfy the needs of those on the lowest rural incomes. This means that the provision of low-cost housing – either directly or through the planning system – would seem to be an obvious means to secure access to housing for local people, notwithstanding the argument that such a conclusion points to inherent inequity in market allocation, or that the 'free' market is free only for the rich (see Chapter 8). Whilst undertaking our case studies, it became clear that many participants had issues with 'social' or 'low-cost' housing believing that:

- Social rented housing, in particular, is often the tenure of last choice and not viewed as desirable in many rural areas, either amongst local politicians or even those households claiming to be in need;
- Truly affordable housing for sale is extremely hard to achieve, particularly in areas of high demand where there is acute competition for development land;
- The provision of social housing can encourage 'welfare migration' with non-local people brought into a village to occupy such housing.

These perceived local problems are in addition to the broad 'policy problems' associated with providing affordable homes through the planning system, which have according to many commentators, resulted in insufficient supply in recent years (Crook *et al*, 2002). We now briefly examine each of these local issues in turn.

Social Housing as the Tenure of Last Choice

In a number of the case studies it was reported that even where *social rented* accommodation was available, it was not a popular choice amongst local people. It is perhaps an issue of national concern that social rented housing has come to be seen as the tenure of last choice, a view that was promoted most vigorously by Margaret Thatcher during the 1980s. This meant that in some case studies, even where it was recognised that local people could simply not access market housing, it was felt that the provision of additional affordable housing was not the answer, because it would be rejected by local communities and their political representatives. The answer lay, instead, in 'addressing' market pressures and bringing these under regulatory control. This might involve 'discouraging' second home ownership, retirement, or general migration. Debates surrounding this issue are discussed in Chapters 7 and 8.

This rejection of social housing was matched in many areas by an expectation that local people should be given the 'opportunity' to buy their own home. Many officers reported that this was a common view held by Members of their local Councils. However, officers contended that using existing market mechanisms, this could not be achieved and that expectations were unreasonable. The general view of officers can be expressed in the following terms: any attempt to control prices by dramatically increasing land release would be unworkable. For a start, many developers would simply hold on to land, sustaining housing scarcity in order to sustain existing price levels. And even if a steep increase in supply could be achieved through land release, and was politically acceptable, any price reductions would benefit incoming households, as much as local people. Indeed, local developers might well advertise their developments in the national press or through London-based agents in order to achieve the best return on their investment. Authorities could respond by placing restrictive conditions on new-build housing, though these often have wider and adverse impacts on the property market (see Chapter 8) and may not prove acceptable to government or to local homebuyers, who may feel aggrieved at restrictions on how they can dispose of their property when they come to sell.

And even if prices could be controlled through an extensive programme of land release and house building, this is unlikely to prove popular with rural communities or with existing home owners; firstly, the character of rural villages might be harmed, and the potential value of existing homes could fall. Vested interests are likely to oppose significant increases in house building in much the same way as restrictions on open market purchasing (by second home buyers and retiring households) would face stiff resistance. The end result is a serious conundrum for local authorities and communities: social housing is frequently unpopular but there is no easy way to give local people preferential access to market housing. Some authorities pointed to the need to promote more 'acceptable' forms of social housing in rural areas including shared-ownership opportunities where the authority or a housing association retains a 'golden share' in perpetuity; similarly, the 'Home Buy' scheme provides a mechanism whereby local people can be helped to access existing village housing. Respondents highlight the positive contribution that such initiatives can make; these are discussed further in Chapter 7.

Unaffordable Affordable Housing

A key difficulty in many rural areas, especially where there are a range of external demands on the housing stock, is that even affordable housing can be unaffordable to many households. Because of strong competition for development land, land cost as a component of total development cost may rise sharply making it difficult for social housing providers to secure development opportunities. And even if they receive grant support from the Housing Corporation (in England, or the Welsh Assembly Government in Wales), these may be insufficient to make homes truly affordable. In the past, the Housing Corporation has provided additional grant support to those providers developing homes in National Parks (by recalibrating Total Cost Indicators to reflect the higher costs of building houses in such locations). These issues are taken up again in Chapter 9. In the case studies, some authorities noted local people cannot secure mortgages even on homes made more 'affordable' through the use of planning gain mechanisms, indeed:

> Even when we do manage to negotiate through the planning system to obtain units, they are still very expensive. We're currently working with local developers to get the units at 80 per cent of their market value – they're still coming out at £68,000 to £70,000. On an average [local] income of £13,000, it's still unaffordable (Housing Officer, Eden District).

The problem in this instance may not lie in the ability of planners to negotiate sufficient gain from new development, or an unwillingness of developers to deliver affordable housing through Section 106 Planning Agreements (see Chapter 8). The problem is simply one of land prices and how much 'gain' a particular development can 'carry' (see Gallent *et al*, 2003), without jeopardising the viability of a market housing scheme. That said, high land values result in inflated house prices, potentially giving developments a greater 'carrying capacity'. There is evidence that some authorities are not doing enough to extract gain from planning permissions: asked about its track-record in delivering affordable housing through the planning system, one authority officer in Wales replied that his authority had '[...] tried that once, but the developer didn't like it, so we didn't push the issue'. Clearly, the unaffordability of some 'affordable' housing relates to the ineffectiveness of local demand, an overheating of the land market in some rural areas, and the lack of enthusiasm that some authorities display for procuring affordable housing through planning, especially where 'social housing' is not apparently favoured (see above).

Insensitive Supply and Welfare 'Migration'

It is extremely difficult, especially in small villages, to tie new affordable housing precisely to local needs. The 'rural exceptions initiative' is one mechanism that can be used to meet very local needs on the back of strong evidence that people living in a village will be forced out if new housing is not made available. The workings of the initiative are described briefly in Chapter 7: it involves a local planning authority negotiating with a landowner to sell land for housing in or adjacent to a small village, that would not otherwise attract planning permission for housing. An 'exceptional' permission is granted where need can be demonstrated and where a housing association agrees to take forward the development; local occupancy in perpetuity is secured through a Section 106 Agreement.

However, from the point of view of social housing providers, there is often greater risk associated with developing two or three units on a very small site. The authority may have established a local need, but this need may comprise young people who claim to want to live locally, but who may subsequently decide to move to a nearby market town to take advantage of social and job opportunities; needs can quickly change, and social providers (that is RSLs) may be worried that either the need identified will not materialise, or the person who the authority thinks will occupy a dwelling will quickly move on, leaving the RSL with a hard to let property on its hands. Hence, because of the tendency of young people to move to larger towns, the RSL will be keener to develop bigger sites there and claim to be following market signals. Perhaps an even more acute problem – and a constant worry for local authorities and RSLs – is that if a very local tenant cannot be found, then they will be forced to look further afield for potential occupants. They may even have to bring people in from larger towns to occupy the homes that the parish or community council – along with local residents – had believed would be occupied by someone from the village. Some authorities noted that when this happens, 'sparks can fly' and confidence in the exceptions initiative – and social housing more generally –

can be undermined. Indeed, this can lead to a perception that social housing provides a 'conduit' for 'welfare migration' of 'problem families' (often people living in the village and needing social housing are seen to have a legitimate need and right, but those who are not known to the local community are treated as welfare migrants). The case studies revealed this to be a particular problem in Wales where non-Welsh speaking tenants are 'introduced' into Welsh speaking communities. The problems of movement and integration were highlighted in Ceredigion:

> [...] there was a *Tai Cantref* [housing association] development around Bow Street [near Aberystwyth] which created quite a furore at the time with people not getting on and the school having problems and things like this. I suppose that can be the problem with any development. I mean it wasn't a huge development, probably 24 houses I think, but even so it's quite a lot, even for a fairly large village like Bow Street. There have been accusations of people being brought in from everywhere, which wasn't quite true. I mean, [...] they weren't actually all living in Bow Street, but they were in Ceredigion previously: these allegations of people being shipped in are not true. But certainly there are difficulties when there is inward movement into an area. In the local community, one or two families integrate quite well. Then again it all depends on the individuals, their home backgrounds and the sort of habits they bring with them I suppose (Housing Officer, Ceredigion).

The crux of the problem in many rural areas is that social housing is often only wanted or accepted where it can be guaranteed that it will only be occupied by people from a particular village: from a community perspective, only the existence of very local need is a justification for building affordable housing; but the local authority performs the role of 'strategic housing enabler' and RSLs often see no problem in moving tenants within their managed stock, decanting smaller households to more suitable properties and bringing larger families into villages where units are more appropriate to their particular needs.

Theme 3: Second Homes and Tourism

Second home use and holiday letting bring tourist money to many areas and some local plans contain policies that favour the conversion of barns and other farm buildings to holiday use. This is the case in North Norfolk where such policies form part of a wider farm diversification strategy. There is a firm belief within many authorities that at least holiday letting – if not second home purchasing for private use – brings benefits to the local economy. This view, however, is tempered by an acknowledgement that granting planning permission for holiday letting can cause resentment amongst local residents where there are housing shortages and where conversions for full-time residential use are unlikely to be permitted.

A key point emerging from the case studies was that many local authority officers were keen to harness the economic potential of holiday letting and wished to make a distinction between private second home ownership and commercial letting: certainly, they did not wish to 'kill off the goose that lays the golden egg' by discouraging the holiday home market. However, many acknowledged that separating holiday from second homes is sometimes difficult. Many private second homes are rented out to visitors and therefore form part of the general accommodation base available to tourists: a second home only becomes a holiday home if it is let commercially for more than 140 days in a year; at this point the owner is liable to pay business rates. But even if the commercial letting period is under this threshold, it can be argued that second homes are indeed part of the local tourist economy, providing further opportunities for people to visit the area and spend money. Indeed, owners, their friends, and paying guests tend to repeat holiday in the area; this may mean that they visit nearby tourist attractions, eat in local pubs and restaurants, use local services and on returning home, encourage others to visit the area. However, on the down side, rental income – when paid – goes directly to the owner and does not stay in the local area. The only direct source of local income comes through Council Tax (assuming the total letting period is under 140 days), and even when the owner pays income tax on rental income, this goes directly to the Inland Revenue. This all suggests that second homes are a weak contributor to the local tourist economy, though their wider economic impacts are discussed at greater length in Chapter 3.

One further point regarding the linkage between second homes and tourism is that the general promotion of an area as a potential tourist destination is likely to heighten its appeal not only to holiday-makers but also to seasonal (and permanent) in-migrants. In other words, glossy brochures sent to London tourist offices or posters with images of the Welsh coastline or Cumbria's Lakes at railway stations promote not only weekend visits, but also more permanent migration flows. The weakness of many rural economies leads many areas to engage in such place-marketing strategies, but these strategies drive the social and cultural changes that many areas otherwise seek to avoid. Many studies of 'sustainable tourism' have little to say on the issue of second home ownership, perhaps because this is often treated separately and as a housing development rather than a tourism concern (the particular concerns of 'sustainable tourism' are set out by Hunter, 1997 and Wall, 1997). It is apparent, however, that many of the potential social changes that can be associated with this form of in-migration run against the defining spirit of sustainable tourism strategies: impacts may be permanent and be characterised by fundamental changes in the social and cultural fabric of receiving communities. These impacts are, of course, offset by the economic gains introduced by tourism and given the loss of agriculture or primary industry, who is to say that the side-effects of tourism and second homes are any more detrimental than the impacts of the economic stagnation that tourism may be compensating for? That said, in tourism planning itself, Godfrey (1998) has argued that there should be greater emphasis on community involvement, and that local authorities would welcome additional integration of tourism planning at the local level. Similarly, the way we plan for tourism should have a clearer *ethical* focus, treating host populations as communities rather than commodities (Hughes, 1995). It is possible that such tourism concerns could provide one focus of the Statements of Community Involvement that will be incorporated in Local Development Frameworks following planning reforms in England and Wales. But again, this issue of impacts – that is, the broader impacts of second homes – was dealt with more comprehensively in Chapter 3.

Theme 4: Additional Pressures on Rural Housing

A number of other issues arose during the course of the case studies. These are dealt with briefly below as they broaden the picture, showing how government policy and wider social changes can bring new pressures to bear on local housing markets.

Household Change

The tendency for people to live alone or to form smaller households was viewed as an added pressure on local housing stocks:

> In the last year we've let 215 properties. The majority of those lettings – the highest group in fact – was to single parents, which is a change on past years (Social Landlord, Radnorshire (Powys)).

The housing stock found in many smaller villages was felt to lack any capacity to adapt to changing social trends: the housing that is available may be too large; similarly, it may be unsuited – in type and location – to the needs of a population that is now living much longer. The frequency of relationship breakdowns also increases the demand for housing. And finally, some authorities noted that they are being called upon to provide for the accommodation needs of the homeless and, more recently, of asylum seekers. There is today a greater diversity of need and demand in many rural areas, which in some instances, overrides the issue of second home ownership.

National Policy

National policy in relation to second homes, investment in affordable housing, planning regulation and so forth will have a dramatic impact on rural areas. Case study participants, however, noted a small number of more particular national policy issues affecting their local areas. In Brecon and in the Yorkshire Dales, it was noted that the siting of military installations may have a major impact on rural housing markets. In both cases, it was suggested that service men and women leaving the armed forces often remained close to where they had been barracked, because they had formed personal ties and put down roots in the local area. Boyle (1995) points out that much long-distance migration in the UK can be explained in terms of the relocation of companies to rural areas; for example, the decision to privatise utilities led to the relocation of large numbers of employees. There is a flow of economic migration to some rural areas (or at least to bigger market towns, and subsequently a trickle down to smaller villages): this pattern was confirmed in Table 4.1.

Other case study respondents noted that decisions taken nationally to improve road and rail links – partially driven by a desire to assist rural economies – often extends travel to work areas (TWAs), and increases commuter pressure. This has certainly been the case in Brecon, where improvements to the A470 has extended Cardiff's TWA and increased housing market activity in and around Brecon. Similarly, the extension of the A55 Expressway along the North Wales coast in the early 1990s had a similar effect on the Lleyn Peninsula.

Authorities also argued that National Park and AONB (Area of Out-standing Natural Beauty) designations both help and hinder areas. National Parks, for example, introduce a housing 'triple whammy': first, they officially define an area of exceptional landscape value, thereby increasing market interest in the area; secondly, they bring further planning restrictions to house building over and above those already applicable to the countryside, and reduce supply. This leads to the third effect: National Parks promote housing scarcity and therefore a premium is placed on owning a property within a Park (buyers are more confident that their investment will rise in value and that open vistas are unlikely to be spoilt by future development). National Parks serve an important purpose, and yet the environmental goals pursued by Park Authorities often override social considerations. In some instances, this may bring these authorities into conflict with social housing providers and with local housing departments, frustrated by the costs and difficulties associated with meeting local housing needs within National Parks.

The Right-to-Buy

The depletion of the council housing stock through the Right-to-Buy was viewed as problematic in all fifteen case study areas. This policy was seen as highly damaging, often generating significant profits for initial purchasers, but reducing the capacity of local authorities to address housing needs, especially in areas where external demand pressures were significant. Research by Chaney and Sherwood (2000) has revealed that although few former council properties become second homes, they are often bought by incomers with the former tenants making large sums of money from the onward sale and subsequently moving to cheaper areas; this may accelerate the process of social change and gentrification in many rural areas. Acknowledging the importance of council housing in many rural communities, government attempted to stave off the loss of rural housing by 'protecting' homes in designated rural areas. Section 19 of the 1980 Housing Act stipulated that areas could apply for such protection: but few outside National Parks or AONBs have been designated and hence the Right-to-Buy caused a stripping away of council homes in many parts of the countryside. In comparison with the scale of loss, other social landlords (RSLs) have made only modest contributions to new social housing supply. This issue is returned to in Chapters 7 and 8.

The sale of council housing was certainly felt to have had a dramatic effect on the supply of more accessible housing in many rural areas. But like many of the issues considered in this chapter, one might question how different rural concerns in fact are from their urban equivalents. In the 1980s, urban sociologists expended much intellectual effort in attempting to define the urban as a distinct object for study (see, for example, Savage *et al*, 2003). Eventually, it was concluded that although 'the urban' offered a useful focus for examining particular aspects of society there was nothing that made it *conceptually discrete* from 'the rural'. Although we might disagree with this conclusion and claim that rural experiences are demonstrably different from urban ones – that is, the sociology of the rural differs from that of the urban – on a more practical level, it is clear that rural housing markets do not operate in isolation: they form part of a wider marker structure. But at times, during the course of the case studies, it became apparent that there was an expectation that rural housing markets *should* work differently. A cynic might argue that some of the expectations were – at best – fanciful, and – at worst – naive. For example, some participants expressed the view – or reported that Council Members were of the view – that local people should *always* be guaranteed access to local housing (to buy or to rent) within their village of choice, and that rented accommodation should *always* be viewed as a temporary solution. Of course, the same ideal aspirations exist everywhere, not least in London and the South East, and there are legitimate concerns over the lack of housing access and choice across the United Kingdom. Frustration with the housing market and housing pressure is not confined to rural areas, though a particular feature of some of these areas is that compromise – moving to a nearby village or even a market town – is not always favoured, and there is a greater determination to ensure that people can live exactly where they wish.

Conclusions

The case studies supported the contention set out in Chapter 3 that housing markets are complex and cannot be reduced down to the opposing interests of incomers and locals; rather, they are the products of, and reflect a range of, economic and social processes. In this context, second homes might be viewed as an aspect of – but not the dominant feature in – at least some rural housing markets. An array of different factors and processes shape housing markets in rural areas: on the demand side, these can include:

- Wider housing pressures stemming from retirement, from lifestyle demand ('down shifting'), from commuting and from teleworking. There are also a range of local demand pressures from people wishing to capitalise on house price inflation, who invest in the buy-to-let market or in holiday letting;
- Ineffective local demand rendering even 'affordable' housing unafford-able; this relates to the strength of the local economy and to the proportion of people locked into low-wage activities;

- The promotion of tourism in the local area, which can be viewed as a double-edged sword: increasing tourist spending, but also encouraging lifestyle migration with its associated impacts on housing demand;
- Social changes in society at large, causing more people to live alone or to form smaller households. This may generate particular housing pressures in rural areas where the existing housing stock is less able to adapt to these changes than the more diverse mix of housing found in towns and cities;
- National policy initiatives including the upgrading of transport infrastructure which may introduce new pressures to some rural areas; similarly, encouraging the relocation of businesses away from built up areas may create new housing demand hotspots away from metropolitan areas.

Supply pressures further complicate this picture. The sale of council housing since 1980 and the promotion of home ownership – firstly by Margaret Thatcher as part of her ideological attack on welfare provision, and today by Tony Blair in his promotion of a 'stakeholder society' – has resulted in social housing being derided as the tenure of last choice. This has made it difficult to gain acceptance for additional social housing in some rural areas. In the case studies, this seemed to be a particular issue in North Wales. And even when affordable housing is provided, highly competitive land markets in some rural areas mean that it can be difficult to bring costs down – through planning gain or direct subsidy – to a level that all local people can afford. Another supply problem relates to the difficulty in providing just enough new housing in the right locations for those judged to be in greatest need. Where social housing becomes occupied by 'non-local' people, confidence in this form of provision appears to be reduced. It also needs to be remembered that rural areas are themselves different, with the clearest division being between more accessible and more remote areas: often people move between small hamlets and large towns at different life stages, adding to the complexity of rural housing markets.

One final but critical point emerging from these case studies is that second homes are more often than not a localised issue. This sets them apart from the broader economic pressures that are more widely felt in the countryside. The general reliance on low paid jobs in many rural areas, for example, may limit housing choice. But this limit may be accentuated in those particular villages where second home buyers, retirees and lifestyle down-shifters have entered the housing market. All case study respondents expressed concern for the lack of housing opportunities available to some first time buyers, though none sought to place the blame solely on second home purchasing: for the majority, this was merely one factor amongst many influencing housing choice. But for a minority, second homes had become the key demand pressure limiting the availability of housing for local people in some villages: in these instances, respondents often supported the need for urgent and immediate action. The possible nature of any action is considered in Part 3 of this book.

Chapter 5

European Experiences: Past and Present

Introduction

In this chapter and the next, attention turns to other European situations. The profiles presented here in Chapter 5 are based either on reviews of literature and secondary data (for Part 1, the European Past), or draw on work undertaken for the Scottish Executive in 2000/01 (for Part 2, the European Present). The latter sought to 'learn' from other European experiences and consider if particular responses to different housing pressures might be reapplied successfully in Scotland. This desire to learn from overseas experiences is not new: we noted in Chapter 1 that second home growth in Europe was already a 'mature' social phenomenon before the 1970s. This fact led many British observers to draw comparisons and consider what 'lessons might be learnt' from experiences abroad. However, these domestic studies tended to recognise that:

> Although reference to foreign experience may provide guidelines, differences in social, cultural, economic and political life-styles are likely to invalidate any clear comparisons or conclusions (Williams, 1974, p.31).

Jim Kemeny (1995) has argued that after the Second World War, 'Western Europe came under the cultural influence of the USA and its English-speaking allies' (Kemeny, 1995, p.3) leading to an 'unconscious assimilation of political and ideological perspectives'. In social research, this assimilation may be manifest as a fundamental misunderstanding of the social and political processes at work in neighbouring European countries. From an Anglo-centric perspective, it is all too easy to commit what Kemeny terms a 'Romeo error' (referring to the mistaken diagnosis of death in the Shakespearean tragedy), applying the same interpretations used in Britain to processes observed abroad (Allen, et al., 1998). In the survey of European experiences presented in this chapter, no attempt is made to draw direct comparisons with the British situation; rather, the purpose is to consider the range of European second home experiences outside the UK, to highlight the observed differences and also to examine how countries have responded to *their own* problems. That said, key differences are noted and in Chapter 6, we provide an analysis of how the second home phenomenon in parts of mainland Europe frequently differ from the situation in the UK.

A European Picture

Attitudes towards second homes vary considerably between different EU member states. These attitudes often reflect cultural differences, the way patterns of second home ownership have developed over time, or the position that such properties occupy in the wider housing market. Despite certain countries having a far higher proportion of second homes within the general stock than is the case in England or Wales, such properties are not automatically seen as a problem. In Sweden, for example, there has been a long tradition of dual property occupation, but low population densities and an abundance of relatively cheap housing have cushioned communities from the types of problems experienced in some parts of Britain. In more recent times, however, changing tastes and new concentrations of second homes on certain west coast peninsulas – often owned by foreign buyers – have brought new concerns and prompted government to act to protect local interests (see Swedish profile, below).

The problems of collating data concerning the number of second homes in the UK pale in comparison to the difficulties of constructing a Europe-wide picture. The European Union has long been interested in formulating new methods to collect data in the 'field of tourism' in order to combat this problem (Official Journal, c236, 1995, p.20). But in the later 1960s, this lack of data was particularly acute. An attempt was made to rectify this situation in 1970 through a survey of 20,000 households across Europe which considered the issue of second home ownership; the results were published in the *Reader's Digest* 'Survey of Europe Today'. It was acknowledged at the time that the survey potentially overestimated the proportion of households with second homes in certain countries (Downing and Dower, 1973, p.20). At the same time, it was not specifically concerned with EU member-states. Table 5.1 presents data on second home ownership in a selection of European countries from a variety of data sources. At the time of writing (2004), Europe-wide data were available for 1970; 1980, 1988 and 1994.

Table 5.1 offers a fragmented picture of second home ownership across Europe. The apparent decline in ownership in some states in the middle columns of the table (notably France and Spain) is likely to be due to overestimation of the phenomenon in 1970 and then underestimation in 1980 and 1988. The lack of data in Germany is largely a result of the administrative changes associated with re-unification. Similarly, the lack of official EU data for Sweden, Austria and Finland (in 1980 and 1988) reflects their recent membership of the Union. What is clear, however, is that the UK (along with Ireland and the Netherlands) has maintained its marginal position in terms of second home ownership. Indeed, The United Kingdom has one of the lowest levels of second home ownership in Europe: the most recent European-wide data suggests that 5 per cent of households have a second home. This compares to more than 20 per cent in Sweden and Finland, and 16 per cent in Spain. Only the more densely populated Netherlands has fewer second homeowners (3 per cent). But these data are approximations and attempt to compare very different types of second homes. The figures for Sweden and Spain, for

Table 5.1   Second Home Ownership in Europe

Country	% of households with a second home			
	1970[1]	1980[2]	1988[3]	1994[4]
Sweden	22	-	-	20+
Finland	7	-	-	20+
Spain	17	-	8	16
Luxembourg	6	-	-	14
Italy	5	4	6	14
Greece	-	-	12	14
France	16	12	9	11
Denmark	10	10	12	10
Portugal	10	-	4	9
Belgium	7	4	5	6
[West] Germany[5]	3	-	-	5
United Kingdom	3	-	3	5
Ireland	2	2	2	5
Netherlands	3	2	1	3
Norway (non EU)	*17*	-	-	-
Austria	8	-	-	-
Switzerland (non EU)	*8*	-	-	-

Notes: (1) *Source*: *Survey of Europe Today* (Reader's Digest, 1970). (2/3) *Source*: European Union (1996) *Social Portrait of Europe* (Luxembourg, Office for Official Publications of the European Communities), p.172. (4) *Source*: European Union (1998) *Social Portrait of Europe* (Luxembourg, Statistical Office for the European Communities), p. 199. (5) The EU had no retrospective data for unified Germany in 1980 and 1988; (-) denotes 'no data available'.

example, include huge numbers of chalets (holiday homes) and it should be noted that these figures do not represent concentrations of *second homes*, but concentrations of *second homeowners*. It may be true that 14 per cent of Luxembourg households have second homes, but many may have properties outside Luxembourg, perhaps in France or further afield in Spain. Likewise, the 1994 figures reflect changes that came about during a boom period at the end of the previous decade. It appears that the UK figure rose 2 percentage points between 1988 and 1994. However, research by Henry Buller and Keith Hoggart in 1994 suggests that many of these new second homeowners actually bought property in rural France (Buller and Hoggart, 1994a).

So although the data presented in Table 5.1 probably do reveal the relative importance of second homes in the domestic markets, they have to be interpreted with some care. Where second home numbers are high (for example in Sweden and Finland) there is also evidence of a strong foreign-buyer market: for example Germans on the Swedish West Coast. But in the UK, the overseas market is less well developed. This means that any 'proportion of total stock' figure would probably be below the 'percentage households' figure given in

Table 5.1. But although the UK – and England more specifically – may have comparatively fewer second homes than Sweden, some communities may experience levels of second home incursion comparable with parts of Sweden. The *Social Portrait of Europe* (1998) says little specifically on the subject of second home ownership, though it summarises the European situation with the following statement:

> On average, 9 per cent of households in the *Europe of the Twelve* (all pre May 2004 EU members minus Sweden, Finland and Austria) possess a second home. Greece, Spain, Italy and Luxembourg are well above the European average. The three former countries are among those with the largest disparities in income distribution in the Union while the latter has by far the highest net monetary income in the EU. Other research has shown that the proportion of households with second homes is very high (around 20 per cent) in Sweden and Finland.
>
> 36 per cent of European households indicated that they cannot afford a second home while the remaining 55 per cent do not want one or do not have one for other reasons. There is a conclusive link with income levels – affluent households (25 per cent) are five times more likely than those with low incomes (5 per cent) to have a second home (in 1994: Statistical Office for the European Union, 1998).

The general conclusion from this review of available data was that second homes are more commonplace in southern EU countries and in Finland and Sweden (European Union, 1998). We return to a Europe-wide analysis of second home ownership towards the end of this chapter. The intention now is to look at different European situations as they have evolved since 1970, at least where data are available. This section is split into two parts: the European Past and the European Present. In the first section, we consider the development of second home concerns from the 1960s to the early 1990s. In the second section, the focus shifts to Europe today, drawing on contributions included in Gallent, Shucksmith and Tewdwr-Jones (2003).

Part 1: The European Past

Belgium (1960s and 1970s)

Throughout the 1960s, Belgium experienced a substantial increase in the number of second homes. By the mid-1970s, there were estimated to be 150,000 rural cottages and in excess of 200,000 chalets built without planning permission. Particular concentrations were developing in the French-speaking area south of the Sambre (Albarre, 1977, p.139). Belgian analyses of second home ownership tend to include urban apartments used by businessmen (that is, "*pieds à terre*" (Clout, 1973, p.750)) and the overall quality of data varies between different Belgian regions. Albarre (1977) claimed that a particularly acute problem in Belgium was the deteriorating relationship between second home owners and local residents, especially farmers (Albarre, 1977, p.140). Brier (1970) highlighted some increases in house prices in certain second home areas which may have been encouraging the process of rural depopulation.

Increases in communal expenditure (on roads, water and electricity supply) were also attributed to the growth in the number of second homes (Brier, 1970). Of particular concern, in terms of social conflict, was evidence that middle-class incomers were often objecting to certain farming practices (either because of the noise or the smell). In Wallonia, owners had a particular dislike for pig farm developments, which corrupted their idealised countryside (Albarre, 1977, p.141).

In many areas, there was evidence of a growing social rift between the incomers and the host population. However, Albarre demonstrated that this rift was not universal and could be bridged if common concerns could be identified and subsequently used to bring together the new and the old population. The commune of Sivry on the French border covered an area of 2,300 hectares and had a resident population of 1,411 at the end of 1971. The undulating landscape was punctuated with small farms divided by distinctive hedgerows; approximately one in eight dwellings was used as a second home, a symptom of the rural depopulation observed in the area since the 1950s and the beginning of the steady decline in the agricultural economy. Throughout the 1960s, a number of urban households purchased vacant properties in Sivry, attracted by the area's rustic character. When the second home owners arrived, they took over not only the buildings but also the hedgerows and recognised the importance these had in maintaining the overall character of the landscape. Schemes for hedgerow conservation (including a competition for the best-kept hedgerow) brought locals and incomers together and promoted an awareness of the interest that incomers had in the rural environment amongst locals and particularly farmers. Albarre claimed that through this process, it was possible to remove some of the obstacles to 'coexistence between various social groups' (Albarre, 1977, p.145). In effect, the incomers came to an area of depopulation (and subsequent neglect) and made an important and significant contribution. A communication channel was established between town and country (built on understanding) which demonstrated how people *can* live together. Albarre notes that:

> Geographers, aware of the increasingly complex interpretation between the urban and rural environments, have encouraged this encounter between farmers and second homers in order to help communication between them, for without this, there would surely be an ineluctable breakdown in the rural environment (Albarre, 1977, p.145).

Patterns of socio-economic change had produced a new social configuration in the Belgian countryside and the divisions between social groups were clearly visible. However, Albarre showed that it is possible to identify common ground and use this as an arena for overcoming social tension by fostering greater understanding. The problems posed by social change are often balanced by the new opportunities offered; it may be the task of both locals and incomers to decide which way the scales should be tipped.

Denmark (1960s and 1970s)

In 1970, there were estimated to be between 140,000 and 145,000 second homes in Denmark, mainly located in coastal areas (a pattern which contrasted markedly with that observed in Sweden and Norway where the majority of second home developments had occurred in the forested and mountainous areas). The parcelling of land for new developments since the 1960s had generated particular concern as public access to beaches was being limited. At this time, half of Denmark's second homes were located in Zealand, with demand coming predominantly from Copenhagen. The development of second homes in Denmark has created a number of planning problems in recent years. Sporadic development in the 1960s was acknowledged as having a detrimental environmental impact; in response, it was recognised that 'recreational' home developments (in groups of roughly 200 dwellings) could limit the impact on the countryside particularly if they were viewed as representing a settlement in their own right and all normal planning guidelines were adhered to. However, some of these 'settlements' had, in the past, been built too close to urban centres and over time, the growth of cities had engulfed these second homes causing a change of use and the creation of poor quality housing ghettos (Bielckus, 1977, p.37). In order to combat this problem, regional plans were used to specify minimum distances away from urban centres for the siting of second homes; similarly, planning guidance was strengthened in order to ensure that no second homes were without adequate water supply or sewage disposal facilities. The measures adopted by the Danish government in the 1960s and 1970s did not seek to limit second home development, rather they sought to ensure that the qualities which attract second homes to an area are not lost through poor planning. At this time, opposition to second home development was in its infancy and the arguments of the anti-development lobby were given little credence.

More recent Danish legislation has focused on the over-riding importance of securing a first home and maintaining the socio-economic viability of host communities. The Danish Government has legislated on both the use of residences and the acquisition of property. First, planning legislation distinguishes between permanent and 'secondary' accommodation. If a new dwelling was granted planning permission on the grounds that it was to be used as a 'permanent' residence, or if a property has been used as a permanent residence over the past five years, then permission must be obtained from the local commune authority before any *change of use* may be implemented. This rule applies for a range of 'use' changes and has been formulated as a response to a growing housing shortage in some parts of Denmark. Danish local authorities have a social responsibility for households seeking accommodation and the control they exert over change of use assists them in this task. The second legislative change relates to the acquisition of property on the part of persons not domiciled in Denmark. Essentially, non-Danish nationals need to apply for a permit from the Minister of Justice in order to acquire real estate. On Denmark's accession to the European Union following the Treaty of Rome, the law was amended to allow citizens of other European member states to acquire real estate with the intention of working and residing in Denmark. This right, however, was not extended to the acquisition of second homes, a point emphasised in the original treaty:

> Property in Denmark – Notwithstanding the provisions of this Treaty, Denmark may maintain the existing legislation on the acquisition of second homes (Treaty of Rome; Protocol 2).

In effect, foreigners must still apply for a permit if they wish to purchase a second home. Social concern has always been central to the second home issue in Denmark. In the 1960s, controls on second home development aimed to ensure and maintain general access to the countryside; the availability of recreational opportunities (to everyone and not just a privileged few) was seen as an important social objective. More recently, attention has focused on the availability of housing for permanent residents with both planning and housing law being used to ensure that housing shortages are not accentuated by second home demand. The Danish strategy in relation to second homes and local interests has been to accommodate outside demand, but only after wider social objectives (leisure and housing) have been achieved.

Finland (1970s)

Williams (1974) has noted that in Finland there has been marked local interest in the second home phenomenon, particularly in the Åland Islands where the Finnish language was becoming virtually unknown because of the presence of non-Finnish second home owners (Williams, 1974, p.36). Åland province has been an area of political controversy for many years and particular border disputes between Finland and Sweden centred on the province in the early part of this century. In the 1920s, the League of Nations assigned power of administration over the territory to Finland with certain conditions of decentralised control. For this reason, Åland has developed its own brand of provincial legislation which places great emphasis on the rights of 'natives' over outsiders (encapsulated in *'hembygdsrätt'*). Åland's law of real estate acquisition, for example, regulates property rights in the province and aims to ensure that all land stays in the hands of people born in Åland. Those not fortunate to have *'hembygdsrätt'* (local property rights) cannot acquire property without a permit and these are only granted to persons connected to Åland by family ties or employment needs. Even where permits are allocated, the property which can be acquired is restricted in type and size.

Clearly, these controls in Åland will restrict all types of property acquisition (including second homes). Similar measures have been implemented in other parts of the country including Northern Savo and are a reflection of the way in which provincial devolution has been administered (a British parallel might be the relationship that the mainland shares with the Channel Islands). Apart from the provincial real estate legislation, there have also been national measures to control the growth of second homes. First, persons not domiciled in Finland for a continuous period of five years require a permit to acquire a holiday residence (whilst no such 'licensing' scheme extends to the purchase of first homes; a move which may have delayed Finland's accession to the EU). Second, legislation has also been implemented which controls the number of farms taken out of farming use. If a person wishes to acquire a farm on which to pursue agricultural activities, he is free to do so. If, on the other hand, the farm is to change use (for example, the farming function is to cease or land is to be sold and the farm residence is to become a second home) then a permit will be required.

The provincial system of Government in Finland has allowed some areas to take quite drastic steps (or at least steps which appear drastic from a British perspective) in order to control the housing and property markets and prioritise local interests. More general controls have also been implemented which seek to ensure open access to first homes and protect the agricultural base where it remains viable. Clearly, however, the most important point here is that the way in which the property market is regulated is a function of peripheral culture and the power wielded by peripheral Government. Where power is devolved, the local or regional perspective is likely (in some instances) to take precedence over national concerns. Where this is not the case (for example in England, Scotland and Wales until very recently) the national perspective prevails and the integrity of national markets is seen to be of greater importance than local interests.

France (1960s and 1970s)

Two phases of historic academic interest in the French second home phenomenon can be identified. The first is associated with the work of Clout in the late 1960s and 1970s and the domestic housing market. The second is more recent, focusing on Hoggart and Buller's concern with British property buyers in rural France during and after the British property boom of the late 1980s.

Clout (1977) notes that the acquisition of second homes in France has a long and varied history and one which follows a pronounced pattern of social democratisation. In pre-Revolutionary France, *châteaux* and country parks owned by the nobility were widespread; these were replaced in the nineteenth century by less grandiose weekend houses owned by rich provincials. Modern patterns of ownership took root in the inter-war and post-war periods and the new 'second homes' comprised country houses used for short periods, holiday homes or furnished flats used for tourist purposes (Clout, 1977, p.47). The French population census (which has collated data regarding second homes since 1962) along with 'Cadastral registers' and other taxation documents today provide the key sources of information regarding second homes across the Channel (Bonneau, 1973, pp.307–320). By 1970, there were 1.5 million second homes across France, although patterns of growth since 1945 have been complicated by the return to first home use of second homes in some northern and southern parts of the country. After the war, some vacation residences in Brittany and Normandy were returned to first home use in order to overcome a shortage of housing created by the devastation of the Allied invasion. In 1962, many southern second homes met the same fate as *pieds noirs* were repatriated from Algeria. Between 1963 and 1966, 25,800 second homes became primary residences, either because of the process of repatriation in the South or because they became overwhelmed by the rapid expansion of many large urban centres (Palatin, 1969, pp.747–57).

Despite these losses, the dominant trend was still one of growth; the construction of new second homes more than doubled between 1963 and 1966 from 10,000 per annum to more than 24,000 (Clout, 1977, p.50). Two thirds of these purpose built homes were located on the coast with the remainder split equally between rural and mountain areas. Psychogios (1980) has noted that in France:

> [...] regional planning corporations have advocated the designation of areas for second home development on the basis that essential utilities could be provided far more cheaply than in dispersed locations and would create far less conflict with farming, forestry and countryside preservation interests (Psyhogios, 1980, p.63).

Hall (1973) has traced the way in which second home developments were 'steered' in the Languedoc-Rousillon area with the creation of new coastal resorts comprising various service provisions and new-built second homes (Hall, 1973, pp.173–75). By 1967, 2.8 million households made use of 1.2 million second homes with 'ownership as opposed to use, [still being] most widespread among affluent strata of French society' (Clout, 1977, p.51). Many owners had relatively high annual incomes and tended to be engaged in professional occupations although in the late 1960s, Clout argued that this pattern was slowly changing (Clout, 1969). Many of the users were the children of older owners who were normally town dwellers (just 2.5 per cent of French second home owners at this time lived in rural cantons). One of the most important points to be raised in Clout's research at this time was the role of *inheritance* in the second home market. In France, it was commonplace for a city-dweller to inherit a rural home from grandparents (Clout, 1977, p.58) and although the national picture was far from clear, anecdotal evidence served to underline Clout's point. In Hérault, 45 per cent of owners had inherited their second home whilst the same was true of 25 per cent of owners in the Paris basin.

By the 1960s, the growth in the number of second homes across France had become the subject of some concern and considerable social comment. Barbier (1968) expounded the economic and social benefits that second homes could bring to importing regions including the local profits derived from sales, the generation of new employment for local craftsmen and the opportunity for rural people to widen their social contact. On top of this, second homes brought the opportunity to anchor dwindling rural populations through an injection of new money. As if by magic, second home owners are drawn to declining regions without the need for any strategic guidance. Cribier (1966), on the other hand, argued that the proliferation of second homes and the subsequent rises in house prices was, at best, producing unbalanced communities and, at worst, accelerating the process of depopulation (Cribier,

1966, pp.97–101). These same arguments became central to the same debates emerging in Britain a decade later.

On reflection, Clout argued that the experience of second home growth in France was 'yet another process' whereby the 'dispersed city' is encroaching on rural space. In the face of second home expansion, 'profound economic, social and visual changes have taken place in many parts of the French countryside and these may be expected to increase in magnitude in future years' (Clout, 1977, p.60). Overall, because the expansion of second home ownership is a component of wider social change, neither the lifestyles of rural nor urban populations can remain unaltered. Clout recognised that the second home phenomenon was not a passing phase in recreational fashion but rather a new and dynamic element of the housing market and perhaps a barometer for socio-economic change, not just in France, but across Europe and beyond. In this early work, he noted that a second home was often viewed as a sound capital investment, not only for the French, but also for the Dutch and the Germans on the Languedoc coast and for the British in the Dordogne and Perigord. Downing and Dower (1973, p.25) pointed out that by the early 1970s, 10,000 Britons owned second homes in Europe and further afield. Areas of growing British interest at this time included southern France, Spain, Portugal and western Ireland. They argued that a rapidly declining rural population on the continent and the way in which foreign governments were keen to attract British tourists meant that:

> [...] property overseas, both old and new, must be seen as a large potential source of supply of second homes for Britons, particularly at the upper end of the income/ education scale (Downing and Dower, 1973, p.25).

In the 1960s and into the 1970s, British buyers remained minor players in the French housing market. However, in the 1980s this situation changed dramatically.

France (1990s)

The work of Hoggart and Buller (1994a, 1994b and 1995) considers the move of British buyers into the French property market and their socio-economic impact. The number of rural properties purchased by Britons rose from 2,000 in 1987 to 14,000 in 1989 and some newspapers have speculated that as many as 200,000 Britons now own properties in France. Growing demand in the late 1980s was stimulated by the widening differential between house prices in the UK (particularly southern England) and the prices being paid for dilapidated rural properties in France. It was also apparent, according to Buller and Hoggart, that a desire to experience a more relaxed French life-style could be attributed to the books of Peter Mayle ('*A Year in Provence*', 1989 and '*Toujours Provence*', 1990). The idealised rural image (and a perception of a loss of rurality in the UK) combined with positive feedback from existing owners to draw many Britons across the Channel. With reference to the earlier work of Clout, Buller and Hoggart point to the fact that although there is a high incidence of indigenous second home ownership in France, this is mainly confined to the coastal and mountain regions and to newer properties (some of which are purpose-built). Clout had earlier argued that inheritance played a major role in determining the distribution of second homes in France; Buller and Hoggart, however, argue that recent French generations have been increasingly cut off from rural origins. In effect, this change along with a continuing pattern of rural depopulation has left the rural property market open to foreign investment. In two recent papers, the authors have disseminated the findings of an interview-based study with 406 British buyers. The first of these (Hoggart and Buller, 1995) considers the impact of British owners on the French property market. In the second, Buller and Hoggart (1994b) examine the social impact of this encroachment.

In Britain, the status attached to rural living and the whole ideal of the rural dream has been questioned most recently by Cloke and Milbourne (1992). The lack of domestic market opportunities (particularly for isolated rural properties) and the erosion of Britain's rural myth (see Newby, 1980a) has meant that:

> It is inevitable that those who wish to acquire a rural haven will either have to compromise on their 'dream' or look to satisfy their desires outside Britain (Hoggart and Buller, 1995, p.181).

Despite the large number of British purchases in France, market competition is limited. French second home buyers tend to acquire properties either through private negotiation (Dourlens and Vidal-Naquet, 1978) or inheritance (although this is declining) and whilst Britons have a preference for old, rustic property, the French are more likely to be in the market for new dwellings. In Normandy, for example, Hoggart and Buller were able to show that only 7.3 per cent of Britons purchased new homes. It should be noted that the work of these particular authors is not devoted entirely to the second home issue; almost half of the buyers interviewed claimed to be living in France *permanently*. However, this does not detract from the value of considering the impact of these acquisitions (many of which were for second home purposes). At the forefront of Hoggart and Buller's study is the argument that the demand from British buyers has been concentrated in areas of economic decline and the properties acquired were often dilapidated. In this context, new investment in these areas was welcomed, particularly as these properties had failed to attract domestic interest. Unlike the situation in Britain, buyers do not compete for mainstream housing and for this reason:

> Local estate agents are able to report that British buyers cause little friction in rural housing markets (Hoggart and Buller, 1995, p.189).

Instead, they have been instrumental in raising rural housing quality and releasing capital for local vendors who may subsequently buy a new home or improve their existing one. In general, British owners have created net quality gains in the rural housing stock although there have been some negative economic impacts. There seems to be little doubt that purchases in France have raised property prices. However, this is not the result of direct market competition, but because French estate agents specifically target British buyers in the hope of achieving higher prices. For this to have a serious impact on the property market, there would have to be competition for the same properties between British and French buyers. What has been observed is a *dual* property market where Britons are offered properties at higher prices than those offered to the French. This phenomenon has been quelled in recent years as a result of the British economic depression.

In effect, the demand for second homes amongst the British almost exists within an autonomous sub-market and Hoggart and Buller argue that the indigenous demand for second homes is likely to have a far more profound effect on the general property market. Similarly, since 1991 the number of Britons acquiring property in France has declined as a result of the economic recession (and the closing of the differential between British and French property prices) and the realisation amongst some buyers that the French rural idyll may not be quite as idyllic as Peter Mayle (1989, 1990) had suggested. But this is not the result of any pronounced hostility on the part of the French; the authors argue that:

> [...] it has to be emphasised that the impact of in-migrant British purchases is quite different from that which is commonly associated with middle class inflows into British rural areas (Hoggart and Buller, 1995, p.195).

In an earlier paper (Buller and Hoggart, 1994b), the way in which British property owners have 'integrated' into French rural communities was examined by the authors. The 'classical' perspective on this kind of social integration is that because the socio-economic make-up of in-migrants tends to differ from the host population, there is an inherent propensity for conflict and the disruption of social relations (see Bonnain and Sautter, 1970; Forsythe, 1980, cited in Buller and Hoggart, 1994b). Newcomers often seek to protect their new home from change by either adopting a protectionist attitude (sometimes manifest as *nimbyism*) or by being critical of existing local practices (as noted by Albarre in southern Belgium). Buller and Hoggart argue that ensuing conflicts might be intensified in France because the British have a very different perception of rurality from the host population (Buller and Hoggart, 1994b, p.199). The ingredients for conflict were certainly present. The British tended to be younger than their French hosts and whilst the French were typically working class, the Britons were higher earning, middle class and petit bourgeois. Similarly, whilst the French saw the countryside as a working landscape, the newcomers tended to adhere to the 'notion that rural space is primarily an aesthetic backdrop for residential location' (Buller and Hoggart, 1994b, p.201). To undermine the situation further, Buller and Hoggart demonstrated that British sensibilities often ran contrary to French rural values. For instance, Britons often registered complaints about the sale of horse-meat and hunting. The French complained that what the British failed to understand is the fact that these are deep-rooted traditions; in the case of hunting, the entire community becomes involved and it is an expression of social unity.

Despite these uncertain foundations, Buller and Hoggart were able to uncover very little evidence of any real social tension. In the communities, the British were often seen as just one component of a larger group of *étrangers* (strangers) and were certainly not as disliked as Parisians (with their easily recognisable cultivated accents and middle class or agnostic views). In fact, 94 per cent of British second home owners felt that they had been welcomed to rural France (Buller and Hoggart, 1994b, p.203). Remarkably, the greatest measure of resentment was observed *between* Britons. Some owners felt that the arrival of more Britons detracted from the French 'rural charm' whilst others found their compatriots distasteful, claiming that they treated the area like a colonial enclave and that this attitude was alienating locals. This was manifest in a 'compatriot fraternity' characterised by Britons who establish their own English-speaking networks and who do not learn French or mix with French people. However, it was clear that because of a lack of any clear social cleavage between British buyers:

> [. . .] factors which separate those who seek English enclaves from those who attempt to integrate with their local community are linked more to value differences and to dissimilar objectives in buying a French home (Buller and Hoggart, 1994b, p.205).

In conclusion, Buller and Hoggart argue that it is difficult for all but the most ardent Francophiles to integrate into French rural communities. The linguistic and administrative barriers faced by many owners have proved too great to overcome and a number have now left France. Despite the friendliness of the French, they are a family-orientated people who may not have time for strangers. However, on a more positive note, it is clear that the motivations of British owners are not conducive to conflict generation; Britons rarely want to 'take over' (in the true nimby tradition) and their social relationships tend to transcend social divisions (something that is not achieved by Parisians and other French buyers). A key factor in promoting good social relations is that fact that there is a distinct lack of cross competition in the property market and the investment brought by the British is often welcomed. For these reasons, the authors argue that:

> No matter what their goals and the limitations they face in achieving these, none of these British groups have socially disturbed their recipient French communities (Buller and Hoggart, 1994b, p.209).

As interesting and enlightening as the findings outlined by Buller and Hoggart are, it must be remembered that no direct comparison is possible with the situation in the UK. Direct competition for mainstream housing and the subsequent social disruption and anxiety contrasts markedly with the situation in France where the demands of Britons have been more easily accommodated and their class differences (and cultivated accents) have often been masked by language barriers and by a greater desire to 'fit in' (on the part of many owners). However, the point raised in the earlier paper (Buller and Hoggart, 1994b) that second home owners are not a homogenous group (even where there is little social differentiation) and many seek social integration in the host area may be applied equally to the domestic scene. It is clear in Wales, for example, that although some English in-migrants fail to recognise differing cultural values because of their Anglo-centric outlook, others are far more receptive to the cultural and linguistic values of the host population.

Greece (1970s and 1980s)

It is probably not surprising that little academic attention has been focused on the second home situation in the EU's (currently) most easterly member state. In 1988, 12 per cent of households owned a second home in Greece; this figure may be viewed as particularly low given Greece's track record in land use planning and Government-promoted moves to extend the social scope of ownership in the 1960s. However, the growth of second home ownership is at least partially rooted in economic prosperity. Robbins (1930) has illustrated that increases in the amount of time spent engaged in leisure activities is a function of higher incomes (Robbins, 1930, pp.123–129) and it is only relatively recently that the amount of leisure time (and real income) has begun to rise in Greece, a country which still had the lowest gross domestic product per capita in the EU in 1992 (Eurostat, 1994, p.11).

In 1980, Psyhogios undertook an empirical study of the second home phenomenon in Nea Makri, an attractive coastal settlement just 33 kilometres from the centre of Athens. A principal factor in the expansion of second home ownership in Greece (and particularly around Athens) was the failure to allow for the recreational needs of urban populations during periods of rapid urban growth during the early years of the twentieth century (Psyhogios, 1980, p.86). More recent rises in real incomes meant an increased demand for leisure activities; this demand could not be accommodated in Athens and so wealthier urbanites began to look further afield. The vast majority of second homes in Greece are concentrated around Athens and Thessaloniki and are mainly coastal (Psyhogios, 1980, p.88). The Census of 1971 revealed that there were between 35,000 and 40,000 second homes in the greater Athens area and of these, 88 per cent were on the coast whilst the remainder were in the uplands. The distribution was driven largely by consumer taste with certain small fishing villages being transformed, by a process of gentrification, into fashionable resorts. These second home resorts are characterised by dwellings ranging from single family houses to multi-rise buildings and by high residential densities.

A serious Greek problem has been the lack of regulatory standards and planning control (Psychogios, 1980, p.94). Second homes have tended to be *purpose-built* and their development is not as closely related to rural depopulation as it is in many other European countries. The lack of planning control is rooted in the way in which successive Greek governments have pro-actively encouraged new development and the social democratisation of second home ownership. In 1967, for example, a Royal Decree stated that *lyomeno* dwellings (demountable vacation houses) could be erected anywhere not covered by a 'master plan'. This move was intended to extend the opportunity of owning a second home to middle and low income families, but instead, it generated a rush in land speculation on the part of developers who subsequently erected more expensive (and profitable) dwellings for higher income groups. Other types of second home development in Greece include multi-rise flats (which have emerged more recently in response to increasing coastal property prices) and villas which attract higher income urbanites and are located in the older, more traditional, vacation areas (Psychogios, 1980, p.97). The pro-development ethos of Greek planning was reflected in Department of Housing Circular 22 (24/4/77) which listed those types of areas suitable for new second home development. The guidelines simply stated that second homes should be sited in areas of maximum recreation potential (that is, with suitable climates and access to water), should be near existing settlements and easily connected to road networks and should avoid coasts with polluted waters. Clearly, these guidelines were geared to the recreational needs of the users and gave little credence to wider socio-economic factors. However, Circular 22 did state that new development should be steered away from forested and rural areas, not because of any concern for the rural population, but because of the difficulties in providing infrastructure support in these areas. Some 'rural' agglomerations had been conceived as micro-towns (Psyhogios, 1980, p.104) which appeared to meet with approval from planners, the conservation lobby and some weekenders. In addition to Circular 22, Decree 947 (26/7/79) stated that designations of these 'suitable' areas could be made in a number of ways. The Ministry of Public Works could make an immediate designation, whilst designations could be proposed by local authorities or made under private application. In effect, it was possible to build second homes almost anywhere, providing they were suited to the needs of the users.

In the study of Nea Makri, Psyhogios claimed that the growth in second home ownership had brought a range of benefits and very few problems. The creation of wealth for local people (through lucrative property sales) had meant that they were advantaged rather than disadvantaged in the property market. There was certainly 'no evidence for any responsibility [on the part] of second home development for local depopulation in the area' (Psyhogios, 1980, p.143) and quite the opposite situation seemed to have developed, with growth in the permanent population running parallel to the growth in second homes. Social tensions were practically non-existent, but this is perhaps not surprising given the economic benefits brought by incomers and the lack of socio-cultural differences between groups. Nea Makri is just 33 kilometres from the centre of Athens; other European studies have examined groups from entirely different regions or even countries. The situation in Nea Makri does not fit easily into the more general cost/benefit models of second home ownership and Psyhogios's interpretation is intended to reiterate the desirability of new development. Given Greece's trailing economic position in the EU, the continuing dominance of the pro-development lobby is to be expected. However, the importance of careful planning for second home demand is still recognised and Psyhogios endorses the argument by Martin (1972) that only by:

> [...] anticipating and by planning for the demand, can the inflow be controlled. If matters are left as they are – to the interplay of market forces – areas will have a settlement imposed on them, dictated solely by wealthy urban interests (Martin, 1972).

In Greece, however, it has been difficult to plan for demand in a co-ordinated way. The main reason for this is the lack of any local input into the planning system. Planning control is entirely in the hands of the national government which has tended to give insufficient attention to the siting of new development. In the 1970s, for example, second homes were zoned in the same area as a proposed international airport and it is a failure of the Greek planning system that all development is deemed beneficial irrespective of siting and local concerns. The belief that second homes have a 'peculiar strength as a potential contributor to the social and economic development of the receiving areas' (Psychogios, 1980, p.158) has underpinned government attitudes towards this type of development. In the 1980s, it was argued that the most significant factor advancing the Greek economy was the 'development of private property (land and housing), especially in areas of second home and tourist demand' (Getimis and Kafkalas, 1992, p.80). However, irrespective of the costs and benefits of second homes, Psychogios argues that all systems of housing priorities should consider 'the supply of a satisfactory first home before the provision of a second' and planning policies should not 'ignore the majority of people for whom second home ownership is but a dream' (Psychogios, 1980, p.161).

Spain (1970s and 1980s)

It has been claimed that the growth in second homes represented one of the most significant changes in the Spanish housing market in the 1970s (Barke and France, 1988; Morris, 1985). There were estimated to be 2 million second homes in Spain by 1981 and even in the early 1970s, 17 per cent of Spaniards had access to a second home leading some observers to comment that 'ownership is almost as much a part of Spanish life as it is that of the French'. As in France, however, many Spanish second homes are owned or used by foreigners. In the 1970s, Spain was experiencing a period of rapid expansion in 'residential tourism' that was largely unaffected by amendments to planning law (particularly, changes to the *Ley de Regimen del Suelo* 1956) which had no real impact until the 1980s. In effect, the 1970s bore witness to Spain's last phase of largely uncontrolled development.

Although the Spanish population census (like others across Europe) has clear flaws where the enumeration of second homes is concerned, it can be estimated that between 1970 and 1981, the number of second homes in Spain rose by 147 per cent from 796,000 to almost 2 million. The 1970s saw a diffusion of domestic-market second homes from larger, more accessible settlements to the smaller, more remote ones (Barke, 1991, p.14). At the same time, new purpose-built (and often foreign-owned) second homes were increasingly being concentrated in the larger settlements. There was a clear distinction between foreign owned second homes and more recent acquisitions made by Spanish nationals; this particular phenomenon and the notion of a dual market was examined by Barke and France (1988) in the Balearic Islands. In terms of the up-turn in the domestic market in the 1970s, two processes were at work. First, *urban* dwellers, experiencing greater economic prosperity since the 1960s, were purchasing inexpensive 'hobby farm' plots in the interior, which often had sheds and farmbuildings which could gradually (in an *ad hoc* fashion, avoiding planning control) be converted into inhabitable dwellings. The second process involved *rural* families moving to urban dwellings but retaining part of their land for recreational use (Barke, 1991, p.14). According to Barke and France (1988), 'it is ironic that such a trend should be under way at a time when urbanisation has been increasing' (Barke and France, 1988, p.144) and large numbers of Spaniards have their principal residences in urban apartment blocks. A predominant concern in Spain has been the growth and distribution of second homes (examinations of impacts have been confined to those areas experiencing extraordinary rates of growth; ibid, 1988) and the importance of landholding in relation to these aspects of the phenomenon. Where landholding patterns involve the ownership of land in fewer hands, development tends to have been more extensive. This has been observed, for example, in the centre north and the west of the country which have experienced the highest rates of growth. However, in terms of the total number of second homes, the area of highest concentration extends 'from west of Madrid through to the Mediterranean coast in the east and including the Balearics' (Barke, 1991, p.15). Provinces adjacent to Madrid have peaks reaching 35 per cent of the housing stock with peaks of just over 30 per cent around Barcelona. These concentrations reflect the presence of foreign buyers. In the north of the country, and particularly in the Basque region, there are far fewer second homes, partly because of the perceived strength of nationalist and separatist feelings. Patterns of ownership are clearly related to the significance of regional tourism; however, the second home phenomenon diffused widely in Spain in the 1970s and now relates largely to the redistribution of the Spanish population (Barke, 1991, p.17).

An important feature of second home growth in Spain has been the dominance of certain coastal regions; a pattern sustained by foreign investment. In Malaga province, for example, the proportion of second homes grew from a base of 8.8 per cent in 1970 to 18.6 per cent in 1981. The cause/ effect relationships often seem clear-cut in Spain with apparently straightforward correlations between economic decline and second home growth or the attraction of coastal regions and foreign acquisitions. However, on occasions, conventional wisdom appears to break down. Away from the coast in Malaga province, although rural depopulation has clearly taken place, few dwellings have been bought as hobby farms and even fewer have been retained by families moving into the urban areas (Barke, 1991, p.18). It appears therefore, that replacement is not always the natural successor to abandonment and where the foreign tourist base is overwhelmingly dominant, even indigenous buyers may gravitate towards it, attracted by recreational opportunities and the vastly superior service infrastructure. In this instance, patterns of acquisition fall outside the classical interpretation and buyers are willing to sacrifice the opportunity of acquiring cheap rural property if the attractions of another, far more expensive and urban-based option, are that much greater. It might be desirable to compare this scenario with the situation here in Britain and consider whether it might be possible to control the demand for rural second homes by increasing the recreational facilities available in exporting regions. However, such a comparison is largely invalidated by the differing socio-cultural contexts and the lack of any appreciation of the value assigned to rural space by various Spanish social groups. It is interesting to note though, that Psychogios (1980) attributed much of the growth in second home demand in Greece to the failure of planning authorities to allow for the recreational needs of urban populations.

In Malaga, second home distributions are associated with new-build rather than abandonment and replacement (Barke, 1991, p.19) and therefore land use planning has played a far more dominant role in shaping development than in many other Spanish provinces. Elsewhere, it is still clear that the second home market is characterised by a dualism whereby foreigners dominate the larger (often coastal) settlements and Spanish ownership is more characteristic of smaller, often remote settlements. These patterns have been underpinned by rural depopulation in the interior and second home tourism on the coast which have generated a division between casual, individual use and large scale, highly capitalised development (Barke, 1991, p.20). The literature examining the second home phenomenon in Spain has been fairly limited in scope and considerably 'underestimates the complexity of the phenomenon and the variety of conflicts resulting from its rapid growth in Spain in the 1970s'. An area of growing concern has been the:

> [...] social and cultural dislocation experienced by local communities where a large influx of temporarily resident strangers takes place, especially if they are foreigners (Barke, 1991, p.14).

To date, little work has been carried out on this aspect of second home growth in Spain, although some clues as to the socio-economic impact of foreign investment might be gleaned from the work of Hoggart and Buller in rural France. However, much of the foreign investment in Spain has been coastal rather than rural and it might be speculated that the types of British visitors spending their holidays in rural France differ markedly from those visiting the Spanish coast. Barke (1991) notes that the full impact of the second home phenomenon has not yet been fully assessed in Spain and it remains to be seen what impact the planning and environmental policies adopted in the 1980s and implemented in the 1990s will have on second home development and in 'meeting the objections of an increasingly vocal indigenous population' (Barke, 1991, p.21).

Sweden (1970s and 1980s)

Bielckus (1977) argued that regulatory measures to control the growth of second homes across Scandinavia became increasingly important in the 1960s in order to safeguard the countryside whilst continuing to accommodate demand. The changing situation in Sweden received considerably more attention than in neighbouring Denmark or Norway. By 1970, there were almost half a million second homes in Sweden (Bielckus, 1977, p.35), owned by 22 per cent of Swedish households (Downing and Dower, 1973, p.20).

The distribution of second homes in Sweden was first mapped in 1938 (Ljungdahl, 1938) and in some respects, still reflected the semi-nomadic tradition of Swedish farmers, moving herds from winter to summer pastures (Bielckus, *et al*, 1972, p.132). Later studies (Larsson, 1969) emphasised the division between urban exporting regions and rural importing regions, showing that two-thirds of all Swedish second homes are owned by people living in blocks of flats. In the 1960s, rural depopulation and the movement away from the land freed 10,000 farms each year and 30 farm houses became available each day. This only partially satisfied a growing Swedish demand and between 1967 and 1970, a further 55,000 plots of land were made available for second home use (Bielckus, 1977, p.38). A particular oddity of the Swedish situation is the concern over the style of second home dwellings. The red-roofed crofter cottages of Dalarna were so popular in the early 1970s, that many were dismantled and moved nearer urban centres. In the 1960s, observers were already noting that the supply of rural dwellings was not inexhaustible and for this reason, the second home aspirations of individuals and the needs of rural communities were not always compatible. As in Denmark (see previous discussion), there were growing concerns that second home ownership and the privatisation of rural land was creating a potential problem in terms of public access. In 1962, the Swedish Government appointed a review commission with a view to establishing an accurate picture of the distribution of second homes and a basis on which to establish coherent planning policies (Williams, 1974, p.15). The subsequent report (Statens Offentliga Utredningar, 1964) revealed that 85 per cent of second homes were located in the central and southern parts of the country. In 1968, the National Swedish Land Survey Board estimated that there were 420,000 second homes, with the principal concentrations around urban centres; in fact, one-third were within 20 kilometres of a settlement with more than 25,000 persons. However, this situation was beginning to change. In 1968, Aldskogius carried out a study of second homes paying particular attention to the types, ages and rateable values of buildings and travel distances from first to second homes. On a regional level, he was able to demonstrate that *new* developments were dominated by owners from outside the importing region, indicating that people were beginning to travel greater distances to their second homes (previously, 65 per cent of Swedes had lived within 50 kilometres of their second home).

An academic concern with second homes in Sweden was juxtaposed with an official concern for land-use planning. The earliest aim of this planning in the 1960s was to 'achieve a balance between vacation housing and provision for

active outdoor pursuits' (Bielckus, 1977, p.42) with public access taking
precedence over the development of second homes. Pressure on the coastline
was seen as a particular problem in this context. The release of land for second
home development was also occurring in a piece-meal fashion which worked
contrary to the objective of long-term effective planning. For example, the
extreme fragmentation of land-holdings around Lake Siljan in Dalarna (a
particular historical phenomenon) was hindering the purchase of appropriate
plots for second homes and causing demand pressure on the existing dwellings
which became much-coveted (Bielckus, 1977, p.43). These types of concerns
generated pressure for legislative change and the control of real estate
acquisition (see below). However, the first moves to control the development of
second homes occurred at the level of regional planning. The earlier
Government research commissioned in 1962 had shown that a large number
of second homes were located in close proximity to urban areas and with the
expansion of these areas, there was evidence of some incorporation of second
homes into primary residential areas. Around Stockholm, former second
homes (many of which lacked proper facilities for waste disposal) were
reverting to first home use, providing poor quality suburban accommodation
for lower income groups. In order to prevent this from happening in future
years, the 1966 Regional Plan for the Stockholm area specified that, by the year
2000, no second home developments would be located within one hour's drive
of the city. By 1968, Aldskogius had already noted that the tendency to acquire
second homes in more remote areas was increasing and therefore, the problems
associated with this particular change of use were likely to diminish as a result
of improving transport infrastructure and regulatory controls.

Other planning measures were also implemented at this time including the
regulation of new development in the open countryside. It was recognised that
many of the problems associated with second homes in the 1960s (particularly
on the Swedish coast) were the legacy of short-sighted planning decisions made
in the 1930s. When the holiday settlement of Herrviksnäs was completed in
1935, for example, its siting prevented general access to the coast; in contrast,
the development of Hanskroka (1956) posed no such problems and the
settlement was far less unit-dense (Bielckus, *et al*, 1972, p.133). Development in
the 1960s and 1970s was rarely permitted within 300 metres of the shoreline. In
the uplands, although dense natural woodland could be used to conceal new
development, it was clear that it should not be used to conceal *poor quality*
development. Increasingly, planning control was used to maintain standards
with plans being rigorously tested before buildings were erected; far greater
emphasis was placed on the provision of adequate facilities for water supply
and waste disposal. By the mid 1970s, typical second home developments
comprised between 100 and 200 dwellings (the 200 limit was rarely exceeded).
In 1974, Williams argued that this move towards developing second homes in
purpose-built 'communities' should be examined with reference to its
'relevance in the British situation' (Williams, 1974, p.35). By the end of the
decade, it was clear that demand for second homes was levelling off. Improved
camp-site facilities across the country meant that an increasing number of
tourists were spending their vacations camping in the mountains; across

Scandinavia (and particularly in Sweden and Norway), vacation chalets for hire were also becoming more popular, providing a cheaper alternative to purchased second homes (Bielckus, 1977, p.44).

On the whole, the Swedish government became far more concerned with the way second home developments were planned and regulated from the 1960s onwards. By the 1970s, far more attention was being paid to infrastructure provision and the striking of a careful balance between conservation and incorporating second homes into the countryside. Increasingly, 'maintenance of the amenity value' became the main concern in the planning system; second homes were an integral part of the tourist industry, but could not be allowed to disrupt recreational opportunities for other tourist groups, either by damaging the environment or by limiting public access to the most attractive areas. Bielckus neatly summarised the situation that had been reached by the mid 1970s:

> In Scandinavia second homes have become a sufficiently widespread phenomenon to warrant specific legislation. Particularly in Sweden, the favourable population-land ratio and attempts at an equitable distribution of economic resources create an environment in which the desirability of second homes as a form of land use need not be questioned at this time (Bielckus, 1977, p.44).

However, another parallel trend had been developing in Sweden for a number of years; this was a trend towards social as well as natural conservation, which emphasised the need for compromise between individuals and society at large. Where this cannot be achieved through planning control, restrictions on the acquisition of real estate for certain purposes are applied. A growing problem in Sweden in recent years has been the demand for second homes from non-Swedish nationals. Where this has created particular problems (such as upward pressure on house-prices) and the demand for 'secondary residences' is high, permits (required under the *Law on the Acquisition of Real Estate* 1992) for acquiring second homes will not be granted to foreigners. To offer additional protection to some communities, the *Law of Option to Purchase Real Estate* 1967 allows communities to purchase properties which come on the market in areas where the demand for second homes is high and where there is a shortage of primary residences. Under this legislation, communes must declare their intention to buy; an intention which can be challenged by the vendor. Where disputes arise, Central Government acts as arbitrator and it is not uncommon for appeal decisions to go in favour of the vendor. Critically, these measures have been shown to be insufficient in many parts of Sweden. On the west coast, for example, heavy demand for second homes (in the mainstream housing stock) is causing the elevation of house prices, leading to an inability, on the part of younger households, to compete in the housing market. For locals in general, higher property values mean burgeoning taxes as their properties are re-assessed in higher tax-bands (the *Law of Assessment of Real Estate* 1979 does not assess individual dwellings and general taxation is based on an aggregate of market values across an area; therefore increasing tax costs are shouldered by all owners, temporary or permanent). In this situation, it is clear that no compromise has been achieved between the aspirations of individuals and the needs of the local communities.

In Sweden, new second home developments have been increasingly well-planned and, arguably, the objective of achieving a balance between conservation and recreation has been met (Jacobs (1972) recognised that there were lessons to be learnt from the Swedish experience). However, the problems brought by competition for existing housing in some areas have been less easy to regulate despite successive moves to control the acquisition of real estate. Legislation designed at the national level may not always have the desired effect at the local level (this has been apparent on the west coast). This final point acts as a reminder that national instruments must be grounded in a thorough understanding of local circumstances.

Norway (1970s)

Far less is known about the second home situation in Norway than in Sweden or Denmark. In 1970, there were estimated to be 170,000 second homes in Norway (17 per cent of households), although Bielckus (1977) concedes that data regarding second homes in Norway is undermined by the problematic way in which tourist accommodation is classified. Accommodation listed as *hytter* (or 'huts') may range from a simple private cabin to a small hotel (Bielckus, 1977, p.37).

Second homes in Norway are often an expression of the desire on the part of Northern people to enjoy light summer months in the south of the country. Therefore a broad pattern of distribution can be identified; however, in the importing region in southern Norway, development tends to be scattered and has taken place with little planning or control in the past. It is only in recent years that Norwegian planning authorities have experimented with planning controls. In Hallingdål, for instance, a two year ban was imposed on hut building in the 1970s whilst the local authority investigated the ways in which new development might be clustered (drawing on experience in Sweden). The definitional problems point to the fact that in Norway, second homes are seen in the broadest context of recreation; they are sometimes examined at the local level (in planning or economic reports) but rarely at the national level. There is little recent research (English) regarding the second home phenomenon in Norway, although Ouren (1969) estimated that an annual growth rate of 10,000 units was likely to be sustained in the 1970s.

Summary: The European Past

Despite the contrasting socio-economic and cultural contexts in which different second home experiences have evolved, it is still useful to list the most salient points, some of which may have some relevance in England, Scotland and Wales (and across Europe generally). Albarre's study of second homes in Belgium demonstrated that the problems posed by social change (of which second homes are a component) are often balanced by the new opportunities offered. In his particular case-study, new opportunities for conservation were generated by the arrival of newcomers. It is the purpose of planning to ensure that such opportunities are maximised and therefore the scales are tipped in favour of rural communities. In Denmark, increasing recreational opportunities is seen as a legitimate planning goal and second homes must be seen in this context. However, second home demand can only be accommodated after wider social objectives have been achieved. Change of use legislation in Denmark attempts to ensure that this is the case. The French experience of second homes through the 1970s and into the 1990s was one of purpose-built resorts and acquisition of properties through inheritance until, that is, the British arrived and began purchasing old derelict rural property, and reminded everyone of the apparent socio-economic benefits that this type of investment can bring. Historical experience shows that where change of use is controlled (or might be controlled in the future), it should be done sensitively. There would be little point in barring the change of use of dwellings that will otherwise remain empty and fall into disrepair. The French situation also acts as a reminder that second home owners are not a homogenous group. The different motivations of second home seekers dictates the social contribution that they might make in host communities; but how might planners allow for these differences?

In Greece in the 1970s and 1980s, it was clear that if second home villages are a desirable option in some areas, they need to be carefully planned. Arguably, however, British planners might learn more from experiences in Sweden than Greece in this respect. One astute point made by Psychogios however, was the recognition that strategies for second homes must invariably take a back-seat to the development of primary residences. In Spain, the dual nature of the second home market (as in France), provides further evidence that residential tourism and the ownership of second homes is a growing international phenomenon. Hoggart and Buller point out that when domestic second home aspirations cannot be realised, demand may drift abroad. From a national perspective, this may have an adverse impact on the balance of payments; from a European and perhaps more altruistic perspective, it may not be seen as desirable to plan in such a way at home as to export domestic problems to other member states. The case in hand is certainly that of German buyers in Sweden. In Sweden, the now 'classical' problems (of house price inflation and social disruption) remain and have, historically, been accentuated by a tax system which appears to 'charge' permanent residents for the number of second homes which they are forced to endure. It appears that real estate acquisition restrictions have failed to close the floodgates on either domestic or foreign purchasers. More success had earlier been achieved in negating the adverse effects of second homes through land use planning and as far as the real estate restrictions are concerned, they appear to represent a policy approach conceived at the national level that does not always operate smoothly at the local level. New planning measures, either in the UK or abroad, could of course suffer the same fate. It would be important in designing any new legislation to ensure a synthesis of both national and local perspectives in order to create a policy framework which is both sensitive and equitable. However, this would be an extremely ambitious goal.

Finally, in Finland, the case of Åland demonstrated how measures (in this case, based on *property rights*) may be implemented that reflect the dominance of the local rather than the national perspective. These, of course, may only be attainable in countries where relatively devolved government structures exist. All policy responses operate in different legislative contexts. In Scandinavia (and particularly in Finland), devolved regional structures emphasise local perspectives and offer more opportunities for prioritising local interests. On the other hand, where centralised government and a dominant free-market ideology prevail, the national perspective is emphasised. Similar differences can also be observed in the same countries today.

Part 2: The European Present

France (2003)

Auclair and Vanoni (2003, p. 73) note that the countryside has played a key political role in France for many years. Public policy has been strongly conditioned by the needs and demands of farming, though the countryside itself has become less dependent on the agricultural economy in recent times. New economic strengths have emerged including tourism, evidenced in part by an increase in the number of second and holiday homes. Some of these are owned by foreign buyers (see above), though an increasing number are now owned by city-dwellers seeking a rural retreat. In the past, it was traditionally rural areas that were feeding urban growth: today, this situation has been reversed and the tide has apparently turned in favour of the countryside. Hence public policy has re-focused on managing growth around the key urban centres and on dealing with decline in the three areas that continue to lose population: Limousin, Midi-Pyrennées and Auvergne.

Growth brings with it demand pressure but this pressure has not been judged as significantly high outside the Paris region (ibid, p.79): the supply of housing in the countryside usually matches demand and average housing costs are typically low. However even 'typically low' costs can be too high for certain categories of household: and there is evidence that younger people do experience difficulty in securing homes of the right type and cost.

The issue of second and holiday homes – that feature so prominently elsewhere in Europe – have been viewed as less important in France (ibid, p.80). However, such properties do play an important role in the countryside and this comes as little surprise given that France claims to have more holiday homes than any other country in the European Union – rising from 600,000 in 1962 to 2.9 million in 1999. In some regions, the numbers of holiday homes are so great that they have a significant impact on the local and regional economy. In Lozere Departement, for instance, one dwelling in every three is a holiday home and these bring a huge and guaranteed influx of visitors to the area. In recent years, growth in the number of such properties has been levelling off and many former holiday homes are being permanently occupied. This is to some extent a result of major infrastructure and transport improvements, which have encouraged some owners to turn their backs on city homes and live full time in the countryside and commute over greater distances. Other former city-based professionals now choose to work from home, though growth in this phenomenon has not been quite as pronounced as was originally predicted. Additional factors leading to the conversion of holiday to permanent homes includes the tendency for some households to abandon expensive urban living and others to settle permanently in their holiday home on reaching retirement age. This transformation of seasonal homes is yet another process resulting in the apparent re-population of the French countryside. The abundance of relatively inexpensive rural property means that this added demand on the rural housing stock is rarely viewed as problematic.

The movement of people into the countryside – whether seasonally or permanently – is generally viewed positively in France. It is seen as a part of the re-vitalisation of economically laggard areas and a welcome relief from agricultural decline. Planning has not sought to influence either this general movement or switches between temporary and permanent dwelling occupancy. However, there is general support for the idea that certain households require assistance and this has been achieved by stepping up the provision of social housing. Such housing is provided via the *Agence Nationale pour l'Amélioration de l'Habitat* (ANAH). Recently, it has also been the strategy of government to build small social housing estates (of between 5 and 40 dwellings) aimed specifically at young people who are experiencing difficulty is meeting market housing costs in the more pressured rural areas (ibid, p.82). Effort is being made to ensure that such estates blend in with existing architecture, are integrated within current settlements, and are not obvious add-ons that end up as concentrations of social exclusion. The current situation in France illustrates that:

- Second and holiday homes may be viewed as a positive force in the countryside;
- But even forces that are generally positive may bring some negative side-effects;
- In France, these negative side-effects are dealt with when and where they arise through supply-led solutions.

Republic of Ireland (2003)

According to Finnerty *et al* (2003, p.129) the Republic of Ireland's current high levels of economic growth – which has tailed off more recently – are putting considerable pressure on housing affordability and access for recently formed and aspiring households. One consequence of this economic growth has been unprecedented demand for and levels of total residential new build, with almost 50,000 new housing units built in 2000. Since the start of the current economic upturn in Ireland, the average price of private new build nationally has more than doubled, rising from approximately £61,000 in 1995 to £133,000 in 2000. While increases have been much more pronounced in the main urban centres of Dublin, Cork, Limerick, Waterford and Galway, house prices have also increased substantially in rural areas.

In many more marginal – but attractive – rural areas, house prices have been elevated by the changing structure of the local housing market. Indeed, 'second and holiday homes substitute for the effects of urban over-spill felt closer to Dublin' (ibid, p.136):

> Reflecting the overall buoyancy of the economy and sustained house price inflation, there is a clear pattern of activity by investors and by those buying second homes, which is making it more difficult for first time buyers and for local authorities to compete for homes and sites. Encouraging the emergence of a pool of residential investors in peripheral rural areas have been certain tax breaks catering to this market, principally the Seaside Resort Renewal Scheme (SRRS). The Seaside Resort Scheme ran from July 1995 to December 1999 and cost an estimated £200m in tax expenditures. It provided tax relief for the construction of, *inter alia*, holiday homes in 12 designated seaside resorts (Finnerty *et al*, 2003, p. 136).

The story is a familiar one: the greater purchasing power of investors or urban households seeking a second home (for recreational or for investment) often pushes prices of even smaller, more modest dwellings out of the reach of local buyers. Given that there are no legal restrictions on the purchase of second homes (or sites on which to build second homes), the problem is particularly acute in more scenic and coastal areas (as is the case in England and Wales, see Chapter 4). The result is that a rising number of homeowners do not reside in these areas for most of the year. In one remote area of County Donegal, for example, it is estimated that almost two-thirds of all out-of-town houses are owned by second home investors from outside the area (ibid, p.136). The strength of outside demand also acts to bid up the cost of building services and of sites, making it more difficult for local authorities to meet unsatisfied housing need:

> This has implications in terms of depopulation, inability to sustain services on a year-round basis and over-stretching of infrastructure at the peak season, and the development of dual communities and social disparities, or social displacement.
>
> This displacement in turn has implications for the sustainability of existing communities and how their needs are met in light of virtually uncontrolled development. Many resort towns and villages become boomtowns during the summer months, but virtually shut down during the low season. Coupled with depopulation of the existing community they can become deserted, alienating, ghost towns surrounded but untouched by the trappings of affluence, and incapable of supporting basic community facilities such as schools, public transport and so on (ibid, pp. 136–137).

Again, the picture presented by Finnerty and colleagues is echoed in the experiences of some rural areas in England and Wales (Chapter 4). In Ireland, the main institutional responses to problems in rural housing continue to lie with the local authorities. As part of the implementation of Ireland's National

Plan each local authority is currently (2003) in the process of producing an integrated 10-year strategy across the areas of health, education, housing and social welfare. The development of this strategy is designed to provide an opportunity for rural local authorities to address the issues of urban encroachment and housing affordability.

According to Finnerty *et al*, a potentially important element in the housing strategies of local authorities is Section V of the Planning and Development Act 2000, which gives authorities the power to acquire at agricultural prices, up to 20 per cent of land for social or affordable housing in new housing developments. Furthermore, a 'Town Renewal Scheme' – which ran from 2000 to 2002 – aimed to counter the trend of people moving out of towns into the surrounding rural areas. The idea is that by making town and city living more attractive, pressure on the countryside can be avoided. This same message is implied in the Urban Task Force's 1999 report for the UK.

But more immediately, many county councils in areas experiencing housing pressure have brought forward an array of zoning and residency conditions for the granting of planning permission for residential developments as part of their County Development Plans (CDPs). These requirements have been justified on the basis of ensuring housing affordability and access for local residents. The County Development Plan for Donegal, for instance, stipulates that priority for new permanent housing in rural areas should be given to members of the 'indigenous rural community' with higher density multiple housing developments being permitted only on serviced areas within defined control points (ibid, p.144).

Country Kerry has also tried to respond to external demand. The County has experienced considerable pressure for holiday/second homes in recent years, particularly in visually sensitive landscapes. The overall result of such development is unsustainable and rapid deterioration of the visual qualities of the natural and scenic landscape, and increasing affordability issues, with local people becoming unable to compete for sites and houses against holiday home speculators in certain parts of the County. The Planning Authority is looking to ensure that such properties:

- Are located in or close to established settlements, villages or towns;
- Are set in well-defined parks or 'satellite units' adjacent to an established settlement, village or town, where the infrastructure is adequate;
- May be subject to an Environmental Impact Statement/Study including a study of social impacts;
- Will not be permitted in the rural landscape (unless renovating or restoring an existing vacant or disused property – conditions apply);
- Will be subject to integration into existing urban structures;
- Must not, by their size or location, dominate the existing fabric of development, nor create 'ghost towns' outside the main tourist season;
- Must be designed and sited so as not to have an adverse impact on the character of the entire settlement, village, town or natural environment;
- Must ensure the retention of existing site features to form part of a comprehensive landscaping scheme; and;

- The Planning Authority will require that adequate facilities, services and infrastructure be provided to cater for the needs of the holiday home development, and may require the developer to provide or contribute to the provision of services and infrastructure additional to those of the immediate needs of the complex. In addition, management and maintenance of such facilities may fall on the management company.

Finnerty and colleagues conclude by adding that '[...] a great deal of controversy has accompanied attempts to tackle "uncontrolled" rural new build, whether for holiday or permanent use. In County Clare a draft proposal allowing anyone to build homes in the open countryside was modified with the addition: "that the purpose of this policy is to facilitate local rural people who have a genuine requirement for housing". Councillors also agreed that "non-locals" would not now be allowed to build homes in areas under high development pressure on the county's west coast and vulnerable landscapes, including much of the Burren' (p.141). This very recent experience in the Republic of Ireland demonstrates the following:

- Emphasis can be placed on controlling new-build housing, with attempts made to direct it towards local need only after demonstrating the potential social impacts of not doing so;
- A concern for understanding why people continue to move away from towns is apparent within policy: there is a need to look at the underlying social/urban trends that drive second home demand;
- Saying who can and cannot build new cottages in the countryside has proven very controversial in Ireland.

Italy (2003)

Padovani and Vettoretto (2003, p.98) note that the 1970s and early 1980s brought with them a wave of counter-urbanisation in Italy. The whole structure of the Italian national economy changed and the most striking feature of this change was the growth of small businesses and firms in Central and North East Italy: the more 'rural' regions. These new peripheral growth areas not only drew in businesses and permanent settlers, but also second and holiday homes. Roughly half of all new house-building in these areas during the 1970s comprised homes that were not permanently occupied (ibid, p.100). This phenomenon had much to do with peoples' desire to maintain links with their places of birth and with the greater value now being placed on environmental assets for tourism development. Having a home in the countryside was for many an important statement of self-identity. This period was characterised by far more building in low-density rural areas.

Second home growth in Italy has continued throughout the last three decades. But in those rural areas with high quality environments and/or significant historical or cultural resources, there has also been a differentiation of tourist activity with a 'soft' or 'intelligent' tourism focused around place-identity, traditional produce and crafts, and which respects local heritage and landscape. Second homes are peripheral to this more 'intelligent' tourism and have been subject to two trends: first a general slowdown in acquisitions and second, a substantial change in the social profiles of those buying properties for this purpose. That said, second homes still bring problems to some tourist areas. In the established tourist areas, with hotels and second homes serving mainly high-income groups, housing pressure is generated by affluent visitors who drive up not only the cost of houses, but all consumption goods. In areas of more recent (seasonal) tourism development, primarily in the low-density coastal areas of the south where illegal building has been rife, there are few comparable pressures. Here, planning regulations have little impact on housing supply (because of weak enforcement and illegal building) and hence the cost of homes. Rather, the effect is to erode environmental quality and degrade those very things that second home buyers and tourists more generally, value so highly.

Second homes in Italy, as elsewhere, are sometimes viewed as a welcome relief from economic decline rather than a problem to be tackled through housing or planning policy. However, the reason for their hitherto low impact on local communities stems from the Italian tradition of weak planning enforcement and illegal house building, particularly in the south of the country. Rural communities tend not to be affected by such outside property acquisitions when there are so few constraints on new house building. Recent Italian experience perhaps illustrates that second homes may only become a problem where they combine with a restrictive planning system and low levels of new house building. As enforcement is standardised across the country, problems stemming from stronger market competition may arise. It looks likely that the response of government will be to increase supply rather than restrict the purchase of homes to locals (Padovani and Vettoretto, 2003, p.109). Italians would probably find the latter move unpalatable given their suspicion of overt state interference and their liking for private enterprise. Overall, the peculiarities of the Italian situation mean that:

- Second homes are viewed as part of a wider economic renaissance: the two go hand-in-hand;
- Community impacts are limited where there has been less land/planning restraint and therefore greater freedom to meet needs whilst also accommodating new demands (do 'high impacts' in Wales occur in areas where insufficient land is released for house building?);
- But a lack of restraint may, of course, bring serious environmental problems.

Spain (2003)

It is generally accepted that Spain has two second-home markets: a coastal (and island) market dominated by foreign chalet buyers and an inland rural market dominated by Spanish nationals. Spanish Census data has, for the past fifty years, differentiated between the privately-used housing stock and dwellings 'rented out for tourist reasons'. However, Census data do not reveal the number of second homes used by their owners for 'tourist reasons' so whilst the explosion in 'chalet type' development can be charted using the Census (See Chapter 7), it is impossible to obtain a detailed national picture of rural, privately owned, second homes.

Coastal chalet development is viewed as a key part of the tourist industry and a driver of the national economy (Valenzuala, 2003, p. 120). Other second homes, particularly those found in the interior and more rural areas, are seen to have both a different role and a different impact. Indeed, the Spanish interior has been subject to very different economic and social processes compared with the coastal regions. Whilst the coast may welcome second or holiday homes, such acquisitions may be more problematic in the interior. The purchase of second homes, either by domestic or foreign buyers, is viewed as a key market pressure – and source of conflict – in certain locations (ibid. p.119). This combines with other forms of external demand – in the form of commuters seeking the perceived benefits of a rural lifestyle – to reduce housing accessibility for the less well-off. And though some areas are facing a deepening rural crisis, others are experiencing both expansion and prosperity. In the latter, the balance between housing supply and demand may become unsettled where there are large numbers of outside buyers. And those workers locked into the agrarian sector may not be able to compete against higher earning incomers in the newer more prosperous sectors. It is commonplace, particular in places such as Galicia, for people to leave the countryside but then in later life to return and purchase second homes either as an investment or for later retirement. Often, this behaviour is replicated by those with no family connection to a particular village but who simply wish to enjoy the relaxation afforded by a weekend retreat.

During the 1990s, the Ministry of Agriculture, Fishing and Food started to exercise new powers, which have brought indirect benefits to the rural housing stock. Mechanisms, for example, were established to support the agrarian labour force and these included grants for young farmers and farm workers for the purchase and improvement of housing (ibid. p.121). Structural Funds provided by the European Union offer another important source of money for dealing with housing problems. A number of different funds have been tapped into. For instance, the European Regional Development Fund (ERDF) has been used to support programmes focusing on difficulties relating to poor infrastructure provision; the funds assist with economic development strategies which will hopefully bring about a better quality of life for many rural areas. Also, the LEADER (*Liaisons Entre Actions de Dévelopment de l'Economie Rurale*, or 'Links Between Actions for the Development of the Rural Economy') programme – conceived as an integrated programme for rural development – assists smaller communities through a range of initiatives and strategies. Recently in Spain, there has been an emphasis on the provision of subsidies for the refurbishment of traditional housing which can then serve as tourist accommodation. The LEADER (and more recent LEADER II) programme has been directed at economic diversification rather than the support of agrarian activities and therefore has the potential to help those communities suffering the consequences of agricultural decline.

There have also been a number of private and self-help initiatives aimed at improving rural housing conditions. Some private companies, for instance, have been pro-active in the rehabilitation of rural dwellings, which are then turned into second homes. In response to local needs, regional government has been more active and successful in intervening in the rural housing market. It has, for instance offered special grants to allow young people, couples or new residents to enter the housing market and subsequently remain in their homes. The programmes created by regional government have also supported dwelling improvement and repairs, ensuring that the condition of rural property reaches an acceptable standard.

Of the three tiers of Spanish government – national, regional and local – it is the regional tier that has greatest influence in relation to housing policy. And the policy that has been developed has taken two broad directions (ibid. p.124). Firstly it has been concerned with permanently occupied dwellings and the industries that sustain the local population. Secondly, it has also been concerned – in equal measure – with that rural housing which supports an 'urban use'; that is, dwellings used as second homes or those seen as supporting the local tourist industry in some other way. Though these directions may seem to address different sets of needs and issues, they are perceived as complementary, both addressing the problems of depopulation and decline though the following strategies:

- The modernisation of rural enterprises (including the promotion of new economic forms);
- Direct housing amelioration, including dealing with issues of supply (of permanent and second homes); and
- Infrastructure and services available to rural communities. (Valenzuala, 2003, p. 124).

Experience in Spain suggests that:

- Economic revitalisation and not restriction is seen as the key to reversing the fortunes of rural communities;
- It is possible to adopt a positive stance towards second and holiday homes (where these are viewed as a positive economic driver) and couple this with complementary support for rural communities through general economic policy and targeted housing support.

Sweden (2003)

Second homes are frequently portrayed as a key issue in the Swedish countryside. The last decade has seen an increasing demand from other European nationals; Danes and Germans have been buying second homes in the south of Sweden and Norwegians on the west coast (Folkesdotter, 2003, p.49). The number of second homes in Sweden is significant: roughly half a million in a country with a population of just 8.8 million and a housing stock comprising only a little over 4 million permanent dwellings. Whilst domestic second home ownership has been a feature of Swedish society for decades, it is the influx of foreign buyers that is often portrayed as more problematic. According to Folkesdotter (p.49), the dramatic increase of German property acquisition in Sweden started in 1991; between 1991 and 1996, 4,000 Germans bought cottages in Sweden. By 2001, there were a total of 5,500 German-owned second homes in Sweden: a figure big enough to cause adverse publicity, but tiny in comparison to levels of German second home ownership elsewhere. Germans own about 300,000 second homes in Spain, 100,000 in France, 80,000 in Italy and 65,000 in Portugal (ibid. p.50).

Folkesdotter argues that Sweden's once largely agricultural countryside has undergone a slow transition and emerged as a 'recreational landscape' (p.50):

> This transition has been marked by second home purchasing, particularly amongst foreign nationals: though any erosion of traditional values is only indirectly linked to this urban encroachment. Its more direct cause is the decline and waning influence of agriculture. The countryside has certainly changed. On the up side, there appears today to be more room for different lifestyles and values. But what of the downside and the potential problems stemming from the higher housing costs? (Folkesdotter, 2003, p.50).

The answer is that in many rural areas, pressure from second home purchasing has resulted in the 'closure and deterioration of commercial and public services and infrastructure'. Seasonal living in some areas has led to the number of rural schools and food stores declining rapidly. However, Folkesdotter suggests that this loss of services is only partially due to the influx of second home buyers; it is also a consequence of past oversupply. However, as well as decreasing the demand for certain rural services, second homes also heap added pressure on others: for example, during the summer months, real difficulties are created for the utilities as demand for fresh water rockets and sewage waste water systems are hit by sudden seasonal demand. There are also additional concerns, peculiar to the Swedish situation. For example:

> Another problem facing local people in the old fishing villages located on these same archipelagos close to the built-up centres of Stockholm and Gothenburg is the recent and significant increase in property tax, which makes it difficult for people to manage their housing costs. This problem results from the general increase in property prices experienced in these areas and therefore the re-allocation of properties into higher tax bands. House price rises have been significant: a consequence of new market pressures (ibid. p.51).

The Swedish government is currently moving to reduce the financial burden on some local households through reform of existing regulations. Official concern for the potential difficulties introduced by second homes – and particularly foreign demand – has ballooned in recent years. One of Sweden's most popular newspapers carried an article in 2001 by the head of the Swedish National Rural Agency, who claimed that many attractive areas risk losing their permanent populations as communities are hi-jacked by wealthy incomers. Three ways of avoiding this situation were proposed: first it is possible to do nothing and simply to accept that displacement and replacement of existing communities is inevitable and unavoidable, but this would of course result in the end of many traditional coastal communities. The second option would involve new legislation to make it harder to turn permanent dwellings into second homes. And thirdly, it might be possible to simply ban the use of new housing for 'recreation'. The Swedish National Rural Agency apparently favours the second approach, favouring further research into the use of planning controls to restrict 'change of use': new legislation '[...] might require buyers to declare whether or not they are intending to live in a property on a permanent basis. Further amendments to the Real Estate Purchasing and Planning and Building Acts are also proposed and would lead to an effective ban on the conversion of permanent to holiday homes' (ibid. pp.53–54). However, Folkesdotter is critical of such an approach:

> Neither current nor past attempts to control holiday homes have been particularly successful. Responsibility for implementing planning policy lies with the municipalities (with the exception of those areas designated as specially protected areas of natural and/or cultural interest) which tend to have quite modest financial and staff resources. The policing of such new policies would require massive resourcing, removing the majority of municipal staff from other tasks. Foreign buyers must make applications to purchase property in Sweden at the current time, though very few of these applications are ever rejected. Over the border in Denmark, a far stricter system of control is in place and restrictive legislation was the product of Danish EC-negotiations in 1972 (ibid. p.54).

However as a result of more recent EU discussions on rights of residence (see Muller, 1999, p102, cited in Folkesdotter, 2003, p.54), it seems unlikely that Denmark will be able to retain its tougher stance towards foreign property purchasing. And given this precedent, it also seems unlikely that Danish-style (see earlier discussion) controls will be introduced in Sweden. In conclusion:

- Sweden has a vast second home market that causes problems in only a minority of areas;
- Fiscal measures can be used to reduce the cost of housing for local groups: this is the opposite approach to the UK, where fiscal measures – in relation to second homes – are seen as a negative tool;
- In the most pressured areas, it might be possible to make second home acquisition more difficult through tighter planning or permit control;
- But enforcement of controls seems to be the key issue and drawback. Can local authorities dedicate the required extra resources to such a measure?;
- Explicit controls on 'foreign' (and perhaps 'non local') buyers can fall foul of EU law.

Conclusions: The European Present

Given that all the countries considered above are very different in terms of their size, population density, and size and nature of their second home markets, a great deal of care must be taken when trying to tease out general lessons. However, it is clear that:

- The extent of second home problems is not determined solely by the size of the second home market. The Netherlands (not examined here, but see Heins, 2003, pp. 60–70) seems to experience difficulties out of proportion with its market, whereas Italy has many more second homes but no well defined community/housing problem stemming from local housing pressures.
- Second homes only appear to become problematic for local communities where they exist in areas of land constraint and planning restriction. Hence in Italy, illegal house building and the flouting of planning law has compensated for the effects of strong external housing demand. Some communities may be more sensitised to the issue, particularly when cultural issues are at stake: these might be linguistic or relate to the erosion/loss of local traditions.
- In areas of planning restriction second homes may cause social problems: in areas without such restriction, their impacts may be more environmental in nature.
- In the Southern European countries, softer approaches to planning mean that second homes are less of a problem. This is not the case where planning is tighter: in the UK, Sweden (and Denmark and Finland).

It is also the case that:

- Many rural areas have declined over the last 100 years as a result of a shift in the focus of production (from agriculture to urban-based industry), the locus of production (from the countryside to town) and the mode of production (from manual labour to mechanisation).
- In this context, tourism and recreation are seen as indicators of an economic renaissance. Second homes may be viewed as part of this renaissance, as in Spain and Italy.
- Most countries have responded positively to second homes: providing support for this kind of development and, at the same time, dealing with community impacts through encouraging new forms of economic development.
- Second homes are responded to at a 'structural' (for example regional) level: they are seen as part of a 'post-productivist' countryside (that is, one where primary production is no longer the core activity) and welcomed. At the same level, governments have attempted to channel growth into communities, harnessing the development represented by second or holiday homes to meet the local needs that would have existed irrespective of the arrival of second homes.
- Local restriction has been a feature of the Netherlands (again, see Heins, 2003) and across Scandinavia. It has met with limited success, is resource intensive and does not address the structural problems that persist.

- The tiers of response tend to be; strategic – managing the consequences of agricultural decline and service-led renaissance; local – support for local tourism (and second homes) and local communities, where low incomes (and the lack of jobs) is the root cause of distress.

Whilst the main purpose of this chapter has been to survey and present a comprehensive account of European experiences, it is useful to examine the different approaches to second homes in different parts of Europe. Indeed, the insights gained in this analysis – and set out as key points above – are taken forward in the development of a possible UK policy framework set out in Chapter 9.

Chapter 6
Mainland Europe and Britain Compared

Introduction

The last two chapters have looked at Britain (represented by England and Wales) and mainland Europe (represented by a number of EU member states) separately. The last chapter ended with a number of 'lessons' that might be taken forward in any future policy framework for dealing with second home – and broader housing demand and supply – pressures in the UK, though we have been careful to emphasise that different national situations vary considerably. At the end of Chapter 5, it was suggested that Southern European countries tend to adopt a more relaxed approach to planning control, therefore creating a market which is more responsive to external and local demand pressures. In contrast, Northern European countries – including the Scandinavian states and Britain – tend towards tighter regulation (through planning controls) which often restricts how easily they can respond to local needs in the light of new external demands on the housing stock. This analysis is presented more fully in Gallent and Allen (2003, pp.208–226), and demonstrates how different countries have traditionally responded to housing market pressures in a variety of different ways. It also shows that although the second home issue in Britain may have unique characteristics, there are parallels with other countries in terms of why 'market pressures' may arise, including the tightness of planning controls.

The aim of this current chapter is to look more closely at the second home phenomenon in Britain and mainland Europe. We approach this analysis with a fairly loose hypothesis in mind: that the second home market in Britain differs in several respects to that found elsewhere in Europe. We have argued previously (Gallent and Tewdwr-Jones, 2001) that whilst second home demand displays 'epidemic' characteristics in Britain, the market elsewhere is more ubiquitous, evenly-distributed and 'endemic'. With this hypothesis in mind, Chapter 7 addresses a fairly basic question: is the second home phenomenon in Britain and the rest of Europe essentially the same? In order to provide an answer, we compare two British (the Scottish Highland and Islands and North Wales) with two continental European regions (Galicia and Sweden's West Coast), examining the market contexts in which second homes are positioned. The analysis presented considers individual local areas; it draws partly on work for Gwynedd County Council undertaken in 1996/97 and partly on a more recent analysis of secondary data and literature.

Britain and Mainland Europe: Shared Concerns?

We began this book with the suggestion that second homes are sometimes viewed as the 'scourge of the British countryside', but added that this view is not universally shared and certainly may not apply in large parts of mainland Europe. Confirming the negative assessment of second homes in Britain, former UK Environment Minister Michael Meacher claimed in 1999, that more affluent households seeking properties for investment or recreation in marginalised rural areas are in fact '[. . .] robbing others of a home' (cited in Gallent and Tewdwr-Jones, 2000). Again, it was noted in Chapter 1 that such views are not uncommon in Britain and that it has been claimed that 'there is no greater inequality in this country [the UK] that some people have two homes while others have none' (Monbiot, 1999).

The last chapter demonstrated – if such a demonstration were needed – that the purchase and use of second homes – as 'weekend cottages' – is not a uniquely British occupation, but occurs across continental Europe (see Chapter 5 for national situations; see also Petersson, 1999). And for reasons that will be discussed in the main part of this chapter, elsewhere second homes are not invariably painted as the wreckers of rural communities, as frequently happens in Britain. The purpose of this chapter is to explain how second homes are viewed elsewhere in Europe, and to consider whether or not the analysis offered by Monbiot (1999) and others has any currency on the continent.

In the opening chapter, it was suggested that the potentially negative impacts of second homes are a consequence of the position they occupy in rural housing markets. In Britain, many properties that are used as second homes are drawn from the mainstream second-hand stock, and pulled out of the reach of local buyers. But in Europe, the situation is frequently very different: second homes used as recreational bases are often purpose-built; and the majority of second homes that are drawn from the mainstream housing stock are used as weekend retreats for those working reasonably close by. In Britain there are two markets: a distinct local market and a national market, and conflict between the two can – and often does – boil over in second home hot-spots. In many parts of mainland Europe, this same division is less prevalent; instead, there is a regional sub-market in which the distinction between urban-rural or local-non-local buyers is impossible to make. This market difference can also be conceived in terms of the 'leisure space' of urban areas. Drawing on the work of Aronsson (1989) and Jansson (1994), Petersson (1999) has argued that 'the leisure space of urban areas can be divided into three categories; the daily leisure space, the weekend leisure space and the vacation space' (p.9). Because the majority of Sweden's 650,000 second-homes are located on the archipelagos near the urban centres of Stockholm and Gothenburg, they occupy a weekend – or even daily – leisure space. In Britain, the principal concentrations are further away from large 'source' towns and cities, hence occupying 'vacation space'. This is another way of conceiving regional differences, but as a framework, it is concerned less with the housing market and more with the purpose that a second home serves. So whilst there are clear overlaps with the housing market perspective, our examination of British and European situations focuses mainly on the 'sub-market' and 'two-market' notion described above.

This broad difference is examined in this chapter using the studies cited in the introduction. The 'working assumption' is made that second homes *are* a problem in Britain (pushing up property prices and forming a barrier to housing access) and the 'two market' (that is, British) and 'regional sub-market' (that is, European) theories are tested through regional comparisons. We also consider whether there are instances, in Europe, of buyers from outside the sub-market area seeking second homes and creating 'British-style' difficulties on the continent. In the past, politicians have been quick to assume that the British and European situations, in respect of second homes, are essentially the same and therefore the only 'learning' to be done related to policy solutions. This issue was explored by Allen *et al* (1998) who focus attention on the transferability of policy tools. In this chapter, the focus is not on 'learning the solutions', but on considering *how* second homes fit into different local or national market situations. This is achieved through a comparison of two British and two mainland European examples. The studies used are brief, but go some way toward answering the basic question: are second homes a *problem* only in Britain?

Britain and Europe: Dual Markets or Regional Sub-Markets?

The comparison provided below draws on four regional examples: two in Britain and two on the continent. The British examples are located in Wales and Scotland and centre on communities that vary in size and economic situation; they could all be described as 'culturally sensitive' (to social change) and economically fragile, and still finding their feet following industrial or agricultural decline. They are areas often described as examples of second home 'hot-spots'. The two European examples (in Spain and Sweden) share most of these characteristics, appear sensitive to change and are transitional in terms of their local economies. The Swedish West Coast examples have in the past, been held up by British policy makers as communities afflicted by the same problems facing more scenic parts of Britain. A strategy, perhaps, designed to mobilise support behind a much wider anti-second home crusade.

Part 1: Britain: Scotland and Wales

The purpose of presenting the following two British case studies is to illustrate how second-homes fit into local housing markets. Their position in the rural housing market determines their importance as a potential barrier to local housing access and is defined by two broad factors. These are:

- The *type of property* purchased and subsequently switched to second home use – the basic question being whether or not this housing might otherwise have been bought by local residents;

- The *characteristics* of second home purchasers and their 'relationship' with their newly-acquired property; are they, for example, distant buyers who use their second homes during odd weekends over the summer, or are they more frequent users living reasonably close by. In the second case, patterns of use may blur the distinction between first and second home, and second home demand may form part of a single sub-regional market rather than an aggressive national market conflicting with local needs.

These two factors are examined in each of the study areas, firstly as a means of defining the essence of the British 'problem' and secondly as a framework for comparing the British and European situations.

The Scottish Highlands

Three areas in the Scottish Highlands and Islands were examined: a cluster of Strathspey villages, Shetland's North Mainland (Yell and Unst), and Sleat Peninsula. These areas are characterised by low-density population coverage, remoteness and a variety of economic activities. They have also been affected by a proliferation of second home purchasing in recent years.

The Strathspey villages are located in the central Highlands, immediately to the west of the Cairngorm mountain range. Comprising Aviemore, Carrbridge, Boat of Garten, and Nethy Bridge, the villages have attracted a significant number of in-migrants over the last 15 years. This growth can, in part, be attributed to the beautiful scenery, the villages' proximity to the snow resorts of the Cairngorms, and the availability of relatively cheap property. Most of the in-migrants are young people or families, attracted to the area from the Scottish 'central belt' and from England. Some of the area's *holiday home* accommodation has been purpose-built (often in the form of 'timeshare' apartments) and is similar in form to numerous chalet developments in Sweden (see Kalbro & Mattsson, 1995). This housing clearly serves a specific tourism purpose and in no way overlaps with the general market.

In contrast, the majority of *second homes* were formerly permanent residences drawn from the mainstream housing stock. They have been created through a *de facto* change of use, switching from serving the local market to a market formed by central belt and English buyers. In some locations, the proportion of second homes within the general housing stock is around 20 per cent. In 1997, it was estimated that there were 292 second-homes and 300 holiday homes in the area, as well as 124 empty properties. The external demand for second homes has raised property prices in the area significantly over the last ten years to levels beyond those of neighbouring areas and the affordability range of many local people. The planning system has also affected prices because of the high conservation value attached to the environment and the strict regulatory policies in place prohibiting development. On the one hand, Strathspey provides a classic example of the British second home problem. Higher-earning incomers have bought a significant percentage of homes and house prices have risen sharply in recent years. However, the higher numbers of holiday homes (commercially let) suggests a fairly strong local economy and there does appear to be a surplus of empty properties. These may be out of reach of local buyers and the owners may be looking for more lucrative uses of their property than renting or selling to locals. But because a whole range of data sources (especially the Census) are notoriously inaccurate in relation to second home numbers (frequently enumerating second homes as empty properties: see Chapter 1), it is probable that some of these 124 empties are in fact second homes. On balance, the 'classic' rural second home processes seem to be at work, with house prices being driven up firstly by restrictive rural planning and only secondly by incomer purchases. In other words, second homes are the manifestation of a problem created fundamentally by the planning system.

The situation in the second Scottish area was slightly different. The North Mainland of Shetland, Yell and Unst, with a population of approximately 4,500, is amongst an island group located beyond the mainland of Scotland. The main centre of administration, employment and service provision is in Lerwick, on the South Mainland, which is home to approximately one third of the population. In-migration has occurred due to the presence of both oil-related activity and several military establishments. Young adults and families figure prominently in the area's population profile. The local economy has been generally buoyant throughout the 1980s and 1990s thanks to the area's proximity to the North Sea Oil fields. Unemployment levels are comparatively low, although *parts* of the North Mainland's economic future remains uncertain at the present time as a consequence of its reliance on crofting, agriculture, quarrying, fishing and textiles. Culturally, the island group differs from the rest of Scotland, resting on Nordic traditions. With continued uncertainty over the future of North Sea oil and the military bases in the medium to long term, alternative economic activities are being sought to provide future stability and security. A total of forty second-homes and 36 holiday homes were noted in 1997 although there were an additional 222 empty properties – some of which may, in the future, be used or purchased by the rising number of seasonal visitors. The total number of second homes is fairly small (only 2.6 per cent of the stock total), though again, it seems likely that many of the empties will become second homes if not already used for this purpose. That said, it is unlikely that second homes will ever come to dominate the housing market, largely because the remoteness of the island makes it attractive only to the most intrepid second homebuyers. Past research has continually re-affirmed that although second home hunters seek some degree of solitude, most gravitate towards properties that are within reasonably easy reach of their first home (Davies & O'Farrell, 1981). So rather than relying on infrequent scheduled flights, they prefer areas with reasonable motorway access – hence the English Lake District (with the M6), North Wales (with the A55 extension), and South West Wales (the M5) are all second home hot spots.

The Sleat Peninsula on the other hand, has more of the characteristics that the British second-home buyer demands. The Peninsula is located at the most southern point on the Isle of Skye, western Scotland. Despite its peripheral location, the area has experienced recent population growth, increased interest in the housing market, and significant infrastructure improvements – including tourism developments – that have opened the area up to economically active outsiders. Perhaps the most significant development – which relates to the access issue highlighted above – has been the opening of the Skye Bridge.[1] The additional development brought by easier access to the island has been cautiously welcomed, though some people see this greater integration into a wider economy as a cultural threat, perhaps ultimately weakening the Island's Gaelic traditions (half of the population speak Scots Gaelic).

There are more than 100 second and holiday homes on Sleat contributing, perhaps, to the significant rises in house prices witnessed during the 1990s. But equally important has been the arrival of an increasing number of retirement migrants to the peninsula, as well as younger people seeking what they anticipate will be an 'alternative lifestyle'. The housing market has been unable to absorb these pressures, and despite the relative strength of the economy (compared to other peripheral Scottish areas), many local households have been forced into temporary accommodation (particularly caravans) or into extended stays with friends and relatives. Some rent second homes during the off-season,

> [...] but then have a major problem when owners want the houses back for themselves, sometimes just for a fortnight, or for summer holiday lets which command much higher rents. This creates a lot of animosity in Skye where incomers can buy into the housing stock and locals find they have to move out in the Spring (www.bambi.demon.co.uk/Skyedata/housing.html).

There is insufficient building land on Sleat, even if planning was to allow a surge in new build activity. Again, it is this combination of external housing demand pressure within a physically and politically constrained rural land market that introduces difficulties for those households seeking homes at a reasonable price. On Sleat, and elsewhere in Scotland, second homes bear the brunt of blame for this situation, not always because they are the most significant component of the housing problem, but because they symbolise the unfairness that locals appear to suffer at the hands of newcomers and an apparently unsympathetic planning system. The situation on Sleat seems to give weight to Monbiot's (1999) analysis of the second home problem.

Gwynedd in North Wales

There has long been concern over the growth in the number of second homes in North Wales (Bollom, 1978) and its apparent association with declining use of the Welsh language in some communities (Cymdeithas Yr Iaith Gymraeg, 1971). Three areas are examined here: Blaenau Ffestiniog, Llanengan, and Pwllheli.

Blaenau Ffestiniog, a town of almost 5,500 people, is the centre of the former slate quarrying area. The almost complete cessation of quarrying activity has brought severe economic repercussions and resulted in a significant out-migration of young people. The town's inability to retain population has impacted upon the socio-cultural profile of the wider area. As 'locals' have moved away, the town has gradually become home to families from urban areas across the border in England, who have been attracted by cheap housing and the promise of a better quality of life for themselves and their children. But despite the lack of jobs in the town (and consequent surplus of housing), the influx of English-speaking people has not been particularly welcome amongst the remaining Welsh-speaking population. Blaenau Ffestiniog is not a natural location for a holiday or second home. The town is located in a valley heavily scarred by its industrial past; it is also one of the wettest places in Britain.[2] In fact, the town's lack of aesthetic appeal resulted in it being left out of the Snowdonia National Park area when the park boundaries were drawn up in 1951. But there are some second and holiday homes – around 200 – in the town, mainly located towards the more attractive Llanffestiniog or above the town and away from the old quarries. Around 10 per cent of Blaenau's housing stock comprises homes used by periodic visitors. As in the Scottish examples cited above, where there is a combination of heavy (permanent) in-migration and second home purchasing, second homes are frequently viewed as the sharp edge of the problem. In Wales, it is usually acknowledged that a lack of jobs means a lack of local housing demand. However, the fact that homes have been purchased by outsiders is viewed as a barrier preventing locals from *returning* to their home area if economic conditions brighten. This means that the potential problems wrought by second homes are viewed in the medium to long rather than in the short term; though a cynic might then argue that such purchasers represent only a hypothetical problem. Will these areas really experience an economic renaissance (based on tourism or on economic diversification) and if they do, will the former population (comprising people who left in search of education and employment opportunities) really find enough in these areas to draw them back? Places like Blaenau Ffestiniog have less of an immediate second home problem than more attractive and economically buoyant areas; but the arguments rehearsed above are fielded as warnings that a longer-term problem could eventually boil over (Cymdeithas Yr Iaith Gymraeg, 1999).

The next area – Llanengan – is arguably a much more appealing second home destination. It is located on the Lleyn Peninsula,[3] opened up just over 10 years ago by the extension past Conway, of the A55. Llanengan – and its main settlement, Abersoch – has become a significant tourist centre in recent years, and experienced a complete reconfiguration of its population in favour of newcomers. Tourism reaps rewards for the few: for the owners of guesthouses or holiday chalets and for some local businesses. But for the younger population, jobs in this sector often hold little appeal and many have left in search of a greater range of opportunities elsewhere. The exodus of young people has been matched by an influx of wealthier retirement migrants; some stay permanently, others seek seasonal retreats. Of all households moving into Llanengan since the 1991 Census, more than 55 per cent originated from outside of Wales. Properties in the area are now advertised in the national press and at estate agents across the border in Chester; they also frequently appear on the Internet. There are job opportunities in Llanengan, but it is often the case that these jobs do not pay enough to enable people to compete in a property market dominated by second home buyers and retired people. The community has the highest proportion of second homes in North Wales: some 400 units, making up 35 per cent of the total housing stock. It is communities like Llanengan that are often used to exemplify the second home problem in Britain: planning constraint is a factor in reducing housing access, and the economic opportunities available will not act as an anchor for the entire population. But the fact remains, or so the argument goes, that the sheer number of second homes – over and above the problem of planning restraint and the rather narrow economic base – reduce the choices (to stay or not to stay, or indeed to buy or not to buy?) available to the local population.[4] Second homes are almost invariably drawn from the general housing stock, and despite other areas facing the same planning constraints, it can be shown that house prices in Llanengan – and similar communities – tower above those found in adjacent communities.[5] Therefore, second homes are heightening the pressures, and reducing the possibilities, facing rural communities.

Britain's Problem – Summary

In relation to the two core factors – which offer some measure of how significant second homes are in local housing markets – the British examples display the following characteristics:

- Types of Property: Second homes (unlike holiday chalets) are drawn from the mainstream or general housing stock and acquired, by their new owners, through a de facto change of use. Competition for these properties in a much wider national market (and the clash between the two – national and local – markets mentioned earlier) has resulted in some price inflation, though hard – as opposed to anecdotal – evidence of this in the case studies cited above was limited.
- Characteristics of Buyers: British buyers tend to live some distance from their second homes (many, in Llanengan for instance, are from Manchester and Birmingham), though they choose locations to which they can gain reasonably easy access. They use properties for brief periods and for recreational purposes. Second homes cluster in tourist areas, forming part of the new tourism-based economy and can be seen (as Coppock, 1977 has pointed out) as a measure of decline in an area's former industries.

The other key characteristic is the way external housing demand pressures in Britain combine with a generally restrictive planning system, and weak rural economies, to create accommodation access problems for local residents. In the two areas examined above, it was often the case that second homes merely symbolised wider problems: these included heavy permanent in-migration, physical constraints on new house building, area-based planning constraints, and economic change. This resulted in one of two situations: second homes being held up (perhaps unfairly) as the root cause of rural problems; or, second homes becoming an 'added burden' on an economy and housing market that already offers little choice to locals. Finally, it is also apparent that different buyers (local and second home) exist within separate markets. Buyers in the larger national market appear to out-gun those whose interests lie solely in the local market. This division – expressed by Rogers (1977) as a distinction that creates 'importing and exporting' places – is at the heart of the British second home problem. These patterns are now compared with circumstances on the continent.

Part 2: Mainland Europe: Sweden and Spain

Within the two mainland European examples discussed below, the same two (buyer and property characteristic) factors are examined. The aim, again, is to consider the nature of the market in which second home demand exists.

West Sweden

Three areas were examined on the Swedish West Coast: Tjorn, Sotenäs, and Årjäng. Tjorn is an island of $167\,km^2$ located roughly 50 kilometres from Gothenburg (but connected by road) and has a population of just under 15,000. The island itself is generally hilly with steep cliffs and fertile valleys stretching inland. Farming, fishing and forestry were once the principal industries of Tjorn and although now in decline, still have an immense impact on the social and cultural life of the island. Its close proximity to Gothenburg and high environmental quality mean that Tjorn has become an attractive area for urbanites, many of whom have started to purchase properties from which to commute back to the city. These are typical Swedish second homes, used almost every weekend by an owner who has to work in the city during the week. Over 45 per cent of the current population have moved into Tjorn during the last ten years and more than half of the island's houses are now *defined* as second or holiday homes. Forty-five per cent is a huge figure even by the standards of some of Britain's most afflicted communities (including Llanengan). But is there a straight comparison here? On Tjorn, the second-home owners are on the island every weekend. They are, for a large slice of the year, part of the ordinarily resident population, supporting services and spending much of their incomes on Tjorn. These are not the summer retreats so often a feature of rural communities in Britain, and in Sweden the clear division between first and second home is considerably more blurred. In this instance, the two are only 50 km apart and given the magnitude of the second home market on Tjorn, it is impossible to separate out buyers from Gothenburg and buyers 'indigenous' to the island. In other words, the notion of divisions (between locals and newcomers, or existing within two conflicting markets) has far less meaning if we seek a straight comparison (in this instance) between Britain and Sweden. The relationship between Tjorn and Gothenburg is probably more akin to the relationship between London and Reading, than London and Llanengan. The real difference is that in Sweden, commuters stay in the cities on weeknights rather than commuting 30 or 40 km to a satellite town. This is a cultural difference, borne from completely different market, physical and planning conditions, which means that despite Sweden having a large number of second homes on paper (see Chapter 5), these homes are very different from those found in Scotland or Wales. Clearly, it can be suggested that Tjorn and Gothenburg are positioned within the same sub-regional market. This is the nature of Swedish second home demand; properties used solely for recreational purposes exist further away from urban centres and are used less frequently. But these tend to be purpose built. Typical Swedish 'second homes' are generally of the type found on Tjorn. Others tend to be 'non-commercial holiday homes', occupying their own particular and closed market (Kalbro & Mattsson, 1995).

Does this mean that comparisons between Britain and Sweden are invalid? Sometimes they probably are, but this is not always the case: the situation in Sotenäs, for instance, is slightly different. Sotenäs, at 140 square kilometres, is one of the smallest authorities in Sweden: it has fewer than 10,000 inhabitants and is located on the Skagerrak coast. The island's residential areas are generally concentrated in small towns and villages, most of which remain 'traditional fishing communities' that have attracted tourists in increasing numbers. Commuting levels have risen following significant in-migration to Sotenäs by middle-class urbanites while out-migration amongst young people has increased. Over 4,300 people have moved to Sotenäs in the last ten years (5 per cent of these from outside the country) whilst just over 3,200 people have left. A third of the total population do not originate from the area. There were 6,697 registered holiday and second homes in Sotenäs in 1994, a huge number when compared to the total population figure of 10,000. The situation in Sotenäs is clearly more akin to the changes observed in Britain, though a great many of the second-home owners are commuters of the type found on Tjorn. However, pure 'holiday buyers' (from Germany) have moved in and there is clear evidence of a social exchange which may, in part, be a result of locals being unable to compete with outside buyers. It is interesting to note that the influx of Germans to the Swedish coast has been at the heart of what many Swedes believe to be their own second home problem.[6] Despite one-seventh of all Swedish households having a second home, this has never been considered a problem in the same way as it has in Britain. In 1977, Bielckus noted that

> [...] the favourable population-land ratio and attempts at an equitable distribution of economic resources create an environment in which the desirability of second homes as a form of land use need not be questioned at this time (p.44).

But the arrival of foreign buyers, who use their second homes solely for recreational purposes and who are absent for much of the year, has sparked a new debate in Sweden. There are clear parallels between this debate and concerns in Wales (and Scotland) not least because the newcomers (like those in Wales) are firstly foreign and, secondly, absent for much of the year. (Sotenäs is thus locked into its own sub-regional market [like Tjorn]; but also displays elements of the 'two market' syndrome. In the latter case, these distant and absent buyers originate from Germany.) That is not to say that feelings in

North Wales would run any cooler if buyers in communities like Llanengan were predominantly from Swansea or Cardiff, but rather that absence and distance (of owners) will invariably mean a reduced social and economic contribution from second homes. Given recent media debacles, Welsh local government is particularly wary of couching second home debates in anti-English or racist language.[7]

The third Swedish area, Årjäng, is located approximately 200 kilometres from Gothenburg on the Norwegian border, and displays more of the characteristics found in Sotenäs. Its population, at 10,000, is sparse and dispersed across 1,417 km^2. The local economy is centred on manufacturing, forestry and farming, with some recent growth in electronics, wood refining and tourism. The area is environmentally sensitive with an abundance of unpolluted lakes: and it is this characteristic – along with free camping, lakeside parks and woodlands, and a range of out-door recreational opportunities – that has provided the catalyst for tourism growth. Significant rationalisation in both the forestry and farming industries has reduced the viability of many smaller communities, and second home seekers have purchased a number of newly vacated properties: a situation that seems to find immediate parallel in Britain. Incomers have tended to be from outside Sweden (particularly from Norway) and have brought with them urban attitudes and values. Friction between local and newcomer groups – the latter attempting to protect the area for their own use and failing to recognise, for instance, Swedish laws permitting free access and the 'right to roam' – would appear to make the parallel with Britain even more striking. Again, Årjäng appears to have the broad split between a local market on the defensive and an aggressive wider market for second homes. The comparison with Britain, however, is imperfect in the sense that there appears to be no wider national Swedish market for these types of second homes. Rather the market draws from the wider regional area, and particularly from Norway and Germany. But still, Monbiot's (1999) local displacement process seems to be at work here: whilst about 4,000 newcomers have moved into the area over the last ten years, 3,700 local residents have moved away. Latest figures indicate the presence of almost 4,000 holiday or second homes in Årjäng.

Sweden's domestic second home market is dominated by the kind of situation found on Tjorn: properties tend to be located within a 'weekend leisure space' (that is, close by; Petersson, 1999) which means that irrespective of which home the owners are using, they

> [...] do not necessarily have to change their social and economic field of behaviour; they can still shop at the same retail stores and maintain their social relations as in everyday life (Petersson, 1999, p. 9; see also Bohlin, 1982).

Hence, second homes exist within regional (or city-regional) sub-markets; are a cultural phenomenon, and the process of displacement (of 'locals') is not an issue. However, Swedes are today concerned about the way in which some areas are being sucked into a wider two-tier market in which local rural populations are increasingly susceptible to the whims of foreign property buyers.

Galicia in Northern Spain

In some ways, the situation in Scandinavia (embodied above in the example of Sweden) is repeated across mainland Europe. The domestic market has never 'created' second home problems. The arrival of foreigners, however, has brought new concerns. This can be illustrated in Spain. It is generally accepted that Spain has two second-home markets: a coastal (and island) market dominated by foreign chalet buyers (Barke & France, 1988; Barke, 1991) and an inland rural market hitherto dominated by Spanish nationals. Spanish Census data has, for the past fifty years, differentiated between the privately-used housing stock and dwellings 'rented out for tourist reasons' (Montero, 1998). However, Census data do not reveal the number of second homes *used by their owners* for 'tourist reasons' so whilst the explosion in 'chalet type' development can be charted using the Census (see Table 6.1), it is impossible to obtain a national picture of rural, privately owned, second homes. But it is this latter market that is examined here.

The Ribeira Sacra Lucense area of Galicia is a scenic landscape dominated by farming, but with huge tourist potential. The local economy is generally weak, based on the existing primary industries and there is high unemployment and large-scale out-migration. Municipality officials plan to revitalise the area with investment based mainly on tourism and complementary industries, capitalising on some important historical centres and the natural environment. Settlements in the area vary in size, ranging from 3,200 people in Pobra de Brollon to 10,500 in Chantada. Most areas suffered significant out-migration, particularly of younger people, in the 1960s and 1970s as a consequence of the steep decline in agriculture. Even today, the percentage of young people under the age of 14 is just 12 per cent, whilst a third of the inhabitants are aged 65 or over. In some areas, this is of particular concern. In Pobra de Brollon, for example, only nine per cent of the population is in the 0–14 age bracket, compared to 27 per cent between 45–64 years, and 33 per cent over 65 years. Some of those former residents who left in the 1960s and 1970s are now starting to return to retirement homes in the region; this is most noticeable in Carballedo and Savina. This type of return movement is not unique to Galicia but has been witnessed across much of rural Spain. (Recent research in the Tierras Atlas in Soria, for example, revealed that seven in every ten in-migrants

Table 6.1   The Growth of Chalet-type, Commercial Second Homes in Spain

	Date				
	1950	**1960**	**1970**	**1981**	**1991**
Dwellings	177,910	255,082	794,373	1,899,782	2,628,817

Source: Montero, 1998: from National Institute of Statistics, Census in Spain, 1950, 1960, 1970, 1981 and 1991.

were returnees (Hoggart and Paniagua, 2001)). The same research also showed that this type of local link could be identified across the full spectrum of groups moving into the countryside, explaining why the newcomer-local conflicts, so well documented in Britain, are less prevalent in Spain).

Agricultural production remains in evidence, though the amount of dairy and cattle farming has declined in recent years. Other industries are present in the form of workshops, textile and footwear production, and vineyards, although all these remain relatively low-key. Unemployment rates vary between seven per cent in Carballedo and 19 per cent in Monforte. Transport connections are good with low journey times to the larger neighbouring towns and cities. In addition to the rail link through the region, the economy has been aided by the construction of a dual carriageway crossing the area from west to east with good links between settlements. The region is culturally and linguistically sensitive, with Galician spoken and taught in local schools. The area is also environmentally sensitive and there is currently a project between the Galician Government and the European Union to declare the Ribeira Sacra and River Sil Canyon as 'Natural Parks' with accompanying environmental protection measures.

Patterns of economic and demographic change, established over the last forty years, have resulted in a rather weak housing market. Land prices have remained low in much of the region, though land and property prices in the main urban centres have risen sharply, driven upwards by the influx of people from the surrounding countryside and the new investment arriving in the wake of the huge infrastructure improvements mentioned above. But back in the small rural communities, patterns of fragmented land holding – and therefore difficulties in land assembly – have meant that even when new house building does occur, this is usually confined to single plots. Thus, there is a significant constraint on new housing supply in the Ribeira Sacra Lucense and as in Britain, this constraint is more legal than physical in its basis. There are also a number of second homes in the area, clustered around some of the more attractive small towns and villages. The most recent figures date back to 1993 when there were 92 such properties in Carballedo, 235 in Pobra de Brollon, 399 in Savina, 628 in Monforte and 642 in Chantada. People living *within* the region own the vast majority of these properties and most of the second home units have either been drawn from the mainstream stock, or converted from old farm buildings or outhouses. Barke (1991) has shown that the number of such second homes in the Spanish interior has risen steadily since the 1960s, and often they are owned by people moving away from the countryside, but who wish to retain a link with their former home community (Barke, 1991, p.14). In some instances, families also retain small plots of land as hobby farms, a phenomenon described most recently by Hoggart and Paniagua (2001) who point out that these 'urban farmers' participate in agriculture on a seasonal basis.

This desire to 'keep in touch' with a more rural, and perhaps 'alternative', lifestyle might be compared with recent trends in Britain. But the market conditions in Spain – and in the Ribeira Sacra Lucense – have much more in common with Sweden. These rural second homes exist in a self-contained regional sub-market. Owners live and work reasonably close by, have strong family ties with the rural areas, and return to their 'second homes' most weekends. Contrasting this situation with that found in Britain, Hoggart and Paniagua argue that:

> The huge number of [second homes in the interior] has not helped transform rural society, as these are components of a family-centred social network, rather than playground objects for the urban middle class (ibid. p. 77).

A large number of people either commute from the surrounding countryside to jobs in cities or (and of more relevance here) become part-time weekly city residents. This means that at the regional level '[...] population movement in rural Spain is becoming more complex, especially in its temporal manifestations' (ibid. p.75: see also Diagram (b), Figure 6.1). The same is true in Sweden where sub-regional areas (with their associated housing markets) are characterised be frequent movement between first and second homes.

Similarities between the two countries also extend to the wider issue of 'residential tourism'. As in Sweden, there is another market for chalets (in this instance, sometimes in large concrete blocks), but this is confined to areas like Malaga, the Balearics or the Costa Del Sol (see Montero, 1998), and has little impact on, or cross-effect with, other housing markets. The purpose-built blocks have also, over the last twenty years, attracted swarms of foreign buyers (some, choosing the lifestyle depicted on BBC Television's '*Eldorado*'). But the regional sub-markets in rural Spain have been left largely untouched by this type of tourist development (Hoggart and Paniagua, 2001, p.76).

The parallel with Sweden then seems fairly exact, though Spain's more 'sensitive' rural communities have not been affected by foreign buyers to the extent that has occurred on Sweden's West Coast. But is this set to change? During the last ten years, more evidence has come to light to suggest that some overseas buyers are no longer content to follow the crowd in search of sun, sand and sangria:

> Nowadays [...] there is evidence that Europe is experiencing new developments in second home ownership patterns. The stage of mature development in many traditional Mediterranean tourist destinations, as well as the environmental stress in many metropolitan areas in Europe, are leading tourists to travel to new and more peripheral areas in Europe (Petersson, 1999, p.7).

A growing number of buyers now want something a little more sophisticated; others are simply turning their backs on the 'sun-lust' of the past (Petersson, 1999). In France, Buller and Hoggart (1994a; 1994b) have charted the movement of British second home seekers into the Dordogne and Provence in the early 1990s. And it now seems that the Spanish interior is experiencing the same process (Valenzuala, 2000; 2003). So whilst the rural second home market in Spain has hitherto taken the form of a closed regional sub-market, this may change in the future, bringing 'British-style' difficulties – of rising property prices, absence and displacement – to yet another part of Europe.

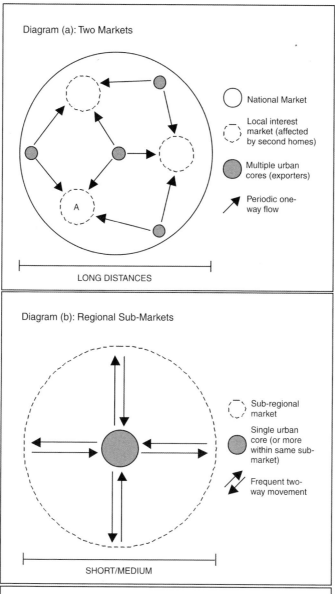

Diagram (a): Two Markets

National Market

Local interest market (affected by second homes)

Multiple urban cores (exporters)

Periodic one-way flow

LONG DISTANCES

Diagram (b): Regional Sub-Markets

Sub-regional market

Single urban core (or more within same sub-market)

Frequent two-way movement

SHORT/MEDIUM

The main argument in this chapter is that British markets follow the structure described in Diagram (a) whilst continental Europe is dominated by city-regional markets (b). In some instances, however, these city-regional markets may be relegated to become a component of a wider pan-European system. At this point, diagram (a) can be used to depict this wider market and diagram (b) becomes just one (albeit bigger) 'local interest market' (See market A, Diagram (a)).

Figure 6.1   Contrasting Housing Markets

Europe's Problems – Summary

Market conditions in these European case-study areas have been shown to display the following broad characteristics:

- Types of Property: Both Sweden and Spain have strong 'holiday chalet' markets (Kalbro & Mattsson, 1995; Barke & France, 1988; Montero, 1998), but these are distinct from the city-regional second home markets examined above. Here, the transition from first to second home use has occurred as rural residents drift to nearby cities in search of work (as in Spain) or the tradition of owning a second home is so culturally entrenched, that is impossible to say that a physical switch in property-use has occurred (as in Sweden). In both cases, second homes within these sub-markets represent part of a particular lifestyle.
- Characteristics of Buyers: Second homeowners tend to live very close to their second homes (as near as 50 km in the Swedish case studies[8]). Properties are used extremely frequently (every weekend in many instances) almost making it impossible to differentiate second from first homes. Again, buyers are living a certain lifestyle and their second homes are an integral part of that lifestyle.

Table 6.2 summarises these and some additional characteristics of the four case study areas, illustrating the main market differences. Finally, a new characteristic is taking root in these more peripheral European regions, and this is the increasing tendency for foreign buyers to enter these hitherto closed

Table 6.2　Case Study Comparison

Case Study	Apparent Source of Demand (1)	Type of Demand (by Source)	Use Pattern	Class of Leisure Space (2)	Market Type
		Demand, use and market characteristics			
Gwynedd	England; Birmingham, Manchester and London	Inter-regional	Infrequent	Vacation Space	Two (national and local market overlaps)
Highlands & Islands	Scottish central belt & England	Inter-regional	Infrequent	Vacation Space	Two (national and local market overlaps)
Galicia	Within Galicia	Local and intra-regional	Frequent	Weekend Leisure Space	Sub-regional
Swedish West Coast	Gothenburg (and Germany)	Local, intra-regional and foreign	Frequent (and infrequent)	Weekend Leisure Space (and Vacation Space)	Sub-regional (and two-market)

Notes: (1) Precise data are unavailable; (2) using the classification employed by Petersson (1999). Distance is the critical factor in determining both market type and class of leisure space.

city-regional second home markets. This structural change in second home markets on the continent – perhaps bringing closer parallels with Britain – is considered in the concluding part of this chapter.

Conclusion

The main argument put forward in this chapter might be best summarised diagrammatically (see Figure 6.1, Diagrams (a) and (b)). Gilbert (2001), in research completed for the Council of Mortgage Lenders, has confirmed that Britain has a significant second home market. The most recent Survey of English Housing (DETR, 1999) suggests that close to a quarter of a million households, in England alone, have access to a second home.[9] European markets are also significant, and in many countries on the continent, the tradition of owning and regularly using a second home has a long history. But Diagrams (a) and (b) attempt to show that the market situations in Britain and Europe are quite different. Britain has less countryside than the Scandinavian states, Spain or France. It is also more densely populated, and these factors mean that there are fewer attractive unspoilt areas to which second homebuyers might gravitate. The severing of links between the urban population and its rural past also occurred much earlier, so the personal links between town and country – critically important in Spain – are less prevalent in Britain. And unlike Scandinavia, the culture of flat living during the week, followed by a retreat to the countryside every weekend (which Petersson, 1999, has argued might be 'regarded as a substitute for counter-urbanisation'), is not part of 'average' British life. Rather, the British attempt to mesh the best of both worlds and plump for suburban living, and then suffer the inconvenience of daily commuting. These are just some of the factors that have conspired to produce very different patterns of second home ownership in Britain and on the continent.[10]

The British situation is characterised by a broad national second home market that produces significant pockets of demand in the most sought after areas (Diagram (a)). Distances between first and second homes are often large, meaning that second homeowners visit and use their properties less frequently. But in many parts of Europe, second homes are positioned within a city-regional or sub-market. They are part of a lifestyle for the many (or a significant minority) rather than a luxury for the few (see Petersson, 1999). Distances between first and second homes are often short, and owners visit their properties far more regularly (Diagram (b)). So are second homes only a British problem? In this chapter, we have attempted to show that some of Europe's second home 'regions' are being drawn into a pan-European market, as Germans head for Sweden's West Coast, Britons to France, and a whole host of foreign nationals to Spain. These are not entirely new processes but began, in earnest, during the 1980s. It is only now, however, that regional and local governments are beginning to recognise the potential problems that property, foreign-owned and empty for much of the year, might bring to small fragile rural communities.

The second home markets identifiable within many continental European countries are demonstrably different from those found in Britain. They are structurally different, comprising buyers whose motivations, and relationships with their property (and host communities), bear little resemblance to those in Britain. The various market differences, described in the main part of this chapter, have meant that second homes in Europe have not been painted in the same negative terms that they have in Britain. But as domestic European markets attract an increasing number of foreign investors, it seems certain that British-style difficulties can only become more commonplace, posing new challenges for those policy makers whose task it is to balance local needs and identity against the pressures wrought by a more integrated and perhaps a more open European market.

Notes

1 A recent socio-economic impact evaluation of the Skye Bridge development (Scottish Executive, 1999) has concluded that the 'second homes market does not seem to have developed as anticipated': that is, there has been no apparent surge in second home numbers. But in the same report, it is conceded that market growth would *not yet* have shown up in official statistics.
2 Rainfall figures on 'members.theglobe.com/blaencwm/index.htm' tell the full story.
3 Gwynedd's most recent UDP shows that 8 per cent of properties on the Lleyn are second homes, whilst a further 6.2 per cent are empty.
4 It was noted in the Gwynedd County Intelligence Report for 1999 that more than 50 per cent of all over 16-year olds in Llanengan are economically inactive.
5 In 1997, nearly 45 per cent of houses in Llanengan fell into the highest (E to H) Council Tax bands, compared to only 17.8 per cent and 23.4 per cent in the neighbouring communities of Buan and Botwnnog respectively (source: Gwynedd Council – www.gwynedd.gov.uk).
6 The movement of Germans (and Norwegians) into the South Coast area (and the north of the country) has increased steadily since the devaluation of the Swedish currency in late 1992. This move increased the affordability of property in Sweden for these nearby foreign buyers.
7 On a Radio BBC Wales programme (January 17, 2001), a Gwynedd councillor expressed the view that the number of English residents in North Wales must be 'monitored and controlled', adding that English residents are a 'drain on the community'. These comments prompted a rather stormy, and unsurprising, political debate in Wales and beyond.
8 Over the last 30 years there has been *some* evidence of a drift outward, in line with general transport improvements. In 1968, the National Swedish Land Survey Board estimated that there were 420,000 second-homes in the country, and one third of these were located within 20 km of a settlement with more than 25,000 inhabitants (Gallent & Tewdwr-Jones, 2000b, p.86).
9 But only half of these properties are in fact 'traditional' second homes in the countryside used as weekend retreats. The remainder are located in towns and cities, and 26 per cent are used for work-related rather than recreational purposes (DETR, 1999).
10 There are, of course, many other factors at work. Buller & Hoggart (1994b) pinpoint some of these and perhaps of relevance here are the language/cultural barriers that prevent less intrepid – or perhaps cosmopolitan – buyers from breaking into a foreign market. This same point is made by Petersson (1999) who argues that the '[...] purchase of real-estate in a foreign country implies the confrontation with another legislation and another language' (p.10).

PART 3
RESPONDING TO SECOND
HOME PRESSURES

Chapter 7

The Evolving Framework

Historical Responses to Second Home Pressures in the UK

The ultimate aim of the three chapters comprising Part 3 of this book is to move towards a practicable and evidence-based framework for responding to second home pressures in the UK. Our intention is that this framework – set out in Chapter 9 – should be grounded in a full understanding of the second home issue, draw on real case study situations (especially those set out in Chapter 4) and recognise what can be learnt from experiences elsewhere in Europe (Chapters 5 and 6). It is also our intention to establish a framework that builds on past policy initiatives and reflects on how this policy has evolved over a period of time. With this in mind, chapters 7 and 8 examine how policy makers in the UK have already experimented with different responses to second home and broader housing pressures in the countryside.

Chapter 4 considered the form that second home pressures take in Wales and England, using research conducted in 2001 and 2002. In chapter 5, we drew on recent work for the Scottish Executive (Shucksmith *et al*, 2000) to consider how a number of European countries have recently been responding to the second homes issue, and to wider housing affordability concerns. And finally, chapter 6 considered how new sources of external demand can create housing pressures where they coincide with planning constraint. The purpose of this first 'framework' chapter is not to consider how effective policy might be formulated within the UK – but to examine some of the *suggestions* put forward in prior studies. The capacity of some of these suggestions to deliver positive outcomes on the ground today is reflected upon using our own research. We consider in this chapter and in chapter 8 how present housing and planning frameworks *might* be used to respond to second homes (reducing their costs and maximising their benefits). This feeds into a view as to how we feel they *should* be used, which is set out in Chapter 9. More than 25 years ago, Dower (1977) suggested that options for controlling the growth in second home numbers and their impacts fall into three broad categories: economic and social development, housing policy options and planning and development control (p.161). Dower's division of options provides a useful framework for this discussion.

Part 1: Economic and Social Development

Clearly, although the growth in second home ownership might be viewed as a complicating factor in processes of socio-economic change in rural areas, it may still be argued that the inability of locals to compete in the housing market (against Shucksmith's 'more prosperous groups': see Chapter 3) is caused by the weak state of the local economy, not by second homes, and therefore emphasis should be placed on boosting economic growth rather than using second homes as a 'convenient scapegoat' (Dower, 1977, p.161). In any economic strategy, second homes will have an important role to play as part of the wider tourist industry. One policy option, therefore, might be to promote second home ownership in such a way as to maximise economic benefits (whilst diverting demand away from existing housing stock). This type of dual strategy exists in Spain and has been described by Valenzuala (2003, p. 124). Such a move, however, would not be without its critics. In the 1960s and 1970s, nationalists in Wales were keen to promote the myth that 'second homes and the whole tourist industry were an unmitigated disaster for the Welsh' (Coppock, 1977, p. 200). Clearly, analysis of the effect wrought by second homes outside the effective housing stock demonstrates that this is not the case and whilst there is a good economic argument for promoting development in some areas, it is also generally accepted that second homes do fulfil a real need (Coppock, 1977, p. 211). Downing and Dower have argued that second homes satisfy recreational benefits and pose the following question to those opponents who argue for prohibitive policy measures:

> If desire for second homes is frustrated, will some other effective outlet for recreational impulses be available: and will its implications be more acceptable on balance than those of second homes? Or if impulses remain frustrated, who will justify the human and societal loss? (Downing and Dower, 1973, p.29).

For this reason and because of the underlying economic logic of promoting second home ownership, control needs to be balanced with a means of satisfying demand. Jenkin (1985) follows this line and argues that a 'policy is needed which attempts to absorb the demand for second homes while at the same time directing that demand away from those communities which are at risk from the intrusions' (Jenkin, 1985, p.70). This would be achieved by identifying sites suitable for purpose-built second home developments and using development control to discourage developments in unsuitable areas; control of the layout and appearance of sites would neutralise the environmental impacts (Jenkin, 1985, p.74).

The success of this strategy, in maximising economic benefits and minimising social costs (through the diversion of demand away from mainstream housing stock) would hinge on two points; first, the attractiveness of purpose built second home 'villages' and second, the willingness on the part of elected assemblies or policy executives to assign specific protection for existing housing (Pyne, 1973, p.52). On the first issue, Davies and O'Farrell have shown that second home seekers will be attracted to developments of fairly high residential density (in the form of 'holiday villages') if these developments are correctly sited (Davies and O'Farrell, 1981, p.108). In their particular analysis, this meant close proximity to the coastline but it would probably also involve proximity to a range of other facilities such as settlements or landscapes of specific interest, inland water surfaces, key tourist attractions and services. Increasing supply in this way might attract people away from static caravans and have a positive environmental impact (Pyne, 1973, p.51).

As Pyne (1973) has noted, diverting demand in the way described above will only be effective if added protection is given to existing housing which is likely to draw the attention of potential second home buyers. The prior studies tend to concede that this would involve change of residential use being brought under planning control; this issue is introduced in Chapter 8 and considered further in Chapter 9. It is clear however that promoting the tourist industry (of which second homes are a part), provides a significant part of a longer term strategy which must be to raise local income levels (Shucksmith, 1983, p.187). Dart's 1977 report in Scotland argued that local government should indicate clear support for tourism in local plans, provide tourist infrastructure (such as roads, harbours, ski slopes and water sports areas) and have a direct hand in second home development and the promotion of the area as a tourist destination (Dart, 1977, p.77). In their earlier report, Downing and Dower (1973) went as far as to advocate direct public provision of second homes, a move that seems somewhat unlikely today (Downing and Dower, 1973, p.36). Encouraging new employers in the area (in all sectors, with the service sector potentially being the most lucrative in many rural areas) will improve employment conditions with increasing demand for labour and higher wage levels. A stronger local economy would generate an upward pressure on both house prices and the supply of new housing and place locals in a far better competitive position in the housing market. All these changes are of course desirable but may not bring a panacea for various socio-economic ailments in the short term. It is clear however, that over-restriction of second home development would run against the tide in terms of sound economic planning which at the end of the day, should seek to maximise rather minimise potential benefits. But it is also true that:

> The basic test of the desirability of second homes must be the local interests and the consideration of rural amenities [...] the positive promotion of holiday villages as a form of tourism will not [on their own] create the economic salvation of rural areas (Williams, 1977, pp.60–63).

The flip-side, however, is that *assaults* on second homes centring on general restrictions on house building – and housing occupancy – may introduce additional economic problems to already marginal rural economies. For example, Pembrokeshire Coast's Joint Unitary Development Plan (JUDP), placed on Deposit in January 2002, included a policy seeking to restrict the occupancy of new housing to persons able to demonstrate an 'essential need' in a total of twenty-six so-called 'sustainable communities' (Pembrokeshire County Council & Pembrokeshire Coast National Park Authority, 2002, Policy 47). A subsequent consultant's report on the workability and likely impact of the policy (Tewdwr-Jones and Gallent, 2002) concluded that this attempt to restrict general market housing to local needs was likely to have both an up and a down side. On the up side, without such a restriction:

[. . .] future house building will have an identifiable impact on tourism. The projected demand for housing could see Pembrokeshire's current land allocations for the next 15 years built upon by the end of 2005. Housing completions at this level have serious environmental and landscape implications. In terms of tourism, the character of the National Park is the essential factor drawing people to the area and sustaining this part of the economic base. Unrestricted house building could have dire environmental and therefore economic consequences, risking the economic viability of some local communities (p. 3).

But, on the other hand, the authors of the report also argue that:

[. . .] house building to serve this part of the economic base (that is holiday homes) will remain important. The development of holiday homes (for example) by local people and local companies has a positive economic impact and will continue under less regulated market conditions (p. 3).

The situation in Pembrokeshire today – where controversy continues to surround the inclusion of Policy 47 in the JUDP – illustrates the difficulty in building economic growth on the back of tourism (within a sensitive landscape) whilst also guaranteeing access to housing for those local people with an essential need. Economies can be adversely or positively affected by second homes: getting the right balance is critical. In Pembrokeshire, attempts to strike this balance have recently resulted in the Park Authority giving planning permission for a new holiday village; there is some hope that this will help divert demand away from the existing housing stock.

Part 2: Housing Policy Options

The housing policy options suggested in previous second home studies tend to be concerned with the provision of housing alternatives (for local residents) in the face of second home demand and general housing shortages or, ways in which housing (or related) policy might be used to curb or even halt the demand for second homes. Because some locals fall into Shucksmith's (1990b) 'low income, low wealth' consumption class, they may not be able to successfully compete for market housing against more prosperous incomers; it follows that one solution is to provide non-market alternatives.

Providing Non-Market Housing

Non-market (and usually rented) housing has traditionally been provided by local authorities and the strategy of building rural council housing was generally successful in sustaining many local communities. However, this situation has now changed and whilst the stock of local authority dwellings has been reduced (typically by a third) by the right-to-buy since October 1980, similar reductions in local authority finance (and the inability of local authorities to invest capital receipts from sales in new development programmes) has meant that the traditional rural role of local authorities in direct provision has become little more than an historical footnote. Local authorities have, in recent years, been asked to play a new housing role; that of development 'enabler' (Goodlad, 1993; Bramley, 1993). Since the creation of the Housing Corporation in 1964 and the establishment of a grant framework in 1974, voluntary sector housing associations – re-branded 'registered social landlords' (RSLs) since 1996 – have come to play an increasingly important role in the provision of 'social' (that is, non-market and 'affordable') housing. By the mid-1980s, these associations were actively engaged in new rural housing schemes across Britain. However, the favourable financial regime brought about by the introduction of the Housing Association Grant (HAG) in 1974 was brought to an abrupt end in the Housing Act 1988. From the following financial year, full public subsidy was replaced by a form of public 'deficit funding' whereby an ever larger part of the cost of new provision would have to be met by the private sector. Over the last ten years, grant rates have been incrementally reduced and these reductions have threatened the affordability of new schemes. In this context, local authorities and associations have been encouraged to 'work together' (see Fraser, 1991; Carmona *et al*, 2001) in order to reduce the cost of provision, sustain supply and ensure that new housing schemes remain affordable. This strategy may involve the transfer of public land or loan sanction from the local authorities to the partner associations. It may also involve the local authority developing 'local housing need strategies' (planning-based, which are written into local plans: see Figure 7.1) which generate additional sources of affordable housing on private development sites (that is, achieving site-specific quotas through planning negotiation) or on rural 'exception' sites (that is, off-plan; Joseph Rowntree Foundation, 1994; Barlow, *et al*, 1994; Gallent and Bell, 2000) which is subsequently developed and managed by a registered social landlord (whose long-term social objectives ensure that housing serves community needs in perpetuity).

However, these partnership strategies have proved problematic, particularly in rural areas where there have been difficulties in securing the necessary input of private finance on exception sites due to the inclusion of Section 106 agreements (RDC, 1995) and where poor development plan coverage has worked against the negotiated strategy (Gallent, 1997b). It can be argued that the synthesis of housing and planning policy (Tewdwr-Jones, *et al*, 1998) generates an inadequate supply of additional rural housing and therefore cannot accommodate all those local residents excluded from the private property market as a result of increased local competition. On the other hand, the contribution of RSLs in providing homes for many rural families should not be underestimated and in this context, the Conservative government's voluntary purchase grant (VPG) scheme for association tenants, introduced in the Housing Act 1996, may prove to be all the more damaging in some rural areas, particularly as it may discourage some landowners from releasing land for housing on some off-plan sites and, like its predecessor in 1980, it may substantially reduce the supply of non-market housing in the countryside. Grants to assist RSL tenants to buy their homes were initially fixed at £13,000, and applied only to existing and not to new tenants. The scheme has now been

Gain and Obligations Mechanism	The negotiation of contributions from developers of affordable housing within market housing schemes, usually on the basis of Section 106 (Town and Country Planning Act 1990) Agreements. Under this more 'general approach', affordable housing is treated as a planning gain and usually specified as a requirement within the Section 106. The inclusion of affordable housing is an obligation negotiated with the developer. It is common for the developer to build affordable homes (a specified number or proportion) and then sell them at discount to a Registered Social Landlord (RSL). The government believes that RSLs are best placed to ensure that such units remain for the use of low-income groups in perpetuity. This gain/obligation approach means that social housing is at least sometimes provided as part of a mixed tenure development and may be funded through planning gain, private sector borrowing and / or public subsidy. Gain – generated at the expense of development value – often replaces some, or all, of the public subsidy.
Exceptions Mechanism	The granting of planning permissions for housing on land not allocated for that particular use within the development plan. The initiative aims to reduce land value and therefore housing unit costs though a mechanism whereby land can be purchased at below full development value. This approach is only to be taken in rural areas, and is to be used for the procurement of a small number of units within or adjacent to existing settlements. It is hoped that landowners can be encouraged to sell land at a price nearer agricultural than full development value if this housing is to be occupied only by people with a local connection and demonstrable need. However, the approach only works where an authority has a clear and up-to-date development plan, which is rigidly applied in development control. Most research has shown that where there is uncertainty over a planning authority development strategy, or its intentions for a particular site are unclear, owners may be less inclined to release land for exception schemes perhaps in the hope that one day, it may be earmarked for market housing and able to command significant value.

Source: Gallent, Mace and Tewdwr-Jones, 2003c

Figure 7.1   Planning and Affordable Housing

subsumed into the Right to Acquire initiative which gives fixed grants not only to RSL but also to local authority tenants. The initiative supersedes the Right to Buy in some areas, but does not apply to properties delivered through Section 106 agreements (see Figure 7.1). However, this difference is likely to be lost on some landowners who will fear that the altruistic release of land at below development value may simply generate large profits for initial occupiers. Permitting tenants to buy social housing has, and continues, to erode confidence in the system.

It can clearly be suggested that it is these types of policy moves over the last 20 years which have reduced housing access chances of rural households rather than the limited influx of second home purchasers. Indeed, Hetherington (2000) has pointed out that more than 100,000 council homes were lost to the Right to Buy in the twenty years between 1980 and 2000; the largest losses were in more attractive rural areas, subject to the biggest pressures from second home and retirement migrants (Hetherington, 2000).

In the light of policy shifts during the last 25 years, few of the suggestions made in the prior studies seem relevant in 2004's political climate. However, back in 1983, Shucksmith did note that the cost of a comprehensive investment package in public and voluntary sector house-building might not prove to be the panacea that everybody hoped for whilst the actual cost would be astronomical. At the same time, such a blanket measure could cause the ghettoisation of tenure classes and social polarisation in some rural communities (Shucksmith, 1983, p.191). It seems however, that the Conservative government did not fall into this particular trap; firstly, by not developing a comprehensive financial package; secondly, by allowing the development of rural housing to continue in an *ad hoc* way, and thirdly, by belatedly promoting policies for tenure diversification. Other suggested policy packages, however, did rely heavily on the promotion of council building as a means of satisfying 'local needs' in the face of outside demands on the existing housing stock (Dart, 1977, p.76). These policy packages also pointed to the potential benefit that might be derived from local authorities purchasing, and municipalising, existing local property that came onto the local market (that is, 'competing' on behalf of those who were unable to compete; this issue is discussed below). Despite recent changes in housing policy affecting local authorities and RSLs, it remains clear that any policy measure designed to control the development of second homes (or any purchases by outsiders) should be augmented with some element of public or voluntary (RSL) provision in rural areas.

'Municipalising' Vacant Properties

The acquisition of empty properties for subsequent letting (or shared ownership sale) to local households is today a viable option in many rural areas, despite Conservative reticence to pursue this strategy in the 1980s and early 1990s. Dower (1977) notes that by 1974, the Labour Government was moving towards encouraging the municipal purchase of vacant properties and development land (the purchase of development land by local authorities was often achieved with the use of compulsory purchase orders before the mid-1980s and the softer policy approach adopted by the Conservatives in the countryside); he added that this strategy could provide a key element in securing additional housing opportunities for rural households (Dower, 1977, p.162). This sentiment was echoed by Jenkin (1985) who argued that when suitable properties came onto the market, the local authority should purchase these properties and let them to families on their own housing waiting lists. The policy could be applied in those areas particularly affected by the growth in the number of second homes in the mainstream housing stock and could extend to acquiring properties from pensioners (and thereafter 'decanting' older single people to smaller, potentially more suitable homes) in order to alleviate the problem of rural under-occupancy (Jenkin, 1985, p.78). Pyne, in his study of Caernarvonshire in North Wales, conceded that such a strategy would be heavily resource-dependent (Pyne, 1973, p.47), involving both the acquisition and renovation of existing housing, a move which would not make any net contribution to the overall rural housing stock (arguments later repeated by the Housing Corporation in England and Tai Cymru/Housing for Wales in the early 1990s). As early as 1983, Shucksmith argued that the acquisition of existing housing on the part of local authorities (like direct new-build) was no longer a realistic proposition (Shucksmith, 1983, p.185). This direct-handed approach was now the task assigned to housing associations (as the Conservative Government's 'third arm' in its housing strategy) who were devoting a growing proportion of their development budgets to acquisition and rehabilitation throughout the 1980s.

By 1987–88, housing associations in Wales devoted nearly 65 per cent of their development programme to rehabilitation, but by 1992–93, this figure had fallen to just 4.6 per cent (Welsh Office, 1993, p.37). This substantial decline was largely due to the way in which grant allocations were calculated after the Housing Act 1988. Before this legislation, associations were able to develop new units or rehabilitate acquisitions and subsequently apply for HAG to cover the full costs (within a certain budget limit). After 1988 however, the costs had to be calculated before schemes went on-site. Also, if budget over-runs occurred, then the association would have to meet these added costs though additional private loan sanctions. In effect, because the cost of new-build schemes was easier to predict, the number of 'rehab' projects decreased in the light of the greater financial risks. In addition, it was generally cheaper to build from scratch (and associations were now forced to be more cost-conscious) and Housing for Wales preferred schemes which were seen to be making net additions to the housing stock. In the early 1990s, the future for this type of acquisition and renovation activity looked bleak; however, government's position has shifted during the last ten years. In 1992, the Conservative government established an 'acquisition initiative' in Wales with a budget of £38 million which allowed some local authorities and housing associations to acquire properties from private ownership, repossessions or newly-built properties which could not be sold in the private market. In 1996, the Government established a rural housing 'challenge fund' of £7.5 million in Wales which was intended to be used to promote 'innovative' methods of affordable housing provision which could potentially include acquisition by associations (Welsh Office, 1996a).

Arguably, these more innovative methods have taken off during the last decades; local authorities and RSLs have not been 'municipalising' private properties in the sense envisaged by Dower in 1977 or Jenkin in 1985, but they – either authorities or RSLs – have been entering into joint purchasing agreements with housing applicants to buy property on the open market under shared ownership arrangements. Prior to 1998, the Housing Corporation in England ran a Tenants' Incentive Scheme (TIS) and a Do-it-yourself Shared Ownership (DIYSO) programme. These allowed existing tenants and new applicants accepted onto the schemes to purchase a part-share in a private property with a local RSL; the RSL retained a 'golden share' (purchased with monies channelled through the Housing Corporation). This is clearly municipalisation of a type. On 31 March 1999, both TIS and DIYSO were cancelled and replaced with 'Homebuy' (Housing Corporation, 1998). The Homebuy scheme operates in England and Wales and is available to existing tenants of a registered social landlord or new applications, approved for the scheme by a relevant RSL. Under the scheme, the applicants finds a property suited to their needs (after being accepted on the scheme); they then purchase the property with a 75 per cent mortgage; the RSL buys the remaining 25 per cent, retaining control of this golden share if the part-owner decides in the future to move on (Housing Corporation, 2004). The current Homebuy initiative is a part-municipalisation of hitherto private housing stock; it works where the applicant is able to finance a 75 per cent share in the property. However, where house prices are very high (including some second home hot-spot areas), even a 75 per cent stake may be too expensive for a large proportion of local buyers; therefore the scheme only assists those households close to being able to afford their own homes; it may not be able to help those on low incomes living in areas where the housing market has been severely affected by commuting, second home and retirement pressures.

Local Authority and RSL Management of Private Properties

Another measure to promote the supply of affordable rural housing has been the municipal *management* of properties remaining in private ownership. The first pilot schemes of this type were attempted in North Wiltshire District in 1976 with private properties being managed (and improved) by the local authority and rented out to local people with particular guarantees and advantages for the owner (relating to the improvement works and the guarantee that the owner can re-gain vacant possession after a set tenancy period). Jenkin (1985) argued that these so-called 'North Wiltshire' schemes could be used as part of a package of measures to combat rural housing shortages (Jenkin, 1985, p.77). A clear disadvantage with this strategy, as Shucksmith pointed out, was the fact that the councils had an obligation to re-house the sub-tenant on the expiration of the sub-tenancy, placing further pressure on the financial resources of the authority (authorities would certainly avoid the situation of having too many sub-tenants and therefore too much potential pressure; Shucksmith, 1983, p.187).

During the last decade, this scheme has been up-dated and 80 local authorities across England and Wales are running 'empty homes' campaigns in partnership with local RSLs. In West Dorset, for example, 7 per cent of properties are vacant (many of these 'empty' properties are second homes) and a 'filling the empties' campaign is trying to ensure that twenty owners each year give up their empty dwellings to local people on waiting lists (*The Guardian*, 26 July 1995, p.29). By mid 1995, the authority had written to 2,353 absent owners and had received 317 replies; the letting of five properties had been agreed whilst negotiation was continuing with a further 24 owners. In 1991, the 'Housing Associations as Managing Agents' (HAMA) scheme was launched and is helping to persuade many owners of the benefits of allowing associations to manage their properties. In return for a small measure of altruism, owners receive grants for renovation work and are guaranteed the vacant possession of the property at the end of the lease. The Empty Homes Agency estimates that 737,000 homes stand empty in the private sector whilst 120,000 families are accepted as homeless by local authorities each year. However, before these 'empty homes' schemes can provide a realistic solution, there is a need to educate owners on the benefits of leasing (many are unaware that assured short-hold tenancies introduced in 1989 allow fixed-term letting) and also to convince rural local authorities that such schemes are applicable outside of towns and cities. However, a majority of current local authority and RSL leasing agreements (with private owners) are being operated in urban areas. A model for these agreements has been established by the London Borough of Hounslow (see Table 7.1), which is currently looking for 'family-sized' accommodation to lease and subsequently let to households on its joint housing register.

Table 7.1   Arrangements for Managing Private Sector Properties: Hounslow

Types of property sought	Hounslow are currently seeking family-sized homes which are unfurnished; other authorities will seek properties that match local needs, gauged through housing need assessments (HNAs)
Rent arrangements	The authority considers issues of location, property condition and size and agrees a rent level with the owner; it then charges the tenant a rent and pays the owner quarterly in advance
Managing and repairing the property	The local authority takes full responsibility for managing the property and will deal with day-to-day repairs; major repairs to the property (drains and so on) can be undertaken by the authority and charged to the owner (with monies deducted from quarterly payments)
Returning the property	The local authority (or RSL) will return the property to the owner on expiration of the lease; any costs associated with securing vacant possession will be met by the authority

Source: Adapted from London Borough of Hounslow: http://www.hounslow.gov.uk/home/a-z_services/h/housingassociationleasingprivatesectorleasing.htm (accessed 08 April 2004).

The real irony in many *rural areas* is that a significant number of these 'empty' properties are in fact second homes and it seems unlikely that part of the cause (of some rural housing problems) could become part of the cure. As a general rule, second home owners wish to maintain access to their properties throughout the year and even the 'winter letting' of some second homes is unlikely to have any significant impact on rural housing problems. Whilst seasonal letting to students might go some way towards alleviating the annual accommodation crisis facing students in some areas, the creation of a 'seasonal homelessness' problem in other areas could increase the burden on local housing authorities.

Community Self-Build

In response to particular housing problems in some rural areas, some agencies have advocated the benefits of community self-build schemes. In relation to second homes and the need to expand housing access opportunities for local people, Shucksmith claims that 'community self-build' offers another way forward (Shucksmith, 1983, p.86). The National Federation of Housing Associations published guidelines for people wishing to become involved in low-cost self-build schemes in the late 1980s (NFHA, 1988a, 1988b). It was clear in these guidelines, however, that this particular option was more suited to towns or key rural settlements where larger groups of people are likely to want to become involved (and can share the various legal and material costs). Because of economies of scale, it is unlikely that a scheme involving just one or two households in a small rural village would be able to get off the ground. Clearly, there are logistical and financial difficulties associated with self-build schemes and Shucksmith argues that the 'difficulties of obtaining finance will prevent self-build schemes making any major contribution in areas of high second home ownership' (Shucksmith, 1983, p.186). As Jenkin points out, self-build is never likely to be a viable substitute for local authority or housing association provision (Jenkin, 1985, p.65). That said, the Joseph Rowntree Foundation (JRF) published a review of self-build activity across the UK in 2001 (Barlow *et al*, 2001): this review found that:

- The number of 'self-build' homes completed each year has risen from around 2,000 in 1978 to an estimated 15,000 in 1999, with a particular increase in the early to mid-1990s.
- Self-build tends to be more prevalent in less urban areas and in areas where the market for speculative house building is relatively small.
- The growth in self-build since 1991 has only partly been driven by changes in the wider land and housing market. Other factors include: relatively well-off households seeking more individual homes; financing becoming more straightforward; and more publicity for the concept.
- There has been a shift in self-builders from those who cannot afford mainstream housing or are not eligible for social housing, to those who want an individual property or a particular location. The average age and income of self-builders has also been rising.

- There is no reliable data on self-build construction costs. However, the most recent market research reports that the average self-build home cost almost £150,000 in 1999, including land. The average UK price for a self-build plot in early 2000 was £44,183, but this covers large regional differences.
- Self-builders often incorporate innovative techniques or design. However, more innovative features are often constrained by planning requirements, concerns over resale values and limited experience of innovation within the construction industry.
- The researchers conclude that the sector is likely to stabilise at around 18,000 homes per year but could grow to provide around 10 per cent of new homes completed each year (around 20,000 homes). However, further expansion will only come with increased awareness and easier production. This will require changes to land provision, planning and finance, and a modernisation of the industry.

Source: Barlow *et al*, 2001: summary provided on JRF website: http:// www.jrf.org.uk / knowledge/findings/housing/951.asp: accessed 08 April 2004.

The JRF study shows that there has been healthy growth in self-build in recent years, especially in the mid 1990s. However, whilst many self-builders 20 years ago comprised households unable to compete for homes in the housing market, today they tend to be wealthier people looking for one-off, architect designed, 'bespoke' properties. Current self-build activity tends to be skewed to the higher end of the market, confirming Jenkin's view twenty years ago, that it is unlikely to be a viable option for those otherwise looking for local authority or housing association properties. However, not all self build homes are expensive. Today, flat-packed solutions offer the possibility of households entering into self-build with less of a financial commitment: a lower skill base is also required and negative attitudes to self build may well have altered with the recent proliferation of DIY and home-improvement programmes on prime-time television. However, some authorities remain concerned over the quality of new housing emerging from such initiatives and argue that a move to self-build of the flat-packed type raises the spectre of low housing quality and illegal development of the type more common in southern Europe (Padovani and Vettoretto, 2003, p.103).

Erecting Tax Barriers to Second Home Ownership

The potential benefits of dissuading people from buying second homes through the erection of tax barriers was an issue introduced at the beginning of this book. In 2001, the DETR consulted on changes to Council Tax regulations affecting second homes and long-term empty properties; in April 2004, it handed local authorities the discretion to charge 90 per cent of the full rate on second homes. We look at this issue a little more closely below. However, Council Tax variations (and increases) are not the only potential means of either reducing the attractiveness of second home ownership, or meeting the 'social costs' that sometimes accompany second home concentrations. In 1973, Pyne argued that a key government option for curbing second home ownership was the imposition of tax penalties (Pyne, 1973, p.40) and in the following year, the Finance Act removed tax relief for mortgages on second homes. Four years later, the Dart (1977) study in Scotland argued that Capital Gains Tax already discourages those purchasers who might consider a second home as an investment whilst the impact of Capital Transfer Tax and Wealth Tax introduced in the earlier legislation was still unknown (although these tax disincentives may have contributed to the decline in demand between 1973 and 1977).

In France, Clout (1969) noted that higher taxes on second homes reflect a recognition of an increased burden on local services (particularly infrastructure), and it is this same recognition that has been used to justify a higher rate of Council Tax on second homes in Wales (from 1998) and England (from 2004). However, in Britain, little public capital expenditure is required to bring a dwelling into second home use and it may be argued that the second home generates an extra use of the possibly underused facilities that are already supplied to permanent residents (Jacobs, 1972, p.48). Whilst the removal of mortgage tax relief may be justified on equity grounds along with the premise that greater levels of consumption should not be rewarded, it is difficult to see how the taxing of ambiguous economic and social impacts might be achieved. That said, government now seems to believe that this is indeed possible and justified, hence its move to give authorities the discretion to reduce discounts on Council Tax. Before turning to look specifically at Council Tax, it might also be noted, that there are other potential tax barriers and disincentives that might be used curb second home demand. It is already the case that capital gains tax is payable on the money derived from the sale of a second home, though this may not act as a disincentive for initial purchase, particularly if the buyer intends to use the property for recreation rather than simply as an investment. However, it might in the future be possible to charge a different rate of stamp duty on properties bought as second homes. In London, the Treasury has already scrapped Stamp Duty (set at a rate of 1 per cent of purchase price up to £250,000 and 2.5 per cent thereafter) on properties purchased in more deprived wards in an attempt to lever investment into such areas. This sets an important precedent, as government has demonstrated a flexibility that might be extended to rural areas, perhaps with stamp duty increased (to 5 per cent?) on properties purchased by non-local households as second homes. This would certainly add substantially to the cost of initial acquisition, though its success would depend on careful usage and local justification. This is an option that we consider further in Chapter 10.

Differential Rates or Council Tax

A number of the past second home studies highlighted the possibility of levying higher rates charges (Council Tax from 1993) from second home owners, again increasing the overall cost of second home ownership. A local authority rating system operated in the UK before the introduction of the Community Charge in 1990, which was itself scrapped in 1993 when the current Council Tax was introduced. The debate in the 1970s focused on increasing the rates levy on second homes; this would have been a controversial move, particularly as second home owners paid full rates at that time but only made partial use of local services (Dart, 1977, p.62): this point was emphasised by Terry Coppock:

> County studies indicate that these owners of second homes bring financial benefits, contributing more in rates than they consume in services and making a considerable local purchases, in turn creating new employment through the multiplier effect (Coppock, 1977, p.147).

Despite such arguments, it was clear that an additional charge could be levied on second homes, the rationale being that '[...] increasing [the] cost of second homes would lead to demand for them falling' (Jenkin, 1985, p.58). The Council Tax discount on second homes (previously 50 per cent of the full charge) was scrapped in Wales in 1998. Arguably, this move severed the connection between services used and Council Tax paid, though it was argued that non-permanent residence exposed local services to the pressure of under-use and therefore the scrapping of the discount was justified. In England, the DETR commenced its consultation on a similar move in 2001. This consultation exercise ran in parallel with work by the Countryside Agency that looked, in part, at the impact of increasing the Council Tax payable on second homes. Housing authorities, planning departments and National Park Authorities were asked for their views on this issue. The overwhelming majority of respondents believed that councils should be given the discretion to levy council tax at the full rate (housing: 93 per cent; planning: 77.6 per cent; parks: 100 per cent). However, it was anticipated that such a move would have only a very small impact on second home demand, with authorities needing to push the tax levy far beyond the current rate to deter second home ownership. Generally, authorities believed that:

- The impact on the second home market is likely to be minimal. The difference between paying £300 and £600 per annum (on a second home valued at £100,000) is of little consequence.
- Similarly, Council Tax is only a small percentage of the total running cost of a second home, and therefore minor tax increases will not affect demand for second homes.
- Extra local income from 100 per cent Council Tax charge on second homes was frequently described as 'useful', though not significant locally.
- A higher Council Tax charge will only dissuade 'marginal purchasers' from buying second homes.

Source: Gallent *et al*, 2002, p. 41.

The study concluded that rural authorities in England 'lost' approximately £50 million per annum as a result of the Council Tax discount on second homes; in authorities where there are large concentrations of second homes, the amount of revenue lost is likely to be locally significant; elsewhere, potential gains were likely to be small. On the back of the 2001 consultation, government decided not to scrap the discount on second homes, but to reduce it to just 10 per cent. The rationale behind this was two-fold: firstly, that there are indeed local costs associated with high concentrations of second homes that should be factored into the local tax system; and secondly, that retention of a small discount with give second owners an incentive to 'register' their second homes, thus enabling local authorities to monitor changes in this part of the housing market. The new regulations came into force on the 1st April 2004 (and are set out in the Local Government Act 2003). Immediately, numerous councils across rural England voted to remove the discount with effect from the 1st April (that is for the beginning of the new billing year; BBC Online, 2004). The issue of ring-fencing Council Tax revenue for rural housing programmes in those areas affected by second home concentrations is taken up in Chapter 9.

Defining Local Property Rights

The final housing policy move that could be used to regulate second home purchasing is also the most radical. Modifying the financial context in which the demand for second homes operates offers an opportunity for indirectly affecting the housing market. But there are, of course, more direct policy options available including the general introduction of property purchase controls (that is, 'licensing' purchases and restricting purchases to certain types of buyer) or the creation of exclusive property sub-markets.

The first of these options is already in operation in the Channel Islands (Pyne, 1973, p.46). Since 1945, Jersey's Housing Committee has been charged to consider all applications of property purchase and land use change, enacting legislation to this effect in 1949; similar measures have been applied in Guernsey since the Housing Control Law of 1969 (Williams, 1974, p.60). Only purchasers meeting specific residency and employment criteria are granted the license to acquire property. However, a number of arguments have been voiced against the extension of such a scheme on the British mainland including the negative economic impact of licensing in some importing regions and the more general effect on the balance of payments as second home buyers seek properties abroad (this is a wider argument against all prohibitive measures). Practically, opponents argue that such a scheme would be extremely difficult to administer over a wide area although this counter-argument is perhaps less damning than the likely impact of such a scheme on personal property rights and the individual's freedom of residence. Indeed, Jersey's Housing Committee has recently been keen to ensure that its own housing law is compatible with legislation adopted on human rights and has thus made recent amendments (Jersey States Assembly, 2004) and conceded that in the future, it may not be desirable to use housing policy as a brake on immigration (Channel Island News, 2001).

Licensing schemes might operate in one of two ways. Firstly, the model employed in parts of Finland (see Chapter 5, this volume) might be adopted, granting particular rights to acquire and occupy property to households with certain characteristics (for example, those having been born in the area, or having lived there for a fixed period of time, as in the case of Jersey). This approach would mean that purchasing rights were simply restricted; and this would affect all property transactions. Secondly, it might also be possible to restrict the use of permanent homes as second homes through planning control. This approach is quite different, and unlike the 'residency rights' model, would not prevent people retiring or migrating permanently to an area. We consider how the housing market might be regulated through planning controls in the next part of this chapter, and then again in Chapters 8 and 9.

The focus here, however, is on 'property rights': controlling who can and who cannot purchase property and reside in an area. The determination of local property rights – and the creation of sub-markets from which non-local buyers are barred – has been proposed in some areas as a means of protecting local interests. In Wales, the Welsh Language Society continues to argue that '[...] the private purchasing market must [...] be controlled so that local people can purchase property at a reasonable price' (Cymdeithas Yr Iaith Gymraeg, 1989, p.1). In the face of rising property prices (this particular document was published at the height of the property boom) in rural areas, the Society has argued that the only answer is to control prices and access to existing housing stock with local people given priority when bidding for new and old housing. On cultural and linguistic grounds, the Society has campaigned for a prioritisation of local interests, despite counter arguments that any and all local housing initiatives '[...] unfairly advantage those on low incomes who, by good fortune, live in rural areas' (Hutton, 1991, p.311). The Society stepped up its campaign for a so-called 'property act' in 1999, publishing an update of its 1992 '*Llawlyfr Deddf Eiddo*' (Property Act Handbook) in which it presented a series of working principles that should be taken forward by the National Assembly for Wales (now the Welsh Assembly Government) in the development of its housing policies: that is

- That houses and property are regarded as a necessity rather than a marketable commodity;
- That local people's access to the existing stock of housing and property is encouraged and ensured;
- That house and property prices reflect the local market; and
- That the planning system protects and serves local communities.

Source: Cymdeithas Yr Iaith Gymraeg, 1999, p. 4.

The proposal is certainly radical: housing would no longer be viewed as a commodity to be bought and sold on the open market; access to housing for those deemed 'local' would be guaranteed; property prices would not be allowed to rise above local wage levels; and the planning system would be re-designed to serve primarily local interests. In the first edition of its Property Act Handbook, the Society proposed that the District Valuers Department in each local authority should set 'fair prices' in the area and that a 'points system' should be extended to the purchase of private property with the principal component being local residence. In practice, someone wishing to sell a property would have to contact the local authority; if there was a need for more rented accommodation in the area then the authority (depending on resources) would purchase the property and let it to local people. If this was not the case then the property could be sold but not with a 'market' value. Instead, a 'banding system' would be implemented whereby local first time buyers have first refusal on the property, people from adjacent areas have second refusal and only if there are no buyers in this local needs 'cascade' could the property be advertised further afield (with price restrictions). The policy's designers claimed this level of control and the creation of such a rural housing

---

Priority for Local People

- To give local people the right to buy a home (or property / business / farm) at a reasonable price from the existing stock of houses and property.
- To give house and property owners the right to sell to a local person without making a loss.
- The aim of this Point (of the proposed Property Act) is to give local people the first opportunity in the private property market, and to gradually bring the market within the reach of local people once again.

The Housing Acts 1980/1985

- The system outlined below is a development of the system established by the Housing Act of 1980 (section 157 of the Housing Act 1985) for the resale of council houses in national parks, areas of outstanding natural beauty and "designated rural areas" (which includes large areas of rural Wales). This Act gives local authorities the right to insist that former council houses are either sold to local residents, or firstly offered to the local authority.

Estate Agents

- Every estate agent will have to be licensed by the appropriate local authority. (Local authorities will also have the right to offer services to buyers or vendors should they wish.)

Defining Local People

- There will be three bands of buyers:–
  Band 1 ("the local band")
  A person who has lived or worked throughout the 3 years prior to buying the property either within the same local authority area as the property, or within the same travel-to-work area, or within 10 miles of the property's location.

Band 2 ("the semi-local band")
(a) A person who has accepted full time permanent employment within the area (as defined above);
(b) A person who has lived in the area (as defined above) for at least 10 years during their lifetime.
Band 3 ("the open band")
This means anyone.

- If couples or families were buying, then only one person would have to satisfy these requirements.

The Process of Buying and Selling Property

- By completing a simple *pro-forma* form, the vendor (or agent) will inform the local authority that the property is for sale. They will receive a certificate from the local authority to prove this, and the solicitor acting on their behalf will present this certificate along with the rest of the documents to the Land Registry when the sale is registered.
- The local authority and local housing providers will be given 5 working days to express an interest in buying the property (in accordance with their strategy). If they have an interest, they must make an offer at its market value within 20 working days.
- If the local authority / housing providers show no interest, or an offer is not received on their behalf, the vendor will be allowed to put the property for sale to those from Band 1. The vendor will decide on the price, and the vendor or their agent will advertise the property for sale. However, local authorities will also have a list of properties for sale, and will have the right to advertise on behalf of vendors who wish them to do so.
- If the vendor does not receive a reasonable offer for the property from a person in Band 1 within 3 months, they may ask for permission from the local authority to offer the property for sale to Band 2.
- Before receiving permission the vendor must present:
  (a) a Certificate from an estate agent or solicitor to prove that the property has been for sale for 3 months and has been reasonably advertised locally (details will need to be supplied);
  (b) a Certificate from a chartered valuer (who may be the same person as above) declaring that the price asked for the property is similar to the sale price of similar properties in the area during the previous 3 months; and that a reasonable offer was not received by anyone from Band 1.
- The district valuer will monitor property prices. Any person who believes that a reasonable offer was refused will also have the right to make a complaint to the local authority.
- The local authority must respond in writing to the vendor within 10 working days, either giving consent to move on to the next band or giving reasons for refusing permission. (The vendor will have the right to appeal to the ombudsman). Any sale without the proper permission will not be legally valid.

- The same procedure as outlined above will be followed in moving from Band 2 to Band 3.
- When the sale is registered with the Land Registry the solicitors of the vendor and the buyer must provide evidence that the buyer complies with the definitions outlined above for Band 1 or Band 2, and also inform the local authority of this.

Source: Cymdeithas Yr Iaith Gymraeg, 1999, pp. 12–13.

Figure 7.2   A Property Act for Wales – Controlling the Housing Market

sub-market offered the 'only long term answer to this worsening [housing] problem' (Cymdeithas Yr Iaith Gymraeg, 1989, p.7): the updated version of this system (Chapter 5 of the current Handbook, 1999) is set out in Figure 7.2.

Clearly, the approach set out in Figure 7.2 would result in tight regulation of the housing market. The authors of the handbook claim that this model would not infringe on property rights, but would simply redistribute those rights to people who have, hitherto, been priced out of the property market; it is claimed that Britain's 'free market' in housing is free only for the rich (ibid. p. 6); an inequity which the Society is seeking to address. However, the model takes as its starting point a very narrow view of both the rural housing problem, and the way in which the housing market operates. Taken to an extreme, and applied to 'local' markets everywhere, the model would erect insurmountable barriers to labour market flows, cause a crash in property prices and probably lead to a new crisis in negative equity. It is also quite wrong to suggest that the rulings set out in the 1980 and 1985 Housing Acts – restricting the onward sale of council housing – could be used as a precedent for regulating private property transactions. Authorities – as vendor – had the power to insert a clause into the sale agreement (restricting onward resale within a certain time period) because they were the original owner of the property and were entering into a legally binding agreement with their secure tenant (as the buyer). Authorities have no such power over transactions between private vendors and buyers.

The principal objective of most radical agendas is to draw attention to important issues and to act as a catalyst for debate. The Welsh Language Society has been involved in the rural housing debate in Wales for several decades, though arguably its hard-line on the rural housing issue and its relative neglect – until very recently – of wider social and economic agendas, has sidelined it in the eyes of many commentators, and alienated it from the Welsh Assembly Government. Indeed, the inference that all migration to rural areas is inherently bad – a view implied in the Property Act model, and challenged by the Countryside Agency in England in recent years – is now as outmoded as Plaid Cymru's suggestion in the 1970s that tourism and second homes are an unmitigated disaster for the Welsh (Coppock, 1977, p.200).

But despite the obvious impracticalities and shortcomings of more radical responses, it is becoming increasingly clear that some means must be found of diverting attention away from some *existing* rural housing and from those communities blighted by unsustainable concentrations of second homes. We do not believe that individuals should or can realistically be granted particular property rights; in many respects, this would be tantamount to handing local authorities the proverbial sledge-hammer to crack a nut. There is no one rural housing market in the same way that there is no one rural economy; therefore, solutions need to be locally designed, robustly justified, and tailored to local contexts. Housing markets are changing as a result of demographic aging, commuting pressures and recreational demands; but they are changing in different ways. Authorities need to be given the means to respond flexibly, a point that we return to in Chapter 10. In the final part of this chapter and in the next, we turn to look at the land use planning system's potential role in managing housing market change in the countryside: 'planning and develop-ment control' was the third of Dower's (1977) list of options for responding to second homes.

Part 3: Planning and Development Control

The potential for using the land use planning system to control the growth of second home ownership and minimise adverse impacts (including the lack of access to affordable homes in areas of strong external demand) is discussed at greater length in Chapter 8. The intention here is simply to introduce the potential of the planning system, with a view to feeding this analysis into the new framework set out in Chapter 9. Two basic issues are considered: firstly, the way in which planning controls can affect the use of *new housing*; and secondly, the opportunities that may exist in the future for affecting the use of *existing housing* through 'change of use' controls.

New Development and Occupancy Controls

A key point to take forward to the next chapter is this: a large proportion of the UK's second homes have been created through change of use – that is, properties are taken from the mainstream existing housing stock and subsequently used as second homes. However, a recent study of the occupancy of new housing in Pembrokeshire Coast National Park (Pembrokeshire Coast National Park Authority, 2002) found that a quarter of new-build homes were being used as weekend cottages, prompting the authority to seek restrictions on occupancy. This demonstrates that whilst the majority of second homes may have formerly been first homes for people living permanently in an area, outside buyers are also attracted to new properties. The planning system is able to restrict the occupancy of new housing, especially when that housing is built by an RSL. However, the planning system cannot control the sale of property from one private individual to another; and it cannot restrict how that property is subsequently used. This means that planning controls are unable to stop people using properties on a temporary basis if that is their wish. This is an important point as some commentators believe that a capacity simply to restrict the use of some new property means that current planning controls are incapable of managing the second home market in areas of high demand. This has resulted in calls for planning reform, handing local authorities the power to distinguish first from second homes in the same way that the system presently distinguishes business from residential premises. If this distinction could be made, then the use of a first home as a second home (and vice versa) would be subject to the success of a planning application. This might mean that authorities could regulate the proportion of dwellings used as second homes within their local area, preventing increases above a threshold of, say, 10 or 20 per cent.

A discussion of how planning can or might be used in the future to address second home and wider housing pressure concerns is continued in Chapter 8. Here, we simply introduce the main mechanisms. First, in terms of *new development*, dwelling occupancy may be controlled by specific local needs policies written into development plans, implemented as planning agreements. For example, these policies may indicate that in certain communities, new housing development will be limited to providing for proven local needs (along the lines of Pembrokeshire's 'essential needs' housing policy for sustainable communities: see above). Also, where housing is provided through a Section 106 agreement (see Figure 7.1 above), this is likely to be subject to a clause in the agreement stipulating that the housing should be retained for local occupancy in perpetuity, affecting for example, who may occupy homes procured through a rural exceptions scheme (again, see Figure 7.1). In the recent past, some authorities have tried to adopt extremely rigid local needs and housing occupancy policies. Ceredigion District Council, in West Wales, included the following policy in a draft version of its Unitary Development Plan:

> The occupation of new dwellings, including the conversion of existing buildings, shall be limited to persons and their dependants who originated from or have lived for a period of five years from the date of occupancy either in Ceredigion or in an area no more than twenty-five miles from its boundary.

This policy was questioned by the Welsh Office (it pre-dated the arrival of the National Assembly Government in 1999) with officials arguing that planning controls should be concerned only with land use and not with the backgrounds of potential occupants. A similar objection to Pembrokeshire's essential needs policy was brought by the Welsh Assembly Government in 2000. However, the view today is not that planning cannot be used to prioritise local needs, but rather that heavy-handed intervention may have unforeseen consequences in the wider housing market, and in the local economy more generally. There is also a view that whilst planning agreements should be used to control the occupancy of 'affordable' housing (procured with some form of direct or planning subsidy), control over housing built for the general market is seen as less desirable.

A series of planning circulars since 1991 have confirmed that a community's need for affordable housing is a material planning consideration (that is Circulars 7/91, 13/96 and 6/98 in England); this gives legitimacy to the use of occupancy control. Also, the much-cited 'Mitchell' case brought before the Court of Appeal in 1993 set a legal precedent, demonstrating that local authorities can give consideration to the characteristics of potential occupiers when determining applications for new housing. These policies can, therefore, be used to ensure that at least some new housing development is for the sole use of local people or key workers and cannot be sold off as retirement or second homes. Binding agreements controlling occupancy are made under Section 106 of the Town and Country Planning Act 1990. We look more closely at their use in Chapter 8.

Existing Housing and Change of Use Controls

Secondly, in terms of *existing housing*, there are no currently available mechanisms for controlling whether a dwelling sold to an outside buyer is subsequently used as a second home. We noted in the 'defining local property rights' section above that – at least theoretically – it is possible to license private property transactions and define who is able to purchase property in a given location. However, such a move is unlikely to attract a great deal of popular or political support, and would probably prove unworkable on a number of fronts (see discussion above). The planning alternative is to bring *change of use* of existing dwellings (from first to second home and vice versa) under planning control. This is not a new idea and has been advocated for more than thirty years (see for instance, Bielckus, *et al*, 1972; Jacobs, 1972; Downing and Dower, 1973; Pyne, 1973; Dower, 1977). The observable trend towards second homes being drawn from the mainstream housing stock through change of use in the 1970s led many observers to call for new legislation making such a use change subject to planning permission (at the time, this may have been possible under the provisions of Section 22 of the Town and Country Planning Act 1971). In 1981, Dafydd Wigley MP – the leader of Plaid Cymru in Wales – introduced a private member's Bill to this effect. In response, the Conservative Government of the time rejected the Bill, arguing that how an occupant chooses to use his or her own home is not a material planning consideration. At the time, it did seem that the policy would '[...] undoubtedly run contrary to the spirit of existing planning law' (Jenkin, 1985, p.57).

That said, the spirit of planning law has changed considerable since 1981. In 1990, the Labour Party's Clive Soley expressed support for such controls (Soley, 1990, pp.38–39) suggesting that a distinction should be made between principal and secondary residences in the 1987 Use Classes Order. The Conservatives were again quick to reject such a move claiming it would be 'spiteful and impractical'. In Chapters 9 and 10, we look again at this option.

Conclusions

This chapter has considered some of the options suggested during the last thirty years for either, directly controlling second homes and venting housing pressures, or for securing an additional supply of affordable housing in those areas most affected by strong external housing demand. The options examined fall into three categories: broad economic strategies, housing policy mechanisms, or planning controls, and involve:

- The promotion of economic growth and diversification in hitherto laggard rural areas;
- Securing additional non-market housing either through planning mechanisms or through direct RSL provision;
- Municipalising vacant properties entirely or entering into shared ownership agreements with those recognised to be in housing need;
- RSL or council management of private empty homes in order to address local needs;
- Promoting self-build initiatives as a means of bring down housing costs in areas of inflated prices;
- The erection of national tax barriers (and disincentives) against external housing demand, with raised revenues being invested in rural housing programmes;
- Local tax disincentives, including raising Council Tax levels on second homes (perhaps beyond the current rate on fully occupied homes);
- Licensing property transactions and stipulating local property rights;
- Controlling the occupancy of new housing through planning mechanisms;
- Restricting the use of previously permanent residences as second homes through reform of the planning system.

Understanding the evolution of these ideas and their potential strengths and weaknesses is a necessary prerequisite to developing a new policy framework. This is set out in Chapter 9. In the next chapter, we examine planning mechanisms in greater depth; these are often considered to be the most practicable means of protecting local interests in the face of overwhelming external housing competition.

Chapter 8

Land Use Planning Mechanisms

Introduction

Inevitably, any framework for addressing second home concerns in the UK will have a planning component. The planning system has widened its field of vision in recent times. Twenty years ago, Circular 15/84 Land for Housing (DoE, 1984) stated that the key objective of planning in relation to new housing development was simply to ensure sufficient supply of land to meet both household demands and the needs of the construction industry. By the time that a second version of Planning Policy Guidance Note 3 (Housing) appeared in 1992, it was accepted that planning's role was certainly wider than that set out in Circular 15/84. Indeed, it was stated that local authorities should concern themselves with the quality of new housing, its design and sustainability, and access to homes for households unable to compete in the open market. These messages were re-affirmed in Circular 6/98 Planning for Affordable Housing (DETR, 1998) and the most recent version of PPG3 (DETR, 2000). That planning should deliver sustainable, balanced communities is a central theme of the current government's Sustainable Communities Plan (ODPM, 2003a) and its consultation draft of Planning Policy Statement 1 (ODPM, 2004). Planning should, therefore, focus not only on the control of land use, but should seek to achieve wider social goals.

This chapter, like the last, examines some of the options for dealing with housing pressures in rural areas with a view to distinguishing what *should* be done through planning from what *could* be done. However, the focus in this chapter is on direct controls over second home demand and use, not on supplying affordable housing through the planning system. The latter subject was addressed briefly in Chapter 7 with the key rural delivery mechanisms summarised in Figure 7.1. A more comprehensive account of how the planning mechanisms in the UK can be used to procure affordable housing can be found in Gallent (2000), Crook *et al* (2002), Adams and Watkins (2002) and Carmona *et al* (2003).

The debate surrounding planning for housing (and for affordable housing) in recent years has been characterised by a widening acceptance that planning does indeed have a social dimension. In policy rhetoric at least, the clearest message is that local planning authorities should use the system to promote greater 'sustainability': this means economic sustainability, connecting housing supply to the needs of the labour market and recognising the wider economic consequences of planning decisions (Barker, 2004); it also means environmental sustainability, ensuring that planning acts to lighten the ecological footprint of development; and it also means social sustainability, combating exclusion, promoting opportunity and creating balanced communities. A move away from the inflexibility of 'land use planning' to 'spatial planning' with its broader array of social, economic, environmental and spatial concerns should be good news for communities where social imbalances are a fact of everyday life. Arguably, many rural areas with high concentrations of second homes fit into this category.

In the 1990s, there was a concern in many rural areas that planning was simply not working in the interests of local people or local economies. In Wales, in particular, the apparently narrow focus of the planning system was a cause of bitterness amongst some rural authorities and language campaigners (see also Chapter 7, this volume). There was a view that whilst planning 'talked the talk' with regards to local community interests, attempts to prioritise these interests were constantly thwarted by central government. Hence, overt policies to prioritise local needs (see the cases of Ceredigion and Pembrokeshire, Chapter 7) in sometimes spurious ways brought local and national state into conflict (House of Commons Welsh Affairs Committee, 1993; Tewdwr-Jones, 1995; Cloke, 1996). Also in Wales, the frustration of many authorities centred on the problems of ensuring access to housing for local people in those areas with a high proportion of Welsh speakers, and where the dual pressures of migration and economic failure had been identified. Today, these concerns continue despite planning's apparently broadened remit generally, and the devolution of power to the Welsh Assembly Government. In both England and Wales (and elsewhere in the UK), concerns centre on the following issues:

- The inadequacy of planning mechanisms to deliver a sufficient number of affordable homes within rural communities given the weight of demand pressure, increasing competition in the land market, and planning constraint (see Crook *et al*, 2002);
- Migration pressures, second home purchasing, retirement, house price inflation and the pressure on local services and schools;
- The inability of current mechanisms to 'manage demand' without simply opening up land to development or pushing local people into social housing.

The last point is critical. Rural housing supply is finite; it is a limited resource with inherent scarcity (Hoggart, 2003). Without controls on the occupancy of new market housing or restrictions on change of use – introduced in the previous chapter – it appears likely that many communities will eventually have either no 'local residents', or 'locals' will only be able to occupy social housing. Gallent, Mace and Tewdwr-Jones (2003a) have demonstrated that this future scenario is a cause of real concern in rural areas, and especially in Wales where some authorities believe that equity demands that local people's access to market housing should be a key objective of planning, and that it is entirely unacceptable that *social housing* should become synonymous with *local housing*.

This chapter is therefore concerned with those planning mechanisms that might be used to guarantee access to market housing. The discussion is centred on three issues: the use of occupancy controls; amendments to the Use Classes

Order; and accompanying political developments. Building on the introduction to this issue presented at the end of Chapter 7, we now focus attention on how planning control may presently be used to regulate the occupancy (and therefore use) of *new housing* and how planning control could potentially, in the future, be used to restrict the number of *existing dwellings* becoming second homes. Again, discussion feeds into the 'new framework for policy' presented in Chapter 9.

Part 1: Controlling the Occupancy of New Housing

Occupancy Controls: Background

In the 1970s, planning agreements – under Section 52 of the Town and Country Planning Act 1971 – were often used by local authorities as a means of securing 'a contribution from developers towards the infrastructure costs' of new housing schemes (Barlow, *et al*, 1994, p.3). By the middle of that decade, some authorities were using legal agreements with developers to procure new council housing units as well as other social infrastructure. Loughlin (1984) revealed that authorities were also using planning agreements (and other conditions) to limit the occupancy of new homes in some rural areas to local residents or key workers. This strategy – aimed at securing local access to new housing – had already been studied in detail by Shucksmith in the Lake District (1981). Where planning agreements are used (often as part of local needs policies written into development plans: see Chapter 7) to procure affordable housing or control market housing, these form part of the planning permission granted to the developer.

The Use of Occupancy Controls

By 1985, more than twenty structure plans in England contained references to specific 'local needs policies' for securing planning gains from development permissions (Bishop and Hooper, 1991, p.13). These policies frequently referenced the need to control the occupancy in new homes to meet local objectives. Four years earlier, Mark Shucksmith (1981) had argued that the housing problems faced by some *rural* communities could be alleviated in three ways; through planning controls ensuring that new dwellings are occupied by local people, by discouraging or preventing houses from being used as retirement or second homes, or by building more council houses and increasing rental stock. Shucksmith examined the operation of the first option in the Lake District between 1977 and 1984 (Shucksmith, 1981; 1990a); this involved the Lake District Special Planning Board (LDSPB; established in 1974) restricting the occupancy of new housing to local people through Section 52 agreements. This use of general occupancy controls in the Lake District in the later 1970s and early 1980s has clear parallels with Pembrokeshire Coast National Park Authorities essential needs housing policy contained in the 2002 deposit of its Joint Unitary Development Plan (see Chapter 7). For this reason, our intention here is to consider the effects of such policies in practice.

In Pembrokeshire, the National Park Authority has suggested that 'it is remarkable that many of our National Parks seem to be at different times recognising quite similar issues, that is the scarcity of housing land, the predominance of second homes and retirement homes and the consequential displacement of local demand' (Evidence for Housing Policy, 2001, Para. 57). Furthermore, the Authority points to the fact that 'the Lake District was first to tackle the issue'. As noted above the Lake District Special Planning Board introduced a new policy in 1977 designed to 'restrict completely all new development to that which can be shown to satisfy a local need' (LDSPB, 1977). The LDSPB asked applicants for residential planning consent to sign an agreement under Section 52 of the Town and Country Planning Act 1971 limiting the future occupancy of the housing to people employed or about to be employed locally, or retired from local employment. This became known as the 'section 52 policy', subsequently evaluated by Shucksmith (1981). The policy that eventually found its way into the Cumbria and Lake District Joint Structure Plan (1980) had the following wording:

> The Board will seek means by which all further housing development can be retained for occupation by local people as full-time residents, except in the case of divisions of existing dwellings or where exceptional site factors apply (LDSPB, 1980).

The similarities in the purpose and intent of this policy and that of the policy contained in the Pembrokeshire Coast National Park's 2002 draft deposit JUDP (to restrict new development to local use) are striking. Like Pembrokeshire Coast's policy, it is designed to ensure that remaining development sites are used for local needs housing: a response to land scarcity. Indeed, the LDSPB argued that there was a pressing need to ensure that 'the diminishing number of sites where new housing will be acceptable are used to maintain rural life' (LDSPB, 1978, p.22). And like Pembrokeshire Coast's policy, the LDSPB's approach faced immediate scrutiny. In the panel report from the 1981 Examination in Public it was argued that:

> It would be an unreasonable use of planning powers to attempt to ensure that houses should only be occupied by persons who are already living in the locality. The objectives of the authority are best served by the use of their powers under the Housing Acts [...].

The panel report added that:

> Planning is concerned with the manner of the use of land, not the identity or merits of the occupiers. Planning permission for a particular use of land otherwise suitable for that use cannot appropriately be refused simply because the planning authority wishes to restrict the user (DoE, 1981, pp.10–11).

These views are mirrored in the Welsh Assembly Government's objection to Policy 47 (Housing in the National Park). The Assembly Government argues that '[...] land allocated in UDPs as housing land should be available to all applicants and not allocated specifically to meet the needs of particular sections of the community' (Welsh Assembly Government, 2002, p.5). We noted above that the 'spirit' in which the planning system operates has moved on at pace since the early 1980s: the need for affordable housing is now a material consideration in the assessment of planning applications and has been – in Wales – since the issuing of DoE/WO Circular 31/91 relating to the provision of affordable housing through planning. The extension of planning powers to cover non land-use considerations is further evidenced by the existence of Technical Advice Note 20 regarding planning and the Welsh language. National Park Authorities, in particular, have a duty to safeguard not only environmental but also cultural heritage: a message emerging from the Edwards Report of 1991 (Edwards, 1991). However, the panel's view of the LDSPB's local needs housing policy (1981) and the objections to PCNPA's proposed policy (2002) are uncannily similar.

There is significant merit in comparing the operation of the Lake District's 'Section 52 Policy' with Pembrokeshire's 'Essential Needs Housing Policy'. Both operate on the same principles and within broadly similar contexts. The Lake District and Pembrokeshire Coast both face the problem of land scarcity; they both endure strong external housing demand pressure (from retiring households, other migrants and from those seeking second homes); and they are both looking for ways to assist local – and particularly young – households. Arguably, the problems being addressed by the LDSPB in the late 1970s (which are still being grappled with today) are similar to those facing the PCNPA at the present time.

The Impacts of Occupancy Controls: the Lake District and Pembrokeshire

Occupancy controls of the type used in the Lakes and proposed in Pembrokeshire exclude commuters, retiring households (and other migrants) and second home purchasers from the market for new housing either generally or within specified communities (Pembrokeshire has designated twenty-six 'Sustainable Communities' where its essential needs policy will be applied). These communities (which are often those enduring strongest external demand) will remain attractive to these categories of non-local purchaser. It is likely therefore that demand will be transferred from the market for new housing to the market for existing housing. It is also possible in some instances that demand will be deflected away from the 'protected communities' to alternative locations. The experience in the Lake District was that those buyers seeking property in the National Park were rarely deterred by the new policy, but instead tended to compete with locals for the existing stock, over which the LDSPB had no control. Within Pembrokeshire Coast's 'Sustainable Communities', it is likely the local needs policy will cause an intensification of competition for existing housing. This is likely to have a range of socio-economic impacts, some relating to the market for new housing and others to the market for existing homes.

(a) New Housing and Development

In order to maximise profit from new house building, developers often build to
the higher end of the market, satisfying demand from those with greater
spending power. In Pembrokeshire Coast, this means that new housing in more
attractive villages, in the open countryside (where new build on existing
footprints has been permitted) and in coastal locations has often been
purchased by non-locals. The exclusion of such buyers within the Sustainable
Communities is likely to have a profound impact on the demand for new
housing: the *market* from outside buyers will be effectively closed. Therefore
the overall market will shrink. In the Lake District, restrictions on occupancy
had a marked impact on the supply of new homes as '[...] builders ceased
speculative residential developments, partly because of the uncertainties raised
by the new policy, but principally because of the greater difficulty of acquiring
suitable land with planning permission' (Shucksmith, 1990, p.122). This means
that occupancy controls may adversely affect the *overall supply* of new housing.

Experience in the Lake District revealed that the combined effects of the
policy on both housing demand (market shrinkage) and housing supply
(limiting the size and number of developments by changing the environment
for house builders) meant that the policy itself had no discernible impact on the
price of new homes. The proposed Pembrokeshire policy is likely to have a
similar impact in the Sustainable Communities: falling demand (for new
property, from outside buyers) and reduced supply will cancel each other out,
resulting in little change in the price of new housing.

A critical problem in the Lakes was that although the policy sought to
prioritise local needs, it made no distinction between relative levels of need. In
other words, there was no mechanism in the policy to ensure that the most
disadvantaged local households occupied new housing: young local people, for
example, were afforded no particular privileges and were often out-competed
for new homes by existing local homeowners. This was partly because of the
greater spending power of existing owners (who can draw on equity from their
current property) and partly because house builders tended to build for this
section of the surviving market, in order to sustain profitability. In the Lake
District, Capstick argued that the policy 'did more to assist existing home
owners [...] than it did to assist new home owners' (1987, p.144).

(b) Existing Housing

The likely effect of occupancy controls on new development is a new, but
lower, equilibrium between housing supply and demand, with negligible impact
on house prices and hence affordability relative to local income levels. The
impact on the market for existing housing is likely to be somewhat different. A
potential homebuyer, perhaps looking to purchase a second home in one of
Pembrokeshire's 26 'Sustainable Communities' is unlikely, after being made
aware of the restriction on occupying new housing, to decide to buy elsewhere
in Pembrokeshire. If they are seeking a particular type of property in a certain
type of community (for example picturesque, coastal, quaint and so on), they

may not be satisfied with a property in Milford Haven, Haverfordwest or one of Pembrokeshire's other larger settlements. The natural response to not being able to buy and occupy new housing is to buy and occupy existing housing. This will result in increased demand for existing homes within those communities where development is subject to occupancy controls, and hence the price of this housing may rise sharply. Jackson *et al* (1994) confirm that constraint on land release will not only change the distribution of house-building activity and the type and timing of housing development but will also increase house prices across a wider area.

The supply of houses already built and occupied tends to be insensitive to changes in house prices: people decide to move not in response to the changing value of their homes but because of changing household circumstances and needs. Shucksmith (1990, p.123) argues that this reality makes the supply of existing dwellings very 'price inelastic'. This means that prices in the existing market will only even out relative to demand if there is a sudden surge in people putting their homes on the market (and hence an increase in supply to balance out demand). Because this is unlikely – for the reasons stated – restrictions on the occupancy of new housing, and hence a re-focusing of aspiration and demand on existing housing, will mean that property values in communities where new housing is subject to occupancy controls are likely to surge upwards. Basically, those seeking homes within the protected communities will look to the second-hand market: the general value of property will rise.

In the Lake District, a substantial increase in property values (in the market for existing housing) deterred some outside buyers from seeking retirement or second homes in the National Park. This was applauded as a success. However, South Lakeland District Council claimed that this led buyers to focus their attention outside of the Park and resulted in an inflation of house prices both in South Lakeland itself and elsewhere on the Parks boundary. In Pembrokeshire, the use of occupancy controls in certain villages may cause inflationary pressure to affect areas in between the Sustainable Communities. Alternatively, outside buyers may look to areas further North (into Ceredigion) or to the east of the National Park. Because prices may rise on the Pembrokeshire Coast, they may also rise throughout South West Wales as the market is affected by the essential needs policy. This inflationary pressure (caused by restricting new supply and the intensification of competition for existing housing) may reduce the affordability of housing more generally.

In summary, Shucksmith concluded that the control of occupancy increased the competition for existing housing stock and caused further house price inflation. The experience in the Lake District – and the above analysis of the potential impacts of a similar policy in Pembrokeshire – reveals that it is difficult to restrict the occupancy of new dwellings whilst responding to local needs (Shucksmith, 1981, p.141). It is also the case, that where such restrictions are placed on new market housing, they are likely to have a broad impact on market processes. This view was shared by the then Secretary of State for the Environment, Patrick Jenkin, who deleted the section 52 policy from the Cumbria and Lake District Joint Structure Plan in 1984 (Jenkin, 1985, p.56).

But even where occupancy controls are only applied to social housing, problems remain. Firstly, these controls may inhibit the capacity of RSLs to attract private finance on rural exception schemes (see Chapter 7, Figure 7.1) further reducing housing access opportunities for local groups (see Rural Development Commission, 1995). And secondly, occupancy controls offer no route into the existing housing stock. This returns us to the point made earlier: that local housing can quickly become synonymous with social housing, much to the frustration of many rural communities and authorities.

However, this conclusion does not lead us to any solution. It remains the case that:

> [...] a considerable body of research reveals a widespread and severe shortage of low-cost housing in rural areas which is recognised as not only a major contributor to rural disadvantage but also as the principal engine of social change in rural England. This is particularly important in excluding indigenous younger households on low incomes, unable to own their own property and with limited opportunities available in the rental market (Joseph Rowntree Foundation, 1999).

The use of planning agreements to regulate the occupancy of some new housing is crucial under certain circumstances. For instance, when authorities negotiate exceptional planning permissions, they need to offer land owners and local communities a guarantee that homes procured in this way will be retained for local use in perpetuity, otherwise confidence in the strategy will be eroded (again, see Chapter 7; see also Gallent & Bell, 2000). More generally, planning controls offer some assurance that the subsidies (for example land value subsidies delivered through planning gain or Social Housing Grant available to RSLs) used to deliver affordable homes will not be lost because initial occupiers of homes are permitted to sell on the open market for huge personal profit. Whatever their shortcomings, occupancy controls guarantee that at least some housing will be retained for local use. However, these controls offer no protection from the aggressive purchasing of existing dwellings for second home use in areas of high demand. Can and should something be done to address this broader concern?

Part 2: Regulating Change of Use in Existing Housing

Change of Use Controls: Background

In the previous chapter, it was argued that assigning property acquisition rights to individuals on the basis of local birth or residency has not, in the past, been seen as a desirable or workable policy response to second home pressures in the UK. An alternative, however, is to use planning control, to regulate the *use* of residential property. This could be achieved, as in Åland (see Chapter 5), by drawing a distinction between dwellings used for a primary, as opposed to a secondary, residential function. This distinction would be retrospective and all existing homes would be classified in this way (in Åland, the *use class* is defined when new dwellings are constructed). In effect, *change of use* would subsequently be subject to planning permission (and controlled by local authorities); that is, consent would be required for a dwelling used as a first home (for the last 5 or so years) to become a second home and vice versa. In the UK, the system could work in the following way:

- All private dwelling houses are currently assigned the classification C3 (in the 1987 Use Classes Order). These could all be reclassified as C3a, apart from those already used as second homes, which would be classified C3b;
- Now, if a purchaser buys a property in a rural area from a permanent resident, but intends to use that property as a second home rather than as their principal residence, then the planning authority will consider that they are making a 'material' change to the use of the property. All switches between use classes in the 1987 Order are considered material changes and are subject to planning control. This means that if the new owner does indeed intend to use their new property (C3a) as a second home (C3b) then they will require planning permission;
- The owner will have to make an application for planning permission to the local authority. This may not be granted where 10 or 20 per cent of local properties were already C3b (second homes), and further increases were likely to have an adverse impact on local services and so on.
- If the application were unsuccessful, the owner could choose to appeal or accept the decision. If they chose to accept the decision, then they might either sell the property on to a local person as a principal home, or rent the property out;
- In practice, it is likely that buyers would investigate local plan policies, and if it were the policy of an authority to deny changes of use from C3a to C3b where there were already high concentrations of second homes, then the purchaser might decide to look for a suitable property elsewhere.

On the face of it, this looks like a fairly robust strategy for regulating second home numbers in rural areas. Indeed, despite his criticisms of occupancy controls, Mark Shucksmith suggested twenty years ago that:

> Planning controls [regulating *use change*] are potentially the most sensitive means of reducing the number of second homes, in that the policy would be operated by local authorities who could apply such restrictions in accordance with local circumstances (Shucksmith, 1983, p.189).

Indeed, permissions might be granted where properties were surplus to general housing needs (and where the benefits of second homes outweighed the costs) but refused where change of use from first to second homes was proven to be driving up house prices and affecting the viability of local services. However, the approach is not without its drawbacks or its critics. Some of the likely problems are discussed under the 'workability' heading later in this chapter.

Change of Use Controls: The UK Debate

The idea of regulating the use of residential property through planning controls is not new, and has been advocated by a number of academics, planning authorities and politicians for several decades. In the early 1970s, it was increasingly apparent that the distribution of second homes in England and Wales was the product of use change; and as the stock of surplus dwellings less favoured by the local market was almost depleted in some areas, second home demand was re-concentrating on mainstream housing of the type sought by local buyers. Competition for housing was intensifying, and concerns over the potential social cost were growing. It was at this time that a number of observers argued that this pattern of use change should be brought under planning control (Bielckus, *et al*, 1972; Downing and Dower, 1973; Dower, 1977; Pyne, 1973; Dart, 1977) by amending Section 22 of the Town and Country Planning Act 1971.

At the beginning of the 1980s, the idea reached the political agenda with the introduction of Dafydd Wigley's Private Member's Bill in 1981. At that time, a number of criticisms were levelled at the possible creation of a separate use class for second homes. The Conservative Government drew attention to the 'infringement to personal liberty' that would arise from restrictions on the use of private property; more specifically, it was argued that determining planning decisions on the basis of future dwelling use, was not a legitimate purpose of the planning process: spending only part of the year in a property as opposed to most of the year is not a 'material consideration' or a 'material use change'. At this time, the notion that planning could do more than simply regulate development had not yet taken root.

But despite Conservative objections, instrumental in the failure of the Bill during its first reading, the concept of change of use as a means of regulating second home numbers in more pressured rural areas received a warmer reception amongst Labour Party members. At the time, the Labour's leadership expressed support for the approach and stated publicly that a future Labour government would introduce such a measure as part of wider planning reforms. The political pledge made in 1981 was clarified in 1990:

> Our proposal is that local authorities [...] would be able to restrict the growth of second homes in the affected areas by ensuring that an existing family home would need planning consent for *change of use* before it could be sold as a second home in much the same way as change of use is required to change a home into an office, for example. The procedure would be subject to appeal. This is the practice in a number of European countries. There is no question of a ban on second homes (Soley, 1990, p.39).

Labour's proposed approach was set out by Clive Soley in a 1990 edition of the housing magazine *Roof*. He went on to explain that the policy would not – and could not – be used in any attempt to reduce the existing number of second homes in rural areas. It was also emphasised that change of use restrictions would be flexible, allowing people to own two or more homes for employment reasons; there would also be a burden of proof placed on authorities before they could implement restrictions. The model to be adopted would follow that described at the beginning of this section. Fresh Conservative criticisms of the proposed policy – and suggestions that it was simply 'spiteful' – were rebuked by its Labour supporters who pointed out that the need for such measures had been accentuated by the Conservative Party's determination since 1980 to rid rural areas of affordable housing, and its prioritising of middle class aspirations and needs well above those of lower income households. Soley added that '[. . .] our villages are a very important part of our heritage and should not be allowed to die on their feet' (Soley, 1990, p.39).

But despite the promises made nearly 15 years ago, the introduction of change of use controls have not figured in the Labour Government's planning reform agenda. Labour's 1997 election manifesto did not deal in this level of detail with regards to planning issues and the rural agenda has since taken a back seat to the government's urban priorities. The Urban Task Force (1999), the Planning Green Paper (2001), the Planning and Compulsory Purchase Bill (2002), and of course the Sustainable Communities Plan (2003a) all point to a strong urban bias in Labour's reform agenda. Government has recently undertaken a review of the Use Classes Order (ODPM, 2003b), but the aim of this is to create a framework that eases the path of mixed use development; the issue of splitting the residential use class has not been part of this review. As a consequence, it has been left to others to push the government on rural housing issues and the more specific question of change of use controls.

In April 1998, the issue was championed once more by a Parliamentary Member of Plaid Cymru. Elfyn Llwyd, Member of Parliament for Meirionnydd Nant Conwy in North Wales, introduced a Private Member's Bill before the House of Commons aimed at amending existing planning legislation in order to protect rural villages in Welsh-speaking Wales from development and housing pressures. His Bill sought to introduce three measures: to impose a time limit of five years on planning permissions awarded by local authorities where the developer had not yet commenced any substantial development; to introduce a third party right of appeal for residents, objectors and others interested in applications for planning permission; and finally to introduce amendments to the Use Classes Order 1987 to classify all housing as primary or secondary residences, bringing change of use under planning control. In relation to the specific issue of second homes, the MP made the following remarks when introducing his Bill to the Commons:

> Such properties [. . .] bring certain social problems: the usual scenario is that they are purchased by those who can, by definition, afford a second home, which often means that they are earning many more times the average salary of those in the local community. They are able to pay the asking price without quibble, and locals are left in the wake wondering when, if ever, they will be able to enter the property market, and buy a house in the community in which, often, they were born and brought up (Elfyn Llwyd MP, Hansard, 28 April 1998, column 148).

The Bill received backing at the first reading and was scheduled to receive a second reading in the House of Commons in July 1998. However, under

Parliamentary rules, it was 'lost' when the House was unable to progress all matters during the allotted day for debate. As a Private Member's Bill, it was never likely to receive Royal Assent. The Plaid Cymru Members were well aware of this: their objective, however, was to draw attention once more to the housing difficulties facing Welsh rural communities,[1] and to government's lack of apparent concern for this issue. By publicising the supposed benefits of change of use controls, Plaid Cymru perhaps hoped to gain support and pave the way for secondary legislation that could be put before Wales' own Assembly once it began sitting in the following year.

Government in the UK is keen to peddle the rhetoric of 'sustainable communities', but tends to deal in principles rather than specifics. It has advocated the creation of sustainable communities in the four Growth Areas in southern England, and designated 'Market Renewal Pathfinder' schemes in the English Midlands and north to tackle the problem of low demand housing, also with a view to creating more sustainable communities (ODPM, 2003). Sustainability in these instances is largely concerned with economic durability, with bringing homes close to jobs, with lightening the environmental footprint of development, and with enhancing the quality of the built environment. It has also referenced the need to promote socially balanced communities and argued that former notions of wealth *redistribution* need to give way today to equality of *opportunity*. The language used by New Labour suggests that it is keen to see greater balance in rural communities, and to ensure that people of different social and economic backgrounds enjoy a range of opportunities. But this language needs to be judged against reality:

> [...] without adequate provision of [...] affordable housing, large parts of rural England risk becoming the near-exclusive preserve of the more affluent sections of society. This risk poses an important challenge to the goal of achieving balanced communities (*Rural Economies*, 1999).

Indeed, more recent work by the Commission for Architecture and the Built Environment (CABE) and the Royal Institute for British Architects (RIBA) forecasts that in twenty years time, some communities may be blighted by social apartheid, with the rich purposely separating themselves from their less well-off neighbours (Early, 2004, p. 4). Even the provision of more affordable housing is unlikely to remedy this situation. Therefore, more drastic steps – including change of use controls – might be warranted. And if government and Westminster chooses to shy away from this path, there are now opportunities to instigate changes to the planning framework in the devolved Welsh Assembly or Scottish Parliament.

In May 1999, the National Assembly for Wales (now re-branded the Welsh Assembly Government) and the Scottish Parliament commenced sitting. The Scottish Parliament possesses both statutory and policy making functions; the Welsh Assembly does not possess *primary* legislative powers – Acts of Parliament will still be debated and passed at Westminster and apply to both England and Wales – but has jurisdiction over policy making and can bring about amendments to *secondary* legislation. This means that amendments to the use classes order (planning *orders* are secondary legislation) can now be instigated in Cardiff to reflect the distinctive problems that exist in Wales; such a move might, for example, be justified as a means of protecting Welsh speaking communities from particular forms of housing demand pressure. However, in the five years since the Assembly was created, it has not brought forward any changes to secondary legislation. There are two factors that may have stayed the Assembly's hand: firstly, the number of second homes in Wales appeared to fall between the 1991 and 2001 Censuses, therefore any 'threat' they posed looks to be receding. And secondly, professional planners – in both the Assembly and within Welsh local government – appear reticent about using planning controls to curb change of use, given the likely problems associated with legally defining a second home for planning purposes, and subsequently enforcing the policy. Earlier in this chapter, we suggested that change of use controls appear to offer a fairly robust means of regulating second homes numbers. But would such a move have the desired outcome – that is more balanced communities – on the ground?

Change of Use Controls: Workability in 2004

Much has changed in the twenty-three years since Dafydd Wigley first proposed new change of use controls in 1981. We saw in the last section that government is increasingly keen to promote planning's role in delivering sustainable communities; also, the transfer of some powers to the devolved administrations possibly increases the likelihood of change of use controls being introduced somewhere, at some point in the future.

As well as these broad changes in the objectives and mechanics of policy making, it is also the case that the spirit and rationale of land use planning has been changing, particularly since the late 1980s. A community's need for a mix of housing types and tenures is now a material planning consideration in determining development applications. In Wales, Technical Advice Note 20 (Planning and the Welsh Language) encourages planning authorities to also consider socio-linguistic issues when assessing applications. The softening and 'socialising' of land use planning can also be observed on the government's planning reform programme: the Local Development Frameworks (LDFs) to be introduced through a Planning and Compulsory Purchase Act, either in 2004 or 2005, will seek to give local communities greater ownership of policies through the process of preparing Statements of Community Involvement. Indeed, Local Action Plans will be developed as a framework for taking forward local agendas. The focus of the planning system is changing: there is now far greater emphasis on community and on the achievement of social goals. But does the rhetoric of community empowerment and social balance increase the likelihood of new powers being handed to local authorities? On the one hand, the planning system is indeed widening its field of vision (as we noted at the beginning of this chapter); but on the other, there is perhaps a parallel move to 'lighten the touch' of planning intervention, to make it more market responsive but also more socially responsible. These two objectives do not always sit together comfortably. For many years now, the focus of debate in rural areas has been on the apparent failure of softer and more indirect mechanisms for helping communities, and on the need for stronger intervention. Could a more interventionist approach – including use change controls – sit with the current objective of delivering sustainable communities? And would they work?

In the late 1980s, Shucksmith and Watkins (ACRE, 1988) laid out the case for the inclusion of a *social* housing use class in the 1987 Use Classes Order, which would aid the delivery of affordable homes in rural areas. At the time, a failure to attract widespread support for the idea hinged on the fact that the Use Classes Order was not designed to be a mechanism of favouring particular types of housing occupants. Instead, it was '[...] intended to be an instrument for allowing changes of use which would constitute development were it not for the Order' (Barlow, *et al*, 1994, p.5). Arguably, a primary-secondary division in the C3 use class would not fall at the same hurdle: all new housing could be given a C3a (primary) designation. This would mean that the planning process (in terms of development control and treatment of the original application) would not be concerned with the characteristics of potential occupiers; it would only be concerned with the use to which a property was put at a later stage. The idea of a *social* housing use class was rejected on the grounds that '[...] it would lead to excessive general interest by planners in the personal circumstances of occupiers of housing' (ibid. p.5). Again, a primary-secondary division is unlikely to face this criticism, so long as all new homes were designated C3a and there were legally enforceable distinctions between C3a use and C3b use. But this is where the problems begin; how easy would it be to define second homes for planning purposes, and then to enforce the policy, ensuring that C3a properties were only used as 'principal homes'?

In Sweden (see Chapters 5 and 6), a significant proportion of 'second homes' are occupied for a large part of the year by the partners and children of businessmen who are employed in nearby cities and live in urban apartments which are 'officially' the family's first home. The distinction, however, is blurred and it is almost as if the rural residence is the first home of half the family whilst the urban apartment is the first home of the working partner. In 1990, the Labour Party suggested that the purchase and use of 'second' homes would not be restricted where the user needed the dwelling for employment purposes (Soley, 1990, p.39). The last Conservative Rural White Paper for Wales claimed that 'geographical location' is becoming 'irrelevant' in the new information age (Welsh Office, 1996a, p. 1). This means that many more people, with access to the internet, can work as easily from home as they can from an office in Manchester, Cardiff or London. In effect, people may have two work locations; one in or close to the city and another far removed, perhaps in a village (Clarke, 2000). But which is the principal residence and which is the second home?

This question would present a real dilemma for planning authorities; the reality of modern living makes it difficult to distinguish first from second homes, but authorities seeking to curtail the demand for 'second homes' would need to have workable definitions splitting C3a and C3b uses. Government (or the Welsh Assembly Government) would probably differentiate on the basis of continual residence within a fixed time period, for example C3a homes would need to be 'permanently occupied' for at least 6 months in any 12 month period by the same household. This definition seems reasonable; if a home were not going to be occupied for this length of time by the same family then the owner would either need to rent the property out, sell it, or apply for planning permission to change to C3b use. The obvious problem that arises is one of enforcement. In work for the Countryside Agency in England in 2002, it was found that many planning authorities already find it extremely difficult to police existing agricultural conditions attached to some local dwellings. These properties were originally built to house farm workers; today they have been sold on to people whose primary business is not agriculture, though 'they may keep chickens'. The issue for one particular English planning authority was how many chickens does one need to be 'engaged in agriculture'? Arguably, difficulties arose in this situation because the wording of very old conditions did not give authorities sufficient grounds to take enforcement action. The wording of the definition of C3a use could be looked at by the finest barristers in the land and made water-tight. But authorities would still need to enforce the system and deal with abuses. If the definition did rely on a 'six month occupancy' measure, then this raises the possibility of enforcement teams having to camp outside C3a properties suspected of being used as second homes. The cost to authorities and to the planning service generally could be massive, and might seriously disrupt progress in government's ongoing reform programme (for instance, getting bogged down in disputes with second home owners might hinder authorities' efforts to become faster and more efficient in delivering planning services).

Another problem relates to the potential loopholes. Having a distinction between C3a and C3b use would not preclude people purchasing buy-to-let properties. This means that someone from London could buy a property in the Cotswolds (for example) as an investment. The planning authority might enquire as to whether the new owner was intending to move to the area permanently, rent the property out, or apply for a change of use permission. Knowing that permission to change use to C3b would be very unlikely in a village where forty per cent of dwellings were already second homes, the owner might simply say that they intended to rent the property to a local family. However, the planning authority has no control over how much rent the new owner asks for; in theory they could advertise the property at any rent level they wished. And if a local tenant could not be found, then the property would simply remain empty; and not being able to find a tenant would not constitute a breach of planning regulations. Therefore the new owner from London could visit his Cotswold investment periodically just to check that that it was okay. To all intents and purposes, the property is a second home, but it retains its C3a use class, and the planning authority is powerless to take action.

When discussing this issue five years ago in *Rural Second Homes in Europe*, we suggested that government would be wary of handing local authorities change of use powers, fearing excessive intervention in the housing market. This probably remains true today. Certainly, any local actions would have to be clearly justified; government would probably tie new planning powers to local assessments of second home impacts, making sure that authorities responded only to local pressures and did not use the controls in a punitive way. If we assumed for a moment that the approach was operable, then it might increase the likelihood of local people being able to access housing; pressured areas may become less pressured; local services might be placed under reduced stress; and more outside money might be spent in local hotels and guesthouses, rather than on buying local property. On the downside, city buyers could simply invest in property abroad; less tourist money might be spent in rural areas; and households could see the value of their homes depreciate. We do not believe any of this will happen. Were change of use controls introduced in an attempt to quell second home demand, then this might have some impact on the market in the period immediately after implementation. On hearing about the new regulations, some potential second home buyers – fearing lengthy and fruitless entanglements with planning authorities – might postpone their purchasing plans. But the large majority of tenacious and intelligent people will see the inherent difficulties in operating and enforcing the policy. Like our hypothetical buyer from London, they will identify the many ways round the controls. Using a residential dwelling as a second home is not like using a dwelling as a bar or restaurant; it is not an obvious switch between residential and commercial use; it is far more subtle. We believe that such an approach would simply not work.

Conclusions

As we noted at the start of this chapter, planning controls are likely to form at least a part of any future framework for addressing housing pressures in rural areas. In this chapter, we have concentrated on how planning has, and might in the future, be used to influence the occupancy and use of new and existing homes. With regards to occupancy and change of use controls, the following key points have been raised:

- Planning authorities commonly use occupancy controls to ensure that affordable homes can be retained in perpetuity for use by local people or key workers. The logic of this approach is clear; too much affordable housing has been lost in rural areas, and mechanisms to protect affordable housing today, in the future, are vital;
- Some authorities (for example in the Lake District) have experimented with the wider use of occupancy controls, placing restrictions on all new market housing. This level of intervention is likely to have wider impacts on the housing market, on house prices, and on housing supply;
- However, some authorities have taken this path, firstly because they believe that market housing should be made accessible to local people (to avoid a situation where social housing becomes the only option for local residents), and secondly because they are frustrated by their inability to influence the occupancy and use of existing homes;

- Planning is about regulating development, not intervening in private property transactions; this state of affairs means that planning has been powerless to prevent sometimes large numbers of local properties being used as second homes;
- Arguably, preventing change of use where second home concentrations are already high, would be consistent with government's desire to deliver sustainable communities;
- However, this strategy would do nothing to deal with the bigger migration pressures facing rural areas: that is retirement and commuting (see Chapter 4); it is also unlikely to bring second home demand to a halt, as many potential buyers will quickly identify the many loopholes that the system is likely to have;
- Promoting greater social balance and avoiding the scenario – of an increasingly 'exclusive' countryside – set out in the Cabinet Office's 1999 *Rural Economies* report, are obviously important objectives. However, the conclusion from this chapter is that these cannot be achieved through planning controls alone.

Indeed, this is an important principle to bear in mind: planning controls should form just one element of a wider policy approach focused on managing not only second home pressures, but the full spectrum of social and economic difficulties facing rural communities. Equally, the planning system has a *positive* role to play in assisting rural areas; it can open up land for development, promote good design that reduces the impact of new housing in more sensitive landscapes, and it can also be used to procure an additional supply of low-cost housing. Planning's role in delivering affordable homes was touched upon in Chapter 7. In this chapter, however, it was noted that some local authorities are frustrated by the pressure to provide affordable housing for local need, believing that this need should be accommodated within the existing housing stock. In short, the purchasing of existing housing for second home use necessitates the building of new low-cost homes: this creates two problems. Firstly, additional development occurs that would not be needed if it were not for second home pressures. And secondly, what might be considered 'core' village housing is taken by seasonal visitors whilst local people become concentrated in social housing. This means that affordable housing development mops up one problem (the lack of housing available to some local people) but creates others.

It is this realisation that has led some planning authorities to call for powers to regulate change of use. Work for the Countryside Agency (2002) revealed that 44 per cent of local planning authorities and 86 per cent of National Park Authorities in England wanted new powers to control the number of local properties becoming second homes (p.40). The Park Authorities, in particular, are pushing hard for stronger planning powers and want to see:

- A new national framework for the use of occupancy conditions that would allow *general* use of conditions to regulate the occupancy of new market housing; indeed, Park Authorities believe that second home and

migration pressures faced in the National Parks are so great, that they should be given special license to intervene in ways that other planning authorities cannot (p. 41);
- Immediate amendment to the Use Classes Order to regulate use change.

However, local authority planning departments were far more circumspect, arguing that:

- Planning is not the correct mechanism for addressing second home pressures and that seeking to control the use of private property would place an additional burden on already stretched planning departments;
- Second homes are a minor planning concern – relative to broader housing, economic and land pressures – and it would be more sensible to formulate a fiscal response;
- It is unclear whether decisions on second homes (for example governing use change) could be made effectively through the planning system;
- Any planning responses need clear and robust legislative backing;
- Planning has only a supporting role to play in addressing these types of housing pressure; rural communities face a broader market problem, often underpinned by weaknesses in the local economy and 'ineffective' local demand for new housing (that is local circumstances do not make it easy for some local people to compete in the housing market, irrespective of external demand pressures).

Planning has only a 'supporting role to play' in addressing rural housing pressures. This is perhaps a surprising conclusion to emerge from planning authorities. The planning system has a pivotal role to play in rural housing markets, in allocating and releasing land for development, in influencing the type of housing delivered and in ensuring good design. But these are all positive roles; the point being made by the surveyed planning authorities, was that negative restrictions on occupancy – controlling, barring, refusing and so forth – should be viewed as only a small part of what planning can do and an even smaller part of the wider policy package needed to address rural pressures. Their role is small for two reasons: firstly, second home pressures are highly localised; they are not a generic or endemic feature of rural housing markets in the UK and therefore new planning powers nationally are unwarranted. Secondly, restrictive planning powers are extremely difficult to operate and enforce; this means that if they are to be used, they should be used only where they are absolutely necessary (and authorities will have to prove very clearly why they are needed). Restrictive planning controls may find a place in a new policy framework, but the role they play will be ancillary to a broader array of positive measures.

Whatever the shortcomings of the planning mechanisms discussed in this chapter, it needs to be recognised that rural communities in many parts of the UK are becoming increasingly polarised, divided and exclusive. CABE's vision of gated communities by 2024 (Early, 2004, p.4) is a real possibility if more is not done by the current government to promote sustainable communities and reduce social exclusion. As we noted earlier in this chapter, the Labour government is keen to 'talk the talk', but little seems to be happening on the ground, particularly in rural areas. Despite second home numbers levelling off during the past decade, many parts of rural England and Wales face increasing migration pressures from retiring households, commuters and those escaping city living (see Chapter 4). How should government and local authorities respond to this challenge? It is to this issue that we turn in Chapter 9.

Note

1   It was not only in Wales that the second home issue was again being debated in 1998. The Lake District National Park Authority (LDNPA: the successor to the Lake District Special Planning Board; see above) was once more proposing local plan policies that would restrict the occupancy of new housing in Cumbria to those living or working in the county. This return to an updated version of the 'Section 52 Policy' of the late 1970s was a response to the growth in second home numbers in the Park, which had risen to 15 per cent of housing stock at this time. The Park Authority knew that it was likely to encounter the same objections that led to the deletion of the previous policy in 1984; for this reason, it was proposed that a local MP would introduce a Private Member's Bill setting our special planning powers for the Lake District that could not subsequently be reigned in the Secretary of State. It never happened, but it did demonstrate the level of concern felt in the Park with regards to the second home and affordable housing issues.

Chapter 9

A New Framework for Policy

Introduction

The objective of this penultimate chapter – the final in our three-part examination of policy options – is to present a possible policy framework for responding to second home pressures – in the context of wider economic and social concerns – in rural areas. The framework builds on the analysis undertaken in previous chapters, especially the British and mainland European case studies presented in Part 2 and the examination of past policy suggestions and restrictive planning mechanisms contained in Chapters 7 and 8 respectively. As well as providing a new framework that mixes housing policy, fiscal and planning tools, it is also our intention to compare what might be done in 2005 with a similar framework offered by Mark Shucksmith in 1983. Comparing potential responses today with suggested policies from the past allows us to consider the evolving – or static – nature of second home pressures in the UK. The new policy ideas set out in this chapter draw on work undertaken for the Countryside Agency in 2002. This study focused on England, though many of the messages emerging from the study are relevant to the wider British situation.

Twenty years ago, *Second homes: a framework for policy* appeared in the journal 'Town Planning Review' (Shucksmith, 1983, pp.174–193). The paper represented an attempt to draw together a range of ideas on how current planning and housing policy – and future policy – might respond to second home concentrations in some rural areas. As we noted in Part 1 of this book, a large number of local studies examining the effects of second homes across rural areas of Britain had been carried out in the previous decade (including those by Bielckus *et al*, 1972; de Vane, 1975; Jacobs, 1972; Pardoe, 1974; Pyne, 1973; South West Economic Planning Council, 1974; and Tuck, 1973), and each had contributed to an expanding body of evidence suggesting that second home purchasing, at the very least, deserved greater attention amongst policy makers. Shucksmith brought together many of the ideas emerging from these studies, but was careful to locate his analysis in the balance of arguments for and against second homes, contending that some:

> [...] see second homes as a flagrant inequality, as conspicuous consumption, or as a factor adversely affecting the rural economy and community; others see them as a natural and desirable form of recreation, and as stimulating the economy and vitality of rural areas (ibid. p.174).

As we have argued throughout this book, second homes continue today to evoke strong emotion and opposing views remain as polarised as ever. It is also the case that, as in 1983, there is a continued failure "[...] to view the phenomenon in a rational framework" (ibid. p.174; see also Gallent, Mace and Tewdwr-Jones, 2003a).

Work carried out for the Countryside Agency aimed to provide 'policy advice on second homes in rural areas' and hence contribute to the creation of such a rational framework. The advice eventually provided to the Agency drew partly on a survey of housing departments, planning departments and National Park Authorities in England. A total of 294 questionnaires were sent out and 119 (or 40.5 per cent) were returned. The survey focused in part on how authorities are already responding to second home pressures, whether they believe current powers should be extended, and which potential new responses they feel might be most appropriate. Questions to the authorities were framed around the most obvious options: building more affordable homes, ending Council Tax discounts, strengthening occupancy controls, introducing change of use powers, or releasing additional land for house building. Authorities were prompted to consider such options, and they were also asked for their own ideas. Using this approach, a possible framework for policy was built on a foundation of local knowledge.

Survey Responses

Just 11 per cent of planning departments surveyed had *already* developed a specific policy or approach towards second homes in their local area, and almost 30 per cent of housing departments claimed to have done so. A third of all National Park Authorities had developed specific approaches, probably because of the relatively greater importance of second home demand in these areas of potentially higher landscape quality. The main approaches noted by the surveyed authorities and departments are listed below:

Housing Departments

- A small number of housing departments (8) had undertaken independent consultations on council tax derived from second homes, assessing the 'loss' of revenue from second homes due to the (pre 2004) fifty per cent discount. Many housing departments saw reducing the discount as a key mechanism for affecting second home demand, or at least ending the inequity that discounts were seen to represent (see Table 9.1);
- A single housing department had drawn up proposals – in partnership with a local National Park Authority – to use planning powers to control the use of properties as second homes, though it was recognised that such an approach would require backing from government;
- Another department had undertaken a local consultation on the range of financial disincentives that might be applied to second homes. The respondent touted the idea of an 'impact levy' that could be used to cost

Table 9.1 The Desired Nature of New Powers

	Housing Departments N = 45	Planning Departments N = 53	National Park Authorities N = 8	Joint Housing/ Planning Departments N = 13
New ways for increasing developers' contributions	57.5	37.2	0.0	46.2
Type specific housing land designations	42.5	60.5	71.4	38.5
Stronger powers over occupancy	45.0	55.8	57.1	30.8
Differentiate second from first homes	32.5	44.2	85.7	30.8
Local discretion over council tax discounts	92.5	74.4	57.1	84.6
National fiscal measures	52.5	51.2	28.6	38.5

Source: Gallent *et al*, 2002, p. 40.

    the social and economic 'problems' that second homes introduced to the local area; however, the respondent did not specify the form that such a levy might take;

- A small number of housing departments recognised that second homes are an important part of the local economy and have positive benefits that need to be maximised; any framework needs to acknowledge that second home demand in an area is not inherently bad;

- Finally, one further department listed the 'use of occupancy conditions designed specifically to limit use of properties as second homes' as a mechanism that could be used, but did not indicate whether this had actually been done. It is probably unlikely that such an approach had been implemented; occupancy controls can be used to prioritise particular needs, but cannot be used negatively to bar specific types of purchasing.

Although nearly a third of housing departments claimed to have developed a particular approach towards second homes; the majority had merely drawn up proposals or consulted on possible future action. However, many ideas were put forward, and all were useful in formulating the new framework for policy.

Planning Departments

Planning department respondents had far fewer ideas than their housing colleagues; however, most recognised that planning controls were often seen as the most logical response to second home pressures; this was a view strongly rejected by many local planning officers (see Chapter 8). Planners tended to argue that housing policy and tax mechanisms were the best means of influencing the level of second home purchasing; certainly, there was far less support for change of use controls than within National Park Authorities (Table 9.1). However, planning departments noted that the following approaches were already being implemented:

- Three planning authorities claimed that permission was only being granted for affordable housing in the local area; this approach meant that no new homes could be purchased by second home buyers;
- Planning authorities also tended to support the idea of scrapping the Council Tax discount on second homes, and a number claimed to be actively lobbying government on this issue;
- But authorities also saw second home development as positive; some claimed to be encouraging 'holiday home' development and conversion as part of a broader farm diversification strategy.

National Park Authorities

The views of National Park Authorities contrasted starkly with those of local authority planning departments. The Park Authorities exhibited:

- Strong support for control of second homes through occupancy conditions applied to new housing and to barn conversions;
- Many also highlighted their desire to see second home use brought under planning control through amendment to the use classes order.

The survey confirmed that direct approaches for dealing with second homes are scarce at the present time, largely because it remains difficult to isolate such properties from the general market and broader housing pressures. Apart from supporting government moves to raise council tax on second homes, authorities have mainly been confined to the use of occupancy conditions in an attempt to ensure that at least some new homes cannot be used as seasonal residences. More radical steps might require primary legislation and of the few authorities commenting on the success of strategies to 'manage' second home pressures, most reported that existing powers are limited to dealing with housing issues in broad terms and do not specifically address second home pressures. As an aside, it can be noted that approaches and views towards second homes need not be negative. They may be seen as a positive contributor to the local economy, and in the case of one authority, the conversion of farm buildings for holiday letting was actively encouraged as part of a wider drive to farm diversification.

The responses above appear to confirm that housing departments, local planning authorities and Park Authorities feel that a wider range of powers should be available for addressing second home concerns; indeed, 87 per cent of all respondents wanted additional powers, none indicated that additional powers were not needed and the remainder had no view on this issue (Gallent *et al*, 2002, p. 39). There was a broad consensus that local authorities should have discretion over council tax rates at the local level. Housing departments were keen to see developer's contributions (planning gain) increased in order to deliver additional affordable housing: planners, however, were more reticent on this issue, perhaps believing that there was no additional capacity for local development to carry additional gain. The National Parks came out strongly in favour of new planning mechanisms: specifically differentiating between housing types in land designations (that is allocating land only for low-cost housing) and differentiating first from second homes. A statistical summary of the responses is set out in Table 9.1.

These results were borne in mind when formulating the new framework for policy. In the next part of this chapter, we re-examine some of the past policy options introduced in Chapter 7. This is followed by the new framework for policy, extending the powers and options currently available to housing departments, planning and Park authorities.

Past Policy Options

Shucksmith's framework for policy (1983) brought together a range of current and future policy options: the current options related to the provision of additional local needs housing, an expansion of council building, a greater use of housing associations in rural areas, 'North Wiltshire' schemes involving the management and sub-letting of private homes by local authorities, and raising local incomes over the long term. The future options were concerned with tighter regulatory controls, differential rates and additional central investment in housing. Each of these can be revisited in the light of more recent experience and particular observations drawn from the Countryside Agency work:

Local Needs

As in 1983, it remains possible for local authorities to allow new house building only when it is justified by local needs. Perhaps the most famous example of such a policy was contained in the Cumbria Structure Plan in the early 1980s (Shucksmith, 1990), but was deleted in a direct move by the Secretary of State, Peter Jenkin, in 1984 (a more detailed account of this policy was provided in the previous chapter). Shucksmith argues in his 1983 paper and again in a more comprehensive account of the policy published in 1990, that the general application of a local needs policy to new house building resulted in a rapid decline in residential permissions and completions and in a deflection of demand to existing housing. This had the effect of reducing the supply of new homes and pushing up the price of existing property. He concluded therefore that such policies are counter-productive and work contrary to local interests (see Chapter 8, this volume).

A policy similar to that contained in the Cumbria Structure Plan has more recently been written into the Pembrokeshire Joint Unitary Development Plan (2002). An examination of the policy undertaken on behalf of the Pembrokeshire Coast National Park Authority reached similar conclusions to those reached by Shucksmith in 1990. In general, it was felt '[...] unlikely that local people (or rather those in greatest need) will secure any competitive advantage in the market for new housing; they may, however, find it harder to buy existing property. Over the long term, this may well lead to a gradual displacement of local people away from [some of the most attractive] communities' (Tewdwr-Jones and Gallent, 2003).

Council Building

The level of disinvestment in public housing and the extent of Right to Buy sales in more attractive rural areas could only have been guessed at in 1983. Today, the experience of the last twenty years has underlined successive governments' lack of confidence in local authorities' role in directly providing and managing new rented housing. The Housing Act 1988 extended the private sale of council housing by introducing a framework for large scale transfers of stock and since the Housing White Paper of the previous year, governments have remained firmly committed to housing association provision funded by a mix of private borrowing, direct subsidy and planning gain. More than 100,000 council homes have been sold in rural areas of England since 1980. Concerns over council housing and the 'Right to Buy' are examined further below.

Housing Associations

In 1983, Shucksmith was able to argue that housing associations represented a 'third arm' in the housing market during the 1970s (p.185) though their influence was less pronounced in the countryside than in urban areas, largely because the Housing Corporation's 'first priority' was to assist inner urban areas. Already by 1983, there were major concerns over the level of public financial support for associations and it was suggested that future private funding initiatives (overseen by the National Federation of Housing Associations – now the National Housing Federation) would be essential if associations were to have a serious impact on housing needs. This was despite the introduction of a relatively generous system of grant funding introduced in the Housing Act 1974. In 1988, this system was replaced by a deficit funding system that reduced the overall public funding element and increased the need to borrow at commercial rates. Since 1988, Housing Association Grant – now Social Housing Grant – has been reduced year-on-year with associations having to borrow increasingly large amounts of money from the banks or, where possible, to bridge shortfalls through planning gain. A major hindrance to housing association activity in second home areas has been spiralling land values which have made it increasingly costly to develop new units (where associations are obliged to compete in an open land market) and therefore reduced the affordability of association homes. One critical problem has been that grant rates (calculated against Total Cost Indicators [TCIs] or the predicted cost of developing a site) do not take sufficient account of local land price variations. This issue is also revisited in our revised framework.

Community Self Build

In 1983, Shucksmith raised the possibility of increasing the modest contribution that self-build makes to rural housing supply. However, the problems associated with raising finance and of individuals being able to commit sufficient time to such projects, led him to dismiss the wider potential of such initiatives. In 2002, follow-up interviews with planning and housing officers revealed continued support for self build initiatives within rural authorities, with some planning authorities arguing that exceptional planning permissions – on land not allocated for housing in local plans – should be granted to those pursuing the self build option. Today, flat-packed solutions offer the possibility of households entering into self-build with less of a financial commitment: a lower skill base is also required and negative attitudes to self build may well have altered with the recent proliferation of DIY and home-improvement programmes on prime-time television. However, some authorities remain concerned over the quality of new housing emerging from such initiatives and argue that a move to self build of the flat-packed type raises the spectre of low housing quality and illegal development of the type more common in southern Europe (Padovani and Vettoretto, 2003, p.103) For that reason, some authorities favoured an alternative approach: the assisted conversion of barns and other redundant agricultural buildings into live/work units, drawing inspiration perhaps from the recent wave of such development in towns and cities. A more comprehensive review of the self build option was provided in Chapter 7.

Management Schemes

Like local authority new build, management schemes of the type considered by Shucksmith have been overtaken by more recent legislative events. In 1974 North Wiltshire District Council pioneered an initiative which brought some private lettings under council management. Owners (and potential landlords), concerned about the security of tenure provisions of the Rent Acts, were reticent about letting their property because of the potential difficulty of recovering vacant possession. The Council's approach was to sub-let on behalf of the owner and hence avoid the provisions of Section 5 of the Rent Act 1968. Put simply, this allowed owners to regain vacant possession of their property with relatively short notice, increasing their willingness to rent out homes to local people.

In order to stimulate the private rental market, government introduced assured short-hold tenancies in 1989. This allowed landlords to let properties for shorter periods and guaranteed vacant possession: hence the impediment to private renting noted by Shucksmith no longer exists. Since 1983, Housing Associations have also experimented with ways of bringing vacant and low quality private properties back into use: the HAMA (Housing Associations as Management Agents) initiative was one such initiative (Balchin, 1995, p.118). The scheme involved owners signing properties over to Housing Associations for a specified period: the association would renovate the property and rent the property to a tenant using its own rent structure: the owner received part of the income plus a returned renovated property at the end of the contract period. However, such schemes tend to work well where rental demand is high but not sufficiently high to encourage owners to undertake their own renovation work. In attractive second home areas, private dwellings are far more likely to be let to holiday makers for short periods: only properties in nearby towns may be appropriate for such management schemes and ensuring that these are available to local people will do little to address need in the surrounding villages and hamlets. Again, see Chapter 7 for a more detailed review of this option.

Local Incomes

As far as options 'currently available' in 1983 were concerned, Shucksmith concluded that '[...] the raising of rural incomes to a level comparable with those in urban areas remains a desirable long-term objective, not only because of its appeal as a solution to the problems arising from second home pressures but as an end in itself: in the short term it offers little help' (p.188). The situation today remains unchanged. By raising local incomes, local demand would become more 'effective' in the market and there would be greater chance of local people being able to compete for housing and, as prices adjusted to local incomes, fewer outside buyers would be attracted by the lure of cheap property. But incomes will only rise if considerably more employment opportunities are attracted to or generated within rural areas. Since 1983, total income from farming has fallen to its lowest level for quarter of a century; jobs in forestry have dropped by 25 per cent since the mid-1980s; there has been little change in the seasonal and casual nature of rural employment; access to jobs remains difficult; and, quite ironically, the only factor driving up average incomes in many rural areas is the proliferation of lifestyle and retirement migrants (Countryside Agency, 2003). The rural economy today is as fragile as it was twenty years ago: the only aspect of the economy that has grown is the uncertainty surrounding its future. Farming's continued crisis (evidenced recently by the Foot and Mouth epidemic), the potential curtailment of some blood sports, and most significantly, EU expansion eastward (from May 2004) and a re-levelling of farm subsidy all suggest that incomes are unlikely to rise without a major restructuring of the rural economy.

Three further measures were discussed by Shucksmith as means of curtailing second home demand and increasing the breadth of housing opportunities for local households: these were regulatory controls aimed at preventing changes of use from permanent to secondary dwellings, the levying of differential rates (now Council Tax) on second homes and greater investment in housing programmes and initiatives. All of these measures form part of our new policy framework and are discussed below. On the whole, Shucksmith's original framework mixes attempts to directly influence the second home market and indirect moves to increase the supply of affordable homes: that is, to provide non-market alternatives for those groups affected by external housing pressures.

A New Framework for Policy

Our own policy framework for addressing second homes and broader housing pressures in the countryside has a similar mix of direct and indirect measures. This similarity is indicative of the almost static nature of the second home issue over the last two decades; outside housing demand within many rural communities continues to be driven by the imbalance between urban and rural incomes, by the prestige attached to a home in the country, and by the scarcity value that planning confers on rural housing. The wider context is also largely unchanged; rural economies endure the same structural weaknesses; the planning system adheres to an almost identical raft of guidelines and objectives; and there continues to be little appetite amongst politicians – or society at large – for banning second homes or seriously infringing on private property rights (despite a 'softening' and 'socialising' of planning's rational in the last 20 years: see Chapter 8). There is also a continued recognition that second homes – and retirement – are merely symptomatic of broader social and economic trends, marked for centuries by an exchange of people and wealth between town and country.

In this context, the policy framework set out below represents a consideration of how:

- the planning system might be used to make this exchange less painful for certain rural areas, and promote balanced communities above social exclusivity in large parts of the countryside; and
- how monetary and taxation policy might contribute to meeting the same aim by decreasing the attraction of second home ownership and also by releasing additional funds to assist in the provision of more affordable homes in rapidly gentrifying parts of the British countryside.

The framework does not represent an assault on second homes, or even an acceptance that second homes are *inherently* harmful to rural communities. Within the framework, they are viewed as part of a gentrifying process that needs to be checked through socially progressive policy tools.

Second Homes and Planning

In the light of the discussion provided above – and in the preceding chapters of this book – our suggested planning framework comprises the following components, each aimed at addressing the second home impacts noted earlier:

- Greater consistency in the use of Occupancy Conditions;
- More housing sites earmarked for affordable housing in local plans;
- Greater consistency in the reviewing of old planning permissions (the regulations affecting review, and the duration of permission and consent, are clarified in the Planning and Compulsory Purchase Bill, Part 4, Section 46, before Parliament at the time of writing);

- Pooling of planning gain, and its use in communities affected by second homes;
- Trialing of experimental options, including a separate use class for second homes.

Occupancy Conditions

Some survey respondents suggested that planning departments and officers sometimes lack the confidence to apply occupancy conditions to new housing, fearing that it will meet with legal challenge and may not stand up to Human Rights legislation. Given recent legislative changes with, for example, regards to Human Rights, it appears that there is a need for government to review its advice to local authorities on the use of occupancy conditions attached to new housing built in the countryside. Under certain circumstances – perhaps where the supply of new homes is limited and demand is strong – the use of conditions might be viewed as a norm rather than an extreme measure. However, conditions should continue to focus on local connection and/or employment (that is the characteristics of those able to occupy a dwelling) and therefore adopt a positive approach to occupancy. Conditions that make reference to occupants who might not live in an area permanently and who should be barred from buying property (that is negative conditions) may be viewed as punitive and subject to challenge. The tone of conditions must of course reflect the need to support and assist both communities and those moving within the job market; they should also draw on good quality housing need assessments, with the use of conditions subsequently viewed as an integral part of an authority's housing strategy. This will require housing and planning departments to co-ordinate their policies and share information on local needs. Nationally, government might review advice on conditions when revising Circulars 6/98 and 1/97; locally, it would be useful for planning authorities to draft specimen conditions based on good legal advice.

Affordable Housing Sites in Local Plans

The rural exceptions initiative – which allows planning authorities to permit affordable housing developments on land not allocated for housing in local plans (see Chapter 7) – does not provide sufficient certainty either in terms of the number of affordable homes delivered or the acceptance that land can only be used for affordable housing (see Gallent and Bell, 2000). Landowners often cling onto sites and will not sell at reduced cost to RSLs, largely because they believe that housing pressures mean that sites will eventually be allocated for market housing. This *hope value* remains a key obstacle to the bringing forward of exception sites, but might be eased if such land could be allocated for *social housing only* within development plans. More generally, government's recent consultation paper on the future of Planning Obligations (DTLR, 2001c) suggested that a move to structured development tariffs would lead to instances where affordable housing is not provided as an on-site gain contribution but rather, tariff money would be used to build affordable housing on earmarked sites elsewhere; despite a rejection of this proposal in the subsequent Planning and Compulsory Purchase Bill (2003), a growing number of authorities are allowing developers to provide payments, specifically for housing, in lieu of on-site contributions. It is also now likely that a 'twin track' approach – on site negotiations or fixed development tariffs – will be introduced. In large towns and cities, this may result in the building of fairly sizeable affordable housing estates, and may go against government's desire to see mixed tenure communities. But in rural areas where such affordable housing sites may be smaller (similar in size to existing exception schemes), they may more easily blend into existing communities and contribute to tenure mixing. Therefore, planning authorities may wish to designate small affordable housing sites (where payments in lieu or tariffs will be directed) within their new Local Development Frameworks (the successors to development plans). The Countryside Agency has already forwarded the idea of Sites for Social Diversity (SSD), identified in Development Frameworks, where existing planning mechanisms or Housing Corporation funding should be targeted and used for the provision of additional affordable housing. There is a strong case for identifying affordable housing sites within local plans, not least in order to match development with need and ensure that affordable housing is targeted where market pressures are most acute. The current exceptions approach delivers fewer than 900 units in rural England each year (Crook *et al*, 2002), largely because it is uncertain and relies on difficult negotiations with landowners. Greater certainty and clarity could be achieved by any of the moves noted above. The current programme of planning reform – which will culminate in a new Planning and Compulsory Purchase Act being ratified by Parliament by 2005 – emphasises the need to generate greater certainty through the planning system: the allocation of sites for affordable housing would contribute to meeting this aim.

Reviewing of Old Planning Permissions

A serious concern amongst many authorities is that a great many existing (unused) planning permissions are out of step with both current socio-economic conditions and with present policy objectives. Greater gains are often required in the form of affordable housing than might have been the case when the permission was originally granted. There is a need for authorities, therefore, to more *actively review* and refuse permissions on renewal to take account of changes in legislation. Government's commitment to providing affordable housing through planning has been stepped up in recent years (see Chapter 8), but some planning permissions in rural areas may be fairly old. This adds to the importance of carefully reviewing permissions to ensure they serve (where applicable) wider social objectives. It is important that data on changing conditions (for example housing needs) is close to hand so those seeking renewal can be informed clearly and quickly of the cost of developing a site.

Pooling and Targeting Planning Gains

A strategy for pooling and targeting planning gains could be especially useful in rural areas, particularly if it were allied with the earmarking of affordable housing sites or the creation of Sites for Social Diversity (see above). The existing planning system based on the negotiation of gains from development is able to generate affordable housing (on sites over the threshold size stipulated in Circular 6/98), but often such housing ends up in larger towns where development opportunities concentrate. There is a clear argument for re-directing at least a portion of these gains to smaller communities, perhaps where housing access is being adversely affected by market distortions (including second home pressures). Presently this could be achieved by requesting payments in lieu of on-site contributions, thus giving RSLs additional funds to purchase small development sites in villages. However, a critical issue is land availability. If no sites are available for development away from bigger towns then the strategy of pooling and targeting funds derived from development will fail. This means that success is dependent on the planning system allocating land for affordable housing in smaller villages and not being constrained by 'urban' strategies such as the sequential release of brownfield sites in larger towns as a priority. There is of course a danger that payments in lieu generated from rural sites and valuable bespoke developments could be directed to urban areas, where needs are seen to be greater and more concentrated. It is essential therefore that clear assessments of housing needs within rural areas are available before such a strategy were implemented.

Trialing of Experimental Options

It was noted in earlier chapters that much attention has focused in recent years – and in the more distant past (see Gallent and Tewdwr-Jones, 2001) on the way the planning system could limit second home ownership, possibly by differentiating between second and first homes. Generally, planners and policy makers are wary of such a move, believing it to be unwarranted and/or inoperable. However, in some areas where there is a demonstrable concentration of second homes (for example in Exmoor National Park), there is often greater support for a more radical approach. Such was the case in some of the case studies explored during this research, where it was believed that neither greater tax burdens nor the provision of additional affordable housing would address the social and economic difficulties created by second homes. Although the general view emerging from the research is that radical or punitive approaches may be unwarranted (see also discussion presented in Chapter 8), and that effective use of existing planning tools (to control occupancy or deliver affordable housing) is the best way of managing second home and general migration pressure, there may be a case for exploring other options in specific localities. Case study work in the Scilly Isles suggested that this is one location that may provide a useful test-bed for more radical approaches as the Isles are exempt from standard legislative instruments (primary legislation must refer separately to the Isles of Scilly) and any experiments in the islands would not set a precedent for the rest of Britain.

Second Homes, Taxation and Spending Tools

Planning is only one policy area that could be used to influence the market for second homes, or ensure that communities do not become the sole preserve of seasonal residents. Taxation and Spending Tools might also be brought to bear on this issue. In this respect, our framework would comprise the following components:

- Adjustment to Council Tax rates and discounts;
- Additional tax levies;
- Capital Gains Tax relief on land sold for affordable housing;
- Extension of Rural Housing Enabler funding;
- Re-weighting of TCI rates to reflect higher land costs in areas affected by second homes.

Council Tax

Authorities accept that an equalization of Council Tax (CT) on principal and secondary residences will not dampen demand for second homes. The rationale of increasing CT on second homes is therefore not grounded in a belief that a higher tax rate will mean fewer second homes, but in a view that the social and environmental impacts of second homes – where proven – should be fairly costed. Additional revenue raised might be used to promote an empty homes strategy, employ an enabling officer (to lead on exception schemes or other housing-planning initiatives), invest in staff training or in the direct funding of new affordable homes. In our research, many planning and housing officers felt that revenue raised above the 50 per cent rate (current at the time of the field work, though this has now risen to 90 per cent) should be ring-fenced specifically for this purpose, though there is of course an inevitable risk that monies could be moved around for other purposes depending on a local authority's spending priorities at any given time. This means changes to current Council Tax rates must be accompanied either with a legal requirement to use additional funds for specified purposes or with government advice on the most appropriate use of these funds (in relation to the 2004 changes, extra revenue will not be ring-fenced for housing, though authorities are being called upon to focus on 'rural issues'). It is likely that housing and planning departments would have to compete for additional funds with other departments. However, if they have undertaken a joint housing need assessment demonstrating the local housing pressures generated by second homes, they are likely to find themselves in a strong position when bidding for the extra cash. Another issue in relation to Council Tax is that owners of second homes need some incentive to register their properties as second homes with the local authority: otherwise the number of such properties in the local area will quickly become hidden and authorities will be unable to monitor changes in the size of the market. Critically, they will not know how much extra revenue is being derived from second homes or the degree of housing pressure that can be attributed to such properties. This would weaken their position if they need to bid for extra cash for new housing projects. Maintaining a discount of 10 per cent below full rate may encourage owners to register their second homes. It appears that government concurs with this view: the future rate for second homes will be set at up to 90 per cent of full Council Tax in England.

Additional Tax Levies

If authorities were able to demonstrate that second home concentrations bring demonstrable harm to rural communities by reducing the viability of services or accentuating social exclusion (issues returned to below), then this may provide the necessary justification for a range of remedial policies. Assessments might, for example, be used to support new discretionary fiscal powers. Beyond increasing the current (pre-2004) rate of council tax on second homes, evidence of an adverse impact on local communities might provide a basis for:

- *Lowering the threshold for the higher rate of Stamp Duty on second homes* (thereby increasing Stamp Duty on this type of purchase) in particular local authority areas. Government has already demonstrated its willingness to alter Stamp Duty in urban areas (Gordon Brown announced in his Autumn statement of 2001 that Stamp Duty in 2,000 wards would be abolished on property sales of up to £150,000) where it believes that the tax is having an adverse impact on property investment and regeneration efforts. At the moment the higher rate (2.5 per cent of value) applies to properties purchased for more than £250,000. In some rural areas, a standard 2.5 per cent (higher) rate on all second homes would raise the cost of initial purchase (from £1000 to £2,500 on a property bought for £100,000). This might act as some disincentive to purchase a second home, though some owners would inevitably find ways around such rules (for example registering properties as first homes for their children in order to avoid the higher tax rate). Another problem is that the tax goes straight to the Treasury so unlike CT could not be used to offset the 'costs' of second homes locally. A more radical option might be to create a much higher 'punitive' rate (of say, 30 per cent), but this could then have a major impact on the property market even if a portion of buyers found loopholes in the system.
- *Maintaining Revenue Support Grant.* Changes to Stamp Duty would inevitably be viewed as negative and punitive, and as potentially harmful to the property market. But a change in the rate of CT (see earlier discussion) would probably court general support. However, there is a hidden danger from such a move. If CT revenue increased in a local area, government could argue that Revenue Support Grant should be lowered in the light of additional revenue being generated from second homes. Such a move should be resisted. The local impact studies are vital in this

context, demonstrating clearly that extra revenue (current RSG rate plus additional tax from second homes) is essential for dealing with the problems (housing affordability and service viability) caused by second homes. These should be used to argue for the maintenance of RSG rates even in the light of more CT revenue being generated – and possibly ring-fenced – to pay for additional or support existing services including the provision of affordable housing.

Capital Gains Tax Relief on Land Sold for Affordable Housing

Granting relief on capital gains tax on land sold solely for affordable housing could reduce the 'hope' value attached to potential exceptions sites, encouraging owners of such sites to sell to RSLs. It could also form part of a wider assault on the problems of providing genuinely affordable housing in the countryside. The hope value attached to exceptions sites is just one problem. With regards to planning and affordable housing more generally, there are gaping inconsistencies in the way affordable housing is delivered on market sites, with some dwellings simply being transferred to RSLs 'at cost' and on other occasions, developers being allowed to provide smaller homes in schemes of larger dwellings in order to meet an 'affordability requirement' (Whitehead, 2002). Fewer than 2,000 affordable homes are being provided through planning in rural England each year. There is a pressing need to increase this figure and as part of a general strategy, scrapping Capital Gains Tax on all land sold for affordable housing would prove useful as long as a system could be closed from potential abuses. For example, some developers might argue that building market homes on such sites would generate a subsidy for the affordable units. But permitting such practice might allow developers to vary the balance in favour of market units if they were not obliged to disclose the development costs or the cost of the option negotiated with a developer (developers could argue that cross subsidy from market housing was the only way to make the site viable). Such possible abuses may reduce the appeal of such a strategy. However, the need to find new ways to fund affordable housing is clear. Research from Cambridge University (ODPM, 2002) argues that there should be:

- A range of tax incentives for organizations involved in the construction of affordable housing;
- Increased revenue for schemes such as the Starter Home Initiative;
- Tax relief for employers that agree to set up savings schemes for first-time buyers;
- Policies aimed at making it more tax efficient for employers playing a direct role in assisting their workers (in accessing housing);
- A reduction in the VAT paid by Registered Social Landlords renovating affordable housing.

Government's response to these ideas has already been positive, with the ODPM committing to look seriously at the options during negotiations with the Treasury. A reduction in VAT on land sold for affordable housing may have seemed like a radical option in the past – open to possible abuse – but with an estimated 3.5 million extra households forming in England by 2016, requiring 4.5 million new homes of which a third will have to be affordable (Barlow *et al*, 2002. pp. 31–33), government seems more prepared now to entertain such options.

Retention of Rural Housing Enabler Funding

Rural housing enablers[1] – who provide an interface been local authorities, RSLs and landowners – are viewed as critical to the delivery of affordable housing. Currently, 50 per cent cost funding is available for enablers for a period of three years; after this period, funding is reduced making it difficult to sustain an effective enabling role. The high up-take on exceptions schemes in rural England relative to other parts of Great Britain has been attributed to the existence of Rural Enablers. Many local authorities believe that this approach deserves continued and increased support. As government looks for new ways to fund and support social housing, it is likely that it will look favourably on an extension of funding for Rural Enablers; the Countryside Agency takes the view that the 50 per cent level of funding to enablers should continue for a period of at least five years (the current maximum is three years). Carmona *et al* (2001, p. 38) emphasise the importance of having someone champion affordable housing schemes, leading different partners through the complex-ities of both the development and planning processes.

Re-weighting of TCI Rates (in Areas of Strong Housing Demand)

Many RSLs find it almost impossible to develop genuinely affordable housing in some rural areas: and often where there are high concentrations of second homes or retired households. There is a strong case for reviewing the Total Cost Indicators (TCIs) used to calculate the grant-eligible elements of development costs on new housing schemes in some parts of rural England. This might be based on local evidence of the impacts of concentrations of second homes on both land and property prices. In the light of such evidence, it might be considered appropriate to press the Housing Corporation for a 'second home' (or more general 'pressured market') multiplier to be used in combination with existing multipliers. This would allow RSLs to bid for additional capital funding to offset the impact of higher land values on their capacity to develop affordable housing schemes. We are not alone in suggesting a revision of TCIs: Bevan *et al* (2001) have argued that '[. . .] for a number of RSLs, the central issue in the provision of affordable social housing [is] the lack of geographical sensitivity in the grant system and in the Total Cost Indicators to provide affordable housing in areas of unmet demand' (p.52).

Supplementary Measures

In order to provide a comprehensive approach to the difficulties faced by some rural communities which, because of the fragility of the local economy, may be more sensitised to second home and retirement pressures, there is likely to be a need to take additional steps to alleviate current pressures. An obvious move would be to protect the remaining stock of council homes. Recent policy debate has focused on a possible suspension of the RTB in some (urban) areas.[2] In rural England, Hetherington (2000) has suggested that most of the attractive council housing, which was not protected from the RTB under earlier restrictions (for example Section 19 of the 1980 Act), has already been sold. In areas attractive to affluent migrants, second home purchasers and retiring households, in seems unlikely ·that the remaining stock of council housing will be significant, though some authorities in the 2002 study reported that some high demand areas have retained useful pockets of council housing. Therefore, where there are strong demand pressures and remaining council homes, there may be an argument for suspending the RTB.

Another step that could be taken (but will suffer the same problem of potentially limited impact) would be to tighten restrictions on the forward sale of former council properties. There may be some tenants who for whatever reason have not yet exercised their RTB, even in the areas of strong demand noted above. Under Section 157 of the Housing Act 1985 authorities can attach a local connection covenant affecting the forward sale of council properties. However, such covenants can only presently be applied on a county-wide basis, and under this arrangement, former council properties (that are sold on) are still achieving prices that might be judged unaffordable in the immediate area. To remedy this situation it might be helpful if local authorities were able set more locally defined covenants (with the possibility to then cascade out to adjoining parishes and then the district and county, where no buyer is found). This should have the effect of further limiting the market for – and so the potential value of – ex-council properties. Such a move might discourage property investment companies – of the type currently operating in London – from extending their activities into rural districts, especially as profits in such areas are more likely to be derived from forward sale as opposed to a lucrative rental market. But broadly speaking, both of these measures (suspension and restriction on forward sale) are likely to bring limited rewards in the majority of high demand areas. Most properties will already have been sold and covenants on re-sale cannot be set retrospectively. It is also the case that imposing such restrictions on remaining council tenants might appear grossly unfair, given the number of households who have already been granted and who have exercised their Right to Buy over the last two decades. Nevertheless, an awareness of the problems caused by RTB should inform future policy, with greater restriction placed on the Right to Acquire in rural England: any further social housing built in the countryside must be retained for local use in perpetuity.

Conclusion: A Better Understanding of Second Home Impacts

Shucksmith's analysis of second home impacts (summarised at the beginning of this chapter) revealed that much of what is commonly understood about second homes is little more than educated guess-work. Their impact on housing access and affordability is difficult to discern mainly because they represent only one component of housing pressure: hence, it may be impossible to state with any confidence that second homes, rather than retirement or commuting, are pushing up house prices. Their impact on local services is equally unclear: the viability of local shops may be threatened by the e-shopping initiates of high street chains, and not by the particular shopping habits of weekend visitors. Indeed, it was suggested by some local authorities that anecdote points to greater use of small shops by weekenders, and a growing tendency amongst local people to travel greater distances to supermarkets. The cause-effect relationships are highly complex and the task facing local authorities is to secure *reasonable* rather than *irrefutable* evidence of the repercussions of second homes.

The starting point needs to be the more effective collection of data at the local level; not only on second homes but on all forms of housing demand. Any analysis of currently available information soon reveals that there are various problems with existing data sources. The Census tends to under-enumerate second homes, with some dwellings that may be second (or holiday) homes listed as simply being empty (see Chapter 1). Census figures also become dated very quickly: the only real advantage of the Census is that it reveals the local geography of second home ownership down to the enumeration district level. The Survey of English Housing – discussed in Chapter 1 – provides useful information on the reasons why people own second homes but has limited use in local monitoring as it only provides a general picture of ownership, disaggregated to the regional level. Council Tax returns offer the most promising method of monitoring numbers and therefore (by using these data in local impact studies) understanding how concentrations of such properties may affect housing affordability and local services. Homeowners can apply for discounts against Council Tax for a variety of reasons, and the new 10 per cent maximum discount on second homes (in England) should make it easier for local authorities to keep track of second home numbers (than it is in Wales where the discount has been entirely scrapped), and to link concentrations to the types of social and economic costs discussed earlier.

But how exactly these costs are measured remains a key question: monetary compensation for affected communities, the pooling of payments in lieu or perhaps even more radical policies will all have to be justified by a *reasonable* demonstration of second home impacts. Any local analysis will need to avoid the assumed linkages of the past: it would be easy for authorities to seek simple cause-consequence relationships, arguing that inadequate access to housing could be linked to the presence of second homes. But as has been emphasised throughout this book, second homes are rarely the sole pressure facing communities:

- Second homes often concentrate in areas of general migration and retirement: how is it possible to isolate the impacts of second homes (on housing affordability) from that of general migration or retirement?
- To what extent can second homes be blamed for housing affordability issues in an area which is failing economically, marked perhaps by a recent closure of major employers or a fall off in agricultural activity?
- How can the impact of second homes on local shops be separated from the effects of 'e-shopping' or the trend towards wider use of super-markets? In some instances, second home owners may be the only users of some local shops and services; it would certainly be necessary to undertake 'control group' analyses in areas where there were no second homes and then compare these to areas with different mixes of external housing pressure;
- How can the inflationary pressure said to be generated by second homes be separated from the effects of housing scarcity created by planning constraint? (for example the impact of a sequential approach to land allocations that favours urban sites).

The likely conclusion from such an analysis is that second homes add to the broader social and economic pressures that many rural communities endure. Where these general pressures are greatest, communities become sensitised to any small additional change in the housing market. Second homes, however small in number, may be seen as the proverbial straw and as the sharp end of a more complex problem. In light of such a conclusion, it might be deemed *reasonable* to take at least some of the steps suggested in this chapter, thereby alleviating some of the problems faced in more pressured rural areas.

Notes

1   Enablers are individuals who work part-time, and are independent of local authorities. Their role is to facilitate the provision of affordable housing: see Joseph Rowntree Foundation, 1995.
2   The ODPM has become concerned with 'abuses' of the current system (especially in London) and with the barriers to regeneration that are created when government funds (for example channeled through SRB) have to be used to buy out leaseholders before local councils and other agencies can embark on wholesale estate renewal. In London, property investment companies have been offering sitting tenants cash sums to buy out their tenancies. Once in control of the tenancy, flats are let out for many times the local authority rent. In areas due for regeneration, renewal schemes have hit the problem of having to buy out leaseholders of former council flats. Because of the current housing boom, even flats on some of the least attractive estates can be worth in excess of £150,000 if they are close enough to the City. The current suspension debate is focused primarily on London, but any steps taken in the capital could be extended to other areas. In London, there seems to be a clear case for taking action.

Chapter 10

Conclusions

Introduction

The new framework for policy proposed in the last chapter should not be viewed as an assault on second homes, but a strategy for addressing the lack of housing opportunities that some people face in the countryside. Over the long term, Shucksmith's (1983) assertion that economic vitality and higher incomes are central to reducing housing stress retains currency; but in the meantime, there is a continued need to stabilise communities by combating the processes of social exclusion.

However, although second homes are at least part of the 'problem', there are a multitude of additional factors resulting in social exclusion in the country-side. On the demand side, purchasing by retiring households, commuter pressures, housing being bought by urban 'down shifters' looking for the slower pace of country life, general migration flows, and ineffective local demand caused by low wage economies in many rural areas are all important. On the supply side, general planning constraints on land release, middle class resistance to new housing development in the countryside, inefficiencies in the planning process, the low quality of some rural housing stock, and a prioritisation of environment goals over social concerns – especially in 'important' landscapes – all have a part to play in driving social exclusion.

Within this context, it is vitally important to 'position' the second home issue and, if necessary, design solutions that address particular second homes concerns as part of a broader response to the full body of housing demand and supply pressures. In this conclusion, we focus on:

- Positioning second homes in the wider spectrum of pressures currently facing rural areas: knowing how second homes fit in the wider picture is a prerequisite for formulating any operable response;
- The key messages emerging from the previous chapters, including what can be 'learnt' from different national situations, and the main elements of any future policy framework in the UK;
- The myths and misconceptions that surround the issue of second home purchasing – especially in the UK – and why such myths are regularly propagated by some local authorities; and finally
- What the future might hold for second homes and second home purchasing in Europe; what is likely to happen to the second home market in the years ahead and what role is property investment likely to have if social welfare regimes sink further into financial deficit?

Positioning Second Homes

Being able to 'position' second homes demands that we understand exactly what purchasers are looking for from their new property and from the area where they wish to buy a second home. The phenomenon of second home purchasing in the UK exhibits 'epidemic' characteristics: second homes are concentrated in particular areas and in certain communities, pointing to the fact that buyers are looking for something very specific. In mainland Europe, the situation appears somewhat different, with owners of second homes tending to have properties in what might be considered 'weekend leisure space' (see Chapter 6), close to their 'first' home. Proximity to where they work seems to be the key factor in where a second home is bought. But in the UK, the factors that lead to a particular purchase choice are perhaps slightly more complex.

Firstly, buyers are often looking for an attractive home in a picturesque village and in a rural setting that fits with a particular pastoral or scenic ideal. This is certainly a key consideration for those purchasing on the Cornish coast or in North Wales. The village of Abersoch, for example, on the Lleyn peninsula fits these criteria exactly and 38 per cent of its housing stock comprises second homes. Secondly, accessibility is important; second home buyers want to be able to get to their properties reasonably easily. This means that they look for good road and rail access. Pembrokeshire is popular because there is good access via the M4 motorway; the Brecon Beacons can be accessed from South Wales via the recently upgraded A470; the Lake District has the M6 passing along its eastern border, and South Cotswolds has an 80-minute train link from London Paddington. Thirdly, price is a consideration. Many – though not all – second home buyers are looking for a bargain and have flocked to areas where house prices tended to be depressed; hence many Snowdonia villages saw a sharp rise in second home demand in the 1970s. This situation arose because of a surplus of small quarriers cottages in villages such as Penmachno and Cwm Machno, abandoned in the 1930s and remaining empty and derelict in the 1960s and 1970s; hence there were bargains to be had.

The key considerations then are *location* (often in areas of natural beauty, and frequently on the coast), *accessibility* and *cost*. Critically, these same considerations provide the rationale for other forms of migration; and location and cost act to heighten planning constraint, and reveal weaknesses in the local economy, respectively. Second home pressures frequently occur in the same places as retirement and commuting, and economic weakness and rigid planning control. Indeed, in an article for the journal Town and Country Planning, we summarised this situation in the following terms:

> It is no accident that second home buyers are frequently drawn to the same villages as retiring households, people commuting to work in nearby towns and cities, or those moving to the countryside for a change of lifestyle. All are seeking the same qualities and advantages that they perceive the countryside can offer (Gallent, Mace and Tewdwr-Jones, 2003b, p.23).

This association of different pressures in many 'second home areas' is explained below:

Location

Those location characteristics that attract second home buyers – quaint villages, stone cottages and dramatic scenery – also attract retiring households, down-shifters and other migrants. Second homes can therefore signify wider demand pressures: they symbolise market 'distortion' but may not be the key component of that distortion. It is also the case that the location characteristics noted above, are most regularly found in National Parks, on Heritage Coasts, or in Areas of Outstanding Natural Beauty. In these areas, planning regulations are tighter and there is often prioritisation of environmental considerations over social concerns; the upshot being that land release for housing is more tightly controlled and the opportunities to deliver additional homes for local need is reduced.

Accessibility

Accessibility to an area also encourages additional housing pressure. Commuters, for example, look to buy in areas that can be reached quickly by road and rail. For example, the community of Bleddington in South Cotswolds District is popular with both second home buyers and commuters. The village has a mainline rail station – at Kingham – close by, which links to London Paddington in 80 minutes (Gallent *et al*, 2002, p.53). Therefore, it serves the accessibility needs of both weekend and seasonal visitors and daily or part-time commuters. Similarly, many urban down-shifters are also attracted to the area, many of whom are looking to escape city living. A cottage in the village of Bleddington will fetch between £200,000 and £300,000; half the price of a typical house in inner London, or the cost of a small flat. Thirty-something down-shifters looking for a complete change in life-style, are likely to find this favourable ratio between London and Cotswold prices attractive.

Cost

More generally, cost is a key factor in attracting second home buyers to an area. Unlike the down-shifters, these buyers may not be looking to release equity from a first home, but are likely to be investing in property using surplus capital. They will want to get the best possible deal for their money. In the past, many second home owners flocked to buy Pembrokeshire cottages and terraced homes in North Wales. These were relatively cheap and abundant. Similarly, rural depopulation in France left a legacy of cheap farm houses available for purchase in Provence and the Dordogne; many of these were bought by British buyers in the early part of the 1990s. People looking to buy second homes want as much as they can get for their money in the most ideal locations; decisions are going to be based on this balance, or trade off, between location and price. But why are prices often depressed in rural areas? In France, rural depopulation was driven by a collapse in some local farming economies; incomes declined and property and land values fell. In North Wales, the failure of primary industries – first slate quarrying and then farming – resulted in the same process. Many people left, reducing the demand on housing stock and depressing prices. Those local people who remained tended to find low paid jobs in marginal industries – including hill farming – but were able to rent or buy homes because of the surplus that existed. However, in North Wales, the second home market took off in the 1970s and has caused housing access problems for local people ever since.

Second home purchasing – and the concentrations that can be observed across England and Wales (see Chapters 3 and 4) – is commonly allied to retirement and commuting, down shifting, planning constraint and economic fragility. Second homes can come to 'symbolise' the difficulties faced by some rural areas. This can be demonstrated in Wales.

Positioning Second Homes in Wales

One of the key objectives of research undertaken for the Welsh Assembly Government in 2001 was to locate second home purchasing and the size of the second home market within the context of other housing and social trends affecting rural Wales and particular communities. A brief summary of this work here allows us to position second homes in this broader context. It draws on an analysis of Census and Council Tax data together with demographic data, population change figures, information on future migration trends and indices of ward-level deprivation. This enables us to examine the association of second homes with deprivation (and language concerns) in Wales, and also to look at the relative 'importance' of second homes next to broader housing and demographic trends.

A particular feature of the Welsh situation (see also Chapter 4) is the importance of the Welsh language in many rural areas.[1] The everyday use of the language declined steadily during the twentieth century, with the Welsh speaking areas contracting into ever fewer strongholds (Aitchison and Carter, 2000). These strongholds tend to be in more rural areas: in Gwynedd, Ceredigion and Carmarthenshire. Gwynedd, in particular, has been a popular destination for second home buyers for several decades; it has also suffered economic difficulties in recent years. In one fairly recent report, *Mapping Social Exclusion in Wales* (National Assembly for Wales, 1999) it was shown that Gwynedd has the third lowest average income in Wales. Many of the second home hotspot areas revealed in Chapter 4 (Wales) also suffer acute income and other forms of deprivation. Figures from the Assembly Government (2000) concerning 'income' and 'multiple' deprivation can be set against 2001 figures for the proportion of second homes found in particular wards: in Table 10.1, second home 'hotspot' areas found amongst the top third most deprived Welsh wards (including urban wards) are identified.

Perhaps the most striking pattern emerging from these data is the association between deprivation and second homes in some of the most pressured north Wales communities, particularly in Gwynedd and across the Isle of Anglesey.

**Table 10.1   Second Home Wards (> 5%) Found in the Top Third Most
Income Deprived Welsh Wards in 2000**

Ward	Second homes in 2001 (%)	Indices of Deprivation 2000, index of multiple deprivation score	Indices of Deprivation 2000, rank of index of multiple deprivation	Indices of Deprivation 2000, income domain score	Indices of Deprivation 2000, rank of income domain
Aberffraw (A)	18.0	35.02	127	32.62	213
Moelfre (A)	15.0	29.49	206	37.29	120
St Dogmaels (P)	14.4	21.90	354	32.27	223
Cynfal & Teigl (G)	10.8	25.28	277	31.24	247
Barmouth (G)	10.5	42.71	79	45.48	39
Talysarn (G)	8.1	46.61	65	44.52	45
Llanaelhaearn (G)	7.7	30.40	196	34.63	171
Pwllheli South (G)	5.9	39.28	100	42.88	58
Deiniolen (G)	5.9	31.86	170	36.00	144
Bowydd & Rhiw (G)	5.4	44.92	74	53.22	15

Note: (G) Gwynedd, (P) Pembrokeshire, (A) Isle of Anglesey. Source: Indices of
Deprivation for electoral divisions in Wales, 2000 (National Assembly for Wales,
Cardiff).

These data provide a snapshot of this association, and demonstrate how a
combination of different concerns (housing and economic) frequently come
together in particular places and may drive much of the political debate that
commonly envelopes the second home issue (see Chapter 1). The fact that
many of these communities are also Welsh language strongholds (Deiniolen
was 84.6 per cent Welsh speaking in 1991; Bowydd and Rhiw, 84.6 per cent,
and Pwllheli South, 81.4 per cent) and considered under threat from a weak
economy and housing pressure, is a source of additional cultural concern,
evidenced by the strength of support for the Welsh Language Society in north
Wales. Abersoch currently has the highest proportion of second homes in
Wales (37.7 per cent of housing stock) and has seen its proportion of Welsh
speakers fall from a level similar to that of Deiniolen thirty years ago to just
over 50 per cent today. An added concern in Gwynedd is the fact that 35 of the
unitary authority's 69 wards fell into the worst decile of all 865 Welsh wards by
housing deprivation (measured by the proportion of households enduring
'poor' or 'inadequate' accommodation) in 2000. Again, it is this coalescence of
substandard local housing, income deprivation, second home purchasing,
retirement migration into the county (see Table 10.2 below) and apparent
cultural sensitivity that has inflamed some local politicians and communities in
recent years (see Gallent, Mace and Tewdwr-Jones, 2003a): second homes are
'positioned' in this complex situation, and for many, come to symbolise the
inequities and weaknesses of the local market. Indeed, second home buyers
perhaps unwittingly exploit these weaknesses: they often stampede to 'bargain'

**Table 10.2   Migration and Projected Population Change (1998 to 2021)
(Thousands)**

			1998	2001	2011	2021	% Change 1998–2021
Anglesey							
Gwynedd		Under 16	129.9	128.9	118.5	115.5	−11.1
Conwy	North Wales	Working Age	387.2	391.0	392.1	403.7	4.2
Denbighshire	Authorities	Retirement Age	140.3	140.8	157.8	157.1	12.0
Flintshire		All Ages	657.9	660.7	668.4	676.3	2.9
Wrexham							
Powys		Under 16	36.3	36.5	34.0	33.6	−7.6
Ceredigion	Mid Wales	Working Age	117.1	119.2	121.7	126.2	7.8
	Authorities	Retirement Age	43.2	44.2	51.9	54.5	26.0
		All Ages	196.7	199.9	207.6	214.3	8.9
Pembrokeshire		Under 16	127.1	124.4	114.9	114.7	−9.8
Carmarthenshire	South West	Working Age	384.2	388.3	387.9	396.7	3.2
Swansea	Wales	Retirement Age	139.0	139.6	151.9	148.9	6.7
Neath Port Talbot		All Ages	651.0	652.3	654.7	660.3	1.4
Bridgend							
Vale of Glamorgan							
Cardiff							
Rhondda Cynon Taff		Under 16	305.7	298.8	269.7	276.8	−9.5
Merthyr Tydfil	South East	Working Age	860.4	875.7	903.6	936.0	8.8
Caerphilly	Wales	Retirement Age	262.1	262.6	288.8	283.6	8.2
Blaenau Gwent		All Ages	1428.1	1437.1	1462.1	1496.4	4.8
Torfaen							
Monmouthshire							
Newport							

properties in picturesque villages, but rarely ask why such property may command such a low price – from an outsiders' perspective – in the local market.

In Wales, there are numerous instances where housing supply restraint (particularly within National Parks), strong demand pressure (including second home purchasing) and linguistic issues coincide. Here, the loudest case for a planning response is made, and there are sometimes calls to halt new development in the hope, perhaps misguided, that this will quell demand or prevent incomers from buying into the local market. In 2001, one particular local councillor from Gwynedd found himself being accused of racism after claiming that the English were no longer welcome in Wales and should 'pack their bags'. His central concern however, was not for second homes, but for recent increases in retirement to Wales: the retired were lambasted as a 'drain on local communities' (BBC News, 19th January 2001). At the very least, the councillor seemed to have recognised the biggest growth pressure facing many areas and to have identified one of the issues rapidly becoming a UK-wide priority.

Many parts of Wales have recently experienced a loss of people in the 20 to 34 years age cohort. The absolute number of people in this group fell by 7.54 per cent in Gwynedd, by 9.98 per cent in Pembrokeshire and by 8.87 per cent in Powys. Relative to overall changes in the population structure, the loss of young people is less spectacular. In the period 1996 to 2000, more people passed the age of 34 than reached the age of 20, so at least part of the absolute loss is a result of demographic ageing. However, there is a clear out-migration issue in Wales and in many rural areas across the UK (Cherry and Rogers, 1994; Bevan *et al*, 2001). But this may not necessarily be a product of any housing shortage brought about by planning constraint or second home pressures: it may result from an aspiration, amongst younger people, to seek better opportunities elsewhere – either education or work related. This was confirmed through interviews with housing department representatives across Wales' 22 Unitary Authorities[2] (and particularly those able to comment on the results of recent housing need assessments: see Tewdwr-Jones *et al*, 2002), though there was also a belief that peoples' priorities change. They may indeed leave for better jobs aged 25, but then might wish to return aged 35. There are barriers to this return, but are they principally housing or employment related? As an aside, housing officers interviewed during the course of five local case studies (ibid. 2002) were commonly of the view that those returning *might* encounter a lack of housing, but at the same time, they *definitely* find it difficult to secure employment at the same wage level that they had previously enjoyed in Cardiff or London. In other words, the main factors causing people to leave may be economic, and these same factors probably deter them from returning.

Yet the key message from published data on Wales does not relate to out-migration of the young, but rather in-migration of older households together with in-situ ageing. In just four years between 1996 and 2000, the above 55 age cohorts increased their membership by 2.78 per cent. This all-Wales average was exceeded in several authorities: notably in Pembrokeshire (+5.21 per cent), Powys (+6.34 per cent) and in Ceredigion (+5.39 per cent).

Ageing is a key feature of Wales' population structure and one product of ageing, namely retirement, will have profound implications for the housing stock, future social needs and local communities. Retirement is one consideration in Table 10.2, which focuses more generally on the components of future population change. The data presented in Table 10.1 were taken from the 1998-based (that is, based on a mid-year population estimate) Population and Household Projections for Wales (National Assembly for Wales, 2000: Table 4, p.6). The results for 2021 take into account the change to a common state retirement age of 65. The key message is that increases in the proportion of people of retirement age, though significant across all of Wales, will be nothing short of spectacular in the Mid Wales authorities. Across all rural authorities, general migration and retirement migration will become significant future contributors to the growth in permanent household numbers. For potential second home purchasers, this may mean that fewer surplus units will be available to those seeking weekend or holiday retreats over the next 25 years. An intensification of competition for existing housing may see second home buyers pushed to other regions or even abroad by more determined and potentially more affluent retirees: such trends are already reported within many local authorities where a levelling out of the second home market has been matched by higher demand from full-time migrant households. But this may be cold comfort to those who fear the more fundamental social reconfiguration of communities that is likely to result from permanent population movements. Whilst second homes may help limit housing choice and cause a 'thinning out' of communities, permanent migration has a clear propensity to bring lasting social change.

Ageing and retirement both emerged as key issues from our demographic analysis: the population projections reveal that Ceredigion and Powys (grouped together as Mid Wales) will see huge rises (of 26 per cent) in the number of people reaching retirement age. North Wales follows some way behind with an increase of 12 per cent.

This brief analysis reveals the 'position' of second homes in many rural areas in the United Kingdom; in particular:

- They are a local and highly concentrated phenomenon (see Chapter 4);
- Their national significance has waned over the last decade (see Chapter 1);
- Population aging is the key social change affecting the entire UK. This process is likely to have profound impacts on housing choices during the next 25 years, with permanent retirement bringing massive social and cultural changes to large tracts of the countryside;
- Retirement in-migration will bring with it a re-patterning of the cultural landscape, introducing new social needs and housing pressures, and providing a source of wider political concern and debate;
- Second homes, on the other hand, will continue to bring localised impacts and may require local attention, especially in areas of economic depression, income deprivation and cultural sensitivity;
- The analysis of the Welsh situation reveals that second homes are frequently allied with issues including: retirement, planning constraint, economic fragility and social sensitivity. This is true throughout the UK.

Rural Second Homes in Europe

Throughout this book, we have tried to locate the second home debate in these wider rural concerns: a key aim has been to avoid contributing to the myth that second homes are a major driver of social and economic change in rural areas. This is neither true in the United Kingdom, nor in mainland Europe. But that is not to say that second home purchasing is not important.

Its importance in the UK derives from the fact that second homes are allied to and often symptomatic of other social and economic features (see last section); in this context they add to the complexity of rural housing markets, and may create a further barrier to local housing access. In continental Europe, there are a wide range of different scenarios: one common scenario, however, is that second homes are an endemic feature of rural housing markets. This is certainly true in Sweden (Chapters 5 and 6) where the division between urban first homes and rural second homes is frequently blurred. In Spain too, the tradition of retaining rural hobby farms in the rural interior might also be viewed as an endemic feature of Spain's housing market (again, see Chapters 5 and 6). However, both of these countries have alternate second home markets: in Sweden, Germans have been buying up second homes on the west coast in recent years. This trend has generated concern amongst some rural populations, which recognise that this phenomenon is different from domestic second home purchasing. Foreign buyers gravitate towards attractive fishing villages; they out-compete local people for housing, and they introduce problems that are more usually associated with the UK's epidemic second home situation. In Spain, the alternate second home market – that is, alternate to the rural market found in the interior – is different again. Here it comprises many hundreds of thousands of holiday chalets built on the coast and in the Balearic Islands. On the one hand, this phenomenon has transformed these locations beyond all recognition. However, this transformation has also been economic and the coastal chalets now form a major element of Spain's tourist economy. These different situations demonstrate the structural differences that exist in second home markets, the problems that external housing demand can introduce, and also the economic benefits that second homes can bring in some circumstances.

As well as noting the key differences between many mainland European and British situations, it was also argued that southern European approaches to land-use planning (particularly that found in Italy) differ significantly from those that proliferate in northern Europe (in Scandinavia and in the UK). Southern European planning tends to be less centralized, geared towards permitting local flexibility, and therefore perhaps more responsive to local housing needs and external demand pressures. Further north, however, far more restrictive planning regimes proliferate: these tend to resist external pressure, but in doing so make it more difficult to satisfy local needs. How these different regimes operate, and their wider impacts on the housing market has not been examined in any great depth in this book, though we have drawn attention to the impacts of restrictive planning controls in the UK (see Chapter 8). This is clearly an issue for further comparative analysis. In particular, are there lessons in flexibility for the UK that might be acquired from a closer examination of planning in Spain and Italy? The strategy towards second homes in Spain, for example, has been to adopt a twin tracking: meeting 'recreational housing' demand whilst also addressing local needs. What might the UK learn from such approaches?

Much of what has been said in this book with regards to policy responses (Part 3) draws on past experiences in the UK and on an examination of restrictive planning mechanisms. The review of the evolving policy framework (Chapter 7) looked at past suggestions and evaluated their potential application today; the examination of planning tools (Chapter 8) concluded that general restrictions on use change and on housing occupancy is likely to have a number of wider consequences in the housing market. This is largely because such responses tackle the symptoms or most obvious symbols (that is second homes) of a troubled housing market and a fragile economy. We have argued that the complexity of rural housing issues demands a positive and balanced response.

Many local authorities in England and Wales share the view that more needs to be done to manage the *full range* of housing pressures now facing particular communities. On the whole, councils do not perceive a straightforward second home problem, but believe that such purchasing is part of a wider challenge facing housing and planning authorities. This challenge is two-fold:

- To find ways to compensate communities for the difficulties that a strong market brings;
- To improve and increase the delivery of affordable housing without too great an increase in the overall volume of new house building.

On the first issue, councils believe that some form of 'impact compensation' is the way forward. If second homes – or levels of retirement purchasing – are proved to be bringing hardship to local homebuyers and communities, then Revenue Support Grant (available to support local services) should be raised. Alternatively, if the impact of second homes can be isolated and is clearly negative, then impact compensation should come directly from second home buyers either through a punitive rate of council tax or through a higher level of stamp duty on properties purchased as second homes (assuming definitional issues can be overcome).

On the second issue, councils agree that more should be done to promote the delivery of affordable housing in smaller rural communities, which often lose out to 'economy of scale' type arguments. This could involve a redirecting of planning gain away from large development sites to villages, or simply greater investment in the Housing Corporation's Rural Programme. It will certainly involve better training for planners and an improved resourcing of rural planning departments, many of which find it extremely difficult to enforce conditions or invest time in negotiations which may deliver very few – albeit very important – homes for local people.

The final outcome of our work for the Countryside Agency (Gallent *et al*, 2002) was a sixteen-point plan for helping communities affected by strong outside housing demand, and particularly by concentrations of second homes. This plan – or 'new framework for policy' – was discussed at length in Chapter 9. This framework is about understanding market change and identifying the presence of different demands, each with its own particular costs and benefits. Admittedly, it is also about creating buffers, but not about preventing incursions by 'outsiders'. The latter would be extremely difficult to achieve and to justify. The answers to many of the problems facing rural communities lie in adopting a positive approach, in harnessing the benefits of migration and social change, and in ensuring that local people – if they wish to do so – can remain to share in these benefits. The principal elements of this framework are summarised below:

- Stronger guidance on the use of occupancy conditions, with the long term objective of achieving greater legal certainty;
- The designation of sites specifically for affordable housing in development plans or Local Development Frameworks, again to increase certainty but also to stack the cards in favour of affordable housing over new build in some instances;
- Additional training for planning professionals, to ensure the maximum benefits are extracted from planning permissions;
- More thorough reviews of planning permissions on renewal to make sure gain requirements are up to date;
- The pooling of planning gains from nearby larger sites to smaller villages;
- The regular adoption of best practice with regards to delivering affordable housing, and working with the private sector and RSLs (see Carmona *et al*, 2003);
- The trialling of more radical solutions – for example change of use controls governing 'conversion' of first into second homes – in some instances;
- An end to the current council tax discount on second homes, but caution over levying 100 per cent in case this prevents councils from monitoring second home numbers (government has since decided to set a minimum discount rate of 10 per cent for this exact reason);
- Research examining the impacts of second homes and how to isolate these impacts from those generated by wider market pressures;
- Local impact assessments to become a pre-requisite to additional powers, such as the pooling of planning gains to second home hot-spots;
- A system of capital gains tax relief on land sold wholly for affordable housing;
- An extension of funding for the Countryside Agency's Rural Housing Enabler Approach;
- A review of the Housing Corporation's Total Cost Indicators in areas of proven strong second home demand;
- Local suspensions of the Right to Buy or tightening of restrictions on resale, again in areas of strong second home demand;
- An improved system of monitoring second home numbers locally, perhaps through regular analysis of discounts granted and by asking those who receive discounts to fill out brief questionnaires on the nature and use of their property; and
- Greater contact between local estate agents and councils to improve the monitoring of shifts in the private housing market.

This framework perhaps provides the logical conclusion for this book; however, before bringing the discussion to a close, two final points need further attention.

Second Homes: Myths and Misconceptions

The first concerns the 'myths' that surround second home ownership. There are many 'minor myths' regarding level of usage, the impact on house prices, the origins of owners (in Wales, they are invariably seen as English, though this is often not the case) or how the market has changed in recent years (opponents of second homes usually see them as a growing problem). But encapsulating all these minor myths is the general belief that second homes in the United Kingdom are the single greatest threat to the survival of many rural communities. This is a point we raised in Chapter 1. At the very beginning of this book, we argued that for local politicians – in particular – the occurrence of second homes 'provides an opportunity to present local problems as being externally driven, caused not by failures in the immediate economy or by misjudged policy interventions, but by the greed and carelessness of outside interests'. There are then a number of logical extensions to this argument: for example, 'that too few housing opportunities cause young people to move away, rather than any lack of diversity in the job market or educational opportunities, or indeed any desire to experience new places. Similarly, house price inflation is associated with second home pressures and not with planning constraints or low levels of house building'.

The argument that we were inferring then – and clarifying now – is that second homes are often convenient scapegoats. Local politicians frequently face very real problems: a declining farming sector, low wages, failing services, unaffordable housing, homelessness, in-migration and out-migration, a gentrification of some villages, and unrest amongst local voters. Sanctioned by the politicians, council officers may have undertaken different monitoring studies, perhaps looking at building land availability, housing occupancy, service usage and local housing needs. They will also have figures from the County or Region setting out projected household growth during the life of their local plan or the County Structure Plan. In other words, authorities will have a reasonable picture of the social changes occurring in the local area. Now, it is likely that these studies reveal a number of trends: declining service use in some communities, incomers occupying a proportion of new housing, rising house prices, more retired people moving into the area, increases in local house prices over recent years, a lengthening housing waiting list, and a rise in the number of second homes bought in certain villages. The politicians are now placed in a position of having to acknowledge the problems, set priorities and formulate a response. In the Welsh example presented earlier in this chapter, data reveals that levels of retirement often far exceed levels of second home purchasing; and yet, second homes are often prioritised as the key challenge. Why should this be the case?

Arguably, there is pressure from local people to focus on second homes. Rows of empty homes – in some communities – are an obvious source of frustration. The local authority may well have identified all the broader trends listed above, but second homes become the talking point locally, with concerns raised in community and parish councils, and eventually with ward members and finally MPs (who might be persuaded to introduce Private Members' Bills to the Commons: see Chapter 8). The other factor leading to this prioritisation is perhaps more cynical. Local politicians recognise that in the short term, at least, economic improvement in the area is likely to be slow; in order to remain in office after the next election, they need a fast explanation for housing problems, and an idea that they can tout to the electorate. Again, returning to the Welsh situation, it has now been clarified that retirement is the biggest pressure facing many rural areas, with second homes not even coming in a close second. But do local politicians want to attribute housing pressures to recently-arrived and locally voting retired households? When a Gwynedd Councillor did just this in January 2001, it provoked a political storm that culminated in the resignation of the leader of Plaid Cymru. The episode was politically damaging because retired people vote locally, and the 'grey vote' is becoming increasingly important in many rural areas. To avoid the wrath of the grey vote, it is much more advisable to blame local housing difficulties on people who do not vote locally: much that goes wrong in the countryside is attributed to the 'greed and carelessness of outside interests'; that is, interests which remain outside and have no local political voice.

Second homes are an obvious symbol; they are also a useful distraction from the more difficult and complex problems that many rural areas face. This is the first of our final key points.

Second Homes: The Future

The second point concerns the future. It was also in Chapter 1 that we suggested that despite a leveling off of second home demand between the UK's 1991 and 2001 Censuses, conditions are being created that favour further expansion of the UK and European second home markets. FDP Savill has recently drawn attention to healthy demand amongst British buyers for mainland European second homes. A combination of cheap flights to many smaller – and often more rural – European destinations, together with a strong Pound and a weakening Euro (that may further weaken when the new ten members join the EU in May 2004), has resulted in increased market activity. The last Survey of English Housing showed that English households own about 450,000 second homes and of these, roughly 230,000 are located in England; the remainder are either elsewhere in the UK or in mainland Europe, especially in France, Spain and Italy. Indeed, although the study by Savills noted some small absolute increase in the size of the second home market in England, it stressed that

> [...] the expansion in these English markets has been relatively limited in numerical terms. The real growth story is being seen in much sunnier locations. This has been for both high value and more affordable stock, in coastal and rural parts of southern France, Italy and southern Spain as well as locations further afield (FDP Savill, 2004).

Another key factor that may drive up second home purchasing in Britain – and property investment more generally – is the anticipated 'failure' of private and state pensions to meet the costs of retirement. Demographic ageing across Europe means that welfare systems may be plunged into crisis over the next ten or twenty years: there will simply be too few people of working age to support those already retired. Many private pension schemes are already responding to this problem by ending 'final salary' schemes to new employees. This will mean that their pensions will be linked to stock market performance and the money they will receive in retirement is extremely uncertain. Clearly, this state of affairs is a cause for serious concern for both national governments and for current workers, who face a number of choices. They might choose to supplement pensions with annuities or ISAs, or some other type of investment. However, the poor performance of the stock market – particularly since the 9/11 attacks on the United States – has revealed that this is not the safest option. However, since 2001, property prices have appeared to move almost independently of stock market trends: whilst the value of the FTSE fell, property prices in the UK continued to rise by between 15 and 20 per cent per annum. This was of course partly a result of the Bank of England's aggressive interest rate cuts following the terrorist attacks in America. But even with rates rising in 2004, the housing market remains resilient.

The rising value of homes in the UK is also attributable to the recent fall in building rates, which dropped to a seventy-seven year low in 2001. The shortage of housing in many locations is also pushing up prices. At the present time, investment in housing seems like the safest option for those concerned about their future financial security. Indeed, the events of the last five years have shaken people's faith in stocks and shares, but not in the security offered by property investment: the adage 'safe as houses' continues to ring true. But what is this likely to mean for the second home market in the UK?

The Centre for Economics and Business Research (CEBR) puts the total number of second homes in the UK at 150,000 units. This is far lower than the Survey of English Housing total, and is derived from Census figures (which are known to under-enumerate second homes: see Chapter 1). The CEBR estimates that this base figure will more than double in the next twenty years: '[...] as wealth spreads, disenchantment with commuting will prompt increasing numbers of people to seek a place in the country as well as the city – or vice versa' (*The Independent*, 11th April 2004). Earlier in this chapter, we suggested that whilst the second home phenomena in much of Europe is 'endemic' in character, there are instances where the more 'epidemic' problems faced in Britain are spreading (that is on the Swedish west coast). However, the conclusions of the CEBR suggest that as mainland Europe imports UK-style problems, the UK may in turn become more 'European'. In Chapter 6, we suggested that second homes in the UK tend to occupy 'vacation space': locations further from first homes that are visited less frequently. In contrast, mainland European second homes tend to occupy 'weekend leisure space': closer to first homes and visited more frequently. FDP Savill's analysis of second home markets that have emerged in the last five years appear to confirm a move from vacation to leisure space, with more people buying second homes that they can use every weekend, together with smaller city homes that they use during the working week:

> The City of London actually tops the list of growth areas, despite it having the highest number of second homes across the country. However, an extension to this trend is Tower Hamlets, which has seen the second fastest expansion in the number of second homes. Encompassing the Isle of Dogs and Canary Wharf, the area has seen a huge growth in financial services employment recently. As in the City, *it has appealed to those looking for a home close to work for use during the week*. Strong price growth in the London market has enabled buyers to trade up the housing market and out of London, using some capital to buy a home in the city. *This trend has supported country house price growth in the markets outside a realistic day commute to London* that is Norfolk, Yorkshire, the more distant parts of the Midlands and the South West (FDP Savill, 2004).

If these trends hold good, then the UK's second home market is perhaps set to become more 'Swedish' with more people owning smaller city homes together with weekend retreats within reasonable commuting distance. Investment in property, driven by increases in personal wealth and concerns over private pensions, may in the future mean that second homes become more endemic; a part of everyday life and embedded in British culture. But will this mean greater acceptance?

Unfortunately, the analogy with Sweden is not necessarily a good one. Although the UK market *might* become more 'endemic', with a greater proportion of households dividing their lives between town and country, structurally the UK and Sweden situations are very different (see Allen *et al*, 1998). The UK has a much greater population density, is smaller in total land area, and has no surplus capacity in rural housing supply. Sweden's housing market can absorb the demands of a dual-property owning population; Britain's – at the present time – cannot. This may result in an endemic market with epidemic consequences: further pressure on rural housing supply and affordability, amplified social tensions and divisions in the countryside, and renewed calls for controls on second home purchasing. The future is not certain, but whatever transpires, second homes are likely to remain an important feature of many rural housing markets, and a focus of debate.

Notes

1   In many parts of Wales great importance is attached to the language issue. And where the lowest income groups are unable to compete in the housing market – because of insufficient housing supply or other pressures – there is an inevitable impact on local communities and their 'cultural' configuration (Phillips and Thomas, 2001). Indeed, Geraint Jenkins has recently argued that '[...] in-migration, especially during the locust years of Thatcherism in the 1980s, has had a calamitous effect on the cultural profile' of many communities and that '[...] any language that is not a community language will surely perish' (Jenkins, 2001, pp.65–66).

2   This chapter does not report the results of our survey of all Unitary Authority housing and planning departments or the results of five local case studies examining market change and policy in Ceredigion, Pembrokeshire Coast, the Lleyn Peninsular, the Brecon Beacons and the area of the former district of Radnorshire. These results are set out in the full report of the research.

Bibliography

Action for Communities in Rural England (1988), *Who can afford to live in the countryside? Access to Housing Land*, Cirencester: ACRE.

Adams, D. & Watkins, C. (2002), *Greenfields, Brownfields and Housing Development*, London: Blackwells Publishers.

Aitchison, J. & Carter, H. (1985), *The Welsh Language 1961–1981: An Interpretative Atlas*, Cardiff: University of Wales Press.

Aitchison, J. & Carter, H. (1986), 'Language areas and language change in Wales, 1961–1981', in Hume, I. & Pryce, W.T.R. (eds.), *The Welsh and Their Country*, Llandysul: Gomer Press.

Aitchison, J. & Carter, H. (2000) *Language, Economy and Society: The Changing Fortunes of the Welsh Language in the Twentieth Century*, University of Wales Press: Cardiff.

Albarre, G. (1977), 'The Impact of Second Homes: A. Second Homes and Conservation in Southern Belgium' in Coppock J.T., (ed.), *Second Homes: Curse or Blessing?* Oxford: Pergamon Press.

Aldskogius, H. (1967), 'Vacation House Settlement in the Siljan Region', *Geografiska Annaler* 49, 2, pp.69–95.

Aldskogius, H. (1968), 'Studier i Siljansområdets fritidsbyggelse', *Geografiska Regionstudier*, 4, Sweden: Kulturgeografiska Institutionen vid Uppsala Universitet.

Allen, C., Gallent, N. & Tewdwr-Jones, M. (1998), 'The limits of policy diffusion: second home experiences in Sweden and the UK', *Environment & Planning C: Government and Policy* 17, 2, pp. 227–244.

Ambrose, P. (1974), *The Quiet Revolution*, London: Chatto & Windus.

Archer, B. (1973), *The Impact of Domestic Tourism*, Bangor Occasional Papers in Economics 2, Bangor: University of Wales Press.

Aronsson, L. (1989), Turism och local utveckling: en turism-geografisk studie. *Meddelanden från Göteborgs universitets geografiska institutioner* B79, Göteborg.

Auclair, E. & Vanoni, D. (2003), 'France', in Gallent, N., Shucksmith, M. & Tewdwr-Jones, M, (Eds), *Housing in the European Countryside: Rural Pressure and Policy in Western Europe*, London: Routledge, pp. 71–85.

Audit Commission (1992), *Developing Local Authority Housing Strategies*, London: HMSO.

Balchin, P. (1981), *Housing Policy and Housing Needs*, London: Macmillan.

Balchin, P. (1995), *Housing Policy: An Introduction*, London: Routledge.

Barbier, B. (1968), *Villes et Centres des Alpes du Sud* in Editions Ophrys, Gap.

Barke, M. (1991), 'The growth and changing pattern of second homes in Spain in the 1970s', *Scottish Geographical Magazine*, 107, 1, pp. 12–21.

Barke, M. & France, L.A. (1988), 'Second Homes in the Balearic Islands', *Geography*, 73, 319, pp. 143–145.

Barker, K. (2004), *Delivering Stability: Securing Our Future Housing Needs*, London: HM Treasury.

Barlow, J., Bartlett, K., Hooper, A. and Whitehead, C. (2002), *Land for Housing: Current Practice and Future Options*, York: Joseph Rowntree Foundation.

Barlow, J. & Chambers, D. (1992), *Planning Agreements and Affordable Housing Provision*, University of Sussex, Brighton, Centre for Urban and Regional Research.

Barlow, J., Cocks, R. & Parker, M. (1994), *Planning for Affordable Housing*, London, HMSO.

Barlow, J., Jackson, R. & Meikle, J. (2001), *The Current State of the Self-Build Housing Market*, York: Joseph Rowntree Foundation.

BBC News (2001), *Apology over 'insults' to English* BBC News, 19th January 2001: http://212.58.226.40/hi/english/uk/wales/newsid_1123000/1123782.stm (accessed 25 January 01).

BBC Online (2004), *Second homes' large discount ends*, BBC Online, 1st April 2004: http://news.bbc.co.uk/2/hi/uk_news/england/devon/3587551.stm (accessed: 08 April 2004).

Barr, J. (1967), 'A two home democracy?' *New Society*, 10, 7th September, 1967.

Bennett, R.J. (1985), 'The impact on city finance of false registration in second homes: the case of the 1981 Austrian Census', *Tijdschrift Voor Economische en Sociale Geografie*, 76, 4, pp. 298–309.

Bennett, S. (1976), *Rural Housing in the Lake District*, Lancaster, Lancaster University.

Bevan, M., Cameron, S., Coombes, M., Merridew, T. & Raybould, S. (2001), *Social Housing in Rural Areas* Coventry: Chartered Institute of Housing and the Joseph Rowntree Foundation.

Bielckus, C.L. (1977), 'Second Homes in Scandinavia', in Coppock, J.T., (ed.), *Second Homes: Curse or Blessing?*, Oxford: Pergamon Press.

Bielckus, C.L., Rogers, A.W. & Wibberley, G.P. (1972), *Second Homes in England and Wales: A study of the distribution and use of rural properties taken over as second residences*, Wye College, London, School of Rural Economics and Related Studies.

Bishop, K. & Hooper, A. (1991), *Planning for Social Housing*, London: Association of District Councils.

Bohlin, M. (1982), 'Second homes in the regional economy: where the cottagers' money goes', *Geografiska regionstudier 14*, Kulturgeografiska institutionen, Uppsala.

Bollom, C. (1978), *Attitudes and Second Homes in Rural Wales*, Cardiff: University of Wales Press.

Bonneau, M. (1973), 'Résidences secondaires et tourisme en Maine-et-Loire', *Bulletin de la Societé Languedocienne de Géographie*, 7, pp. 307–320.

Bontron, J-C. (1989), 'Equipement et cadre de vie', Brun, A. (ed.), *Le Grand Atlas de la France Rurale*, Paris: de Monza.

Bowen, E.G. & Carter, H. (1975), 'Some preliminary observations on the distribution of the Welsh language at the 1971 Census', *Geographical Journal*, 140, pp. 43–142.

Boyle, P. (1995), 'Rural in-migration in England and Wales 1980 – 1981', *Journal of Rural Studies*, 11, 1, pp. 65–78.

Bramley, G. (1991), *Bridging the affordability gap in Wales: a report of research on housing access and affordability*, Cardiff: House Builders Federation and Council of Welsh Districts.

Bramley, G. (1993), 'The enabling role for local authorities: a preliminary evaluation', in Malpass, P. & Means, R., (eds.), *Implementing Housing Policy*, Buckingham: Open University Press.

Brier, M.A. (1970), *Les Résidences Secondaires*, Paris: Dunod Actualités.

Brody, H. (1973), *Inishkillane: change and decline in the west of Ireland*, London: Allen Lane.

Buchanan, R. (1985), 'Rural housing: romantic image in need of repair', *Radical Scotland*, 17, pp. 22–23.

Buller, H. & Hoggart, K. (1994a), *International Counterurbanisation: British Migrants in Rural France*, Aldershot: Avebury.

Buller, H. & Hoggart, K. (1994b), 'The Social Integration of British Home Owners into French Rural Communities', *Journal of Rural Studies*, 10, 2, pp. 197–210.

Burby, R.J., Donnelly, T.G. & Weiss, S.F. (1972), 'Vacation home location: a model for simulating residential development of rural recreation areas', *Regional Studies*, 6, 4, pp. 421–439.

Cabinet Office (1999), *Rural Economies*, London, The Stationery Office.

Capstick, M. (1987), *Housing Dilemmas in the Lake District*, University of Lancaster: Centre for North West Regional Studies.

Carmona, M., Carmona, S. & Gallent, N. (2001), *Working Together: A Guide for Planners and Housing Providers*, London: Thomas Telford.

Carmona, M., Carmona, S. & Gallent, N. (2003), *Delivering New Homes: Planning, Processes and Providers*, London: Routledge.

Champion, A.G. (2000), 'Flight from the Cities?', in Bate, R., Best, R. & Holmans, A. (eds) *On the Move: The Housing Consequences of Migration*, York: York Publishing Services, pp. 10–19.

Champion A.G., Fotheringham, S., Rees, P., & Stillwell J. (1988), *The Determinants of Migration Flows in England: A Review of Existing Data and Evidence*, A report for the DETR, Newcastle: Department of Geography, University of Newcastle-upon-Tyne.

Champion, A. & Townsend, A.R. (1990), *Contemporary Britain: A Geographical Perspective*, London: Edward Arnold.

Chaney, P. & Sherwood, K. (2000), 'The resale of right-to-buy dwellings: a case study of migration and social change in rural England', *Journal of Rural Studies*, 16, pp. 79–94.

Channel 4 (2004), http://www.channel4.com/life/microsites/A/a_place_in_the_sun/ (accessed 05 April 2004).

Channel Islands News (2001), *Housing Law Change*, 16th January 2001: http://www. islandlife.org /news2001_jsy.htm (accessed: 08 April 2004).

Chartered Institute of Housing (1992), *Housing: the first priority*, Coventry: CIH.

Chartered Institute of Housing (1999), *Response to DETR / MAFF discussion paper: rural England*, Coventry: CIH.

Clark, G. (1982), *Housing and Planning in the Countryside*, Chichester: Research Studies Press.

Clarke, M. (2000), *Teleworking in the Countryside: Home-based Working in the Information Society*, Aldershot: Ashgate.

Cloke, P. (1985), 'Wither rural studies?' *Journal of Rural Studies*, 1, 1, p. 2.

Cloke, P. (1996), 'Housing in the open countryside: windows on "irresponsible planning" in rural Wales', *Town Planning Review*, 67, 3, pp. 291–308.

Cloke, P. & Milbourne, P. (1992), 'Deprivation and lifestyles in rural Wales: rurality and the cultural dimension', *Journal of Rural Studies*, 8, pp. 359–371.

Cloke, P., Milbourne, P. & Thomas, C. (1994), *Lifestyles in Rural England*, Salisbury: Rural Development Commission.

Cloke, P., Phillips, M. & Rankin, D. (1991), 'Middle-class housing choice: channels of entry into Gower, South Wales', in Champion, T. & Watkins, C., (eds.) *People in the Countryside: Studies of Social Change in Rural Britain*, London: Paul Chapman Publishing.

Cloke, P. & Thrift, N. (1987), 'Intra-class conflict in rural areas' *Journal of Rural Studies*, 3, pp. 321–333.

Clout, H.D. (1969), 'Second homes in France', *Journal of the Town Planning Institute*, July, 1969.

Clout, H.D. (1972), *Rural Geography, an Introductory Survey*, Oxford: Pergamon.

Clout, H.D. (1973), '350,000 second homes', *Geographical Magazine*, 45(10), p. 750.

Clout, H.D. (1977), 'Résidences Secondaires in France', in Coppock J.T., (ed.), *Second Homes: Curse or Blessing?* Oxford: Pergamon Press.

Coppock J.T. (1977), 'Second Homes in Perspective', in Coppock J.T., (ed.), *Second Homes: Curse or Blessing?*, Oxford: Pergamon Press.

Coppock J.T. (1977), 'Issues and Conflicts', in Coppock J.T., (ed.), *Second Homes: Curse or Blessing?* Oxford: Pergamon Press.

Coppock, J.T. (1977), 'Social Implications of Second Homes in Mid- and North Wales', in Coppock J.T., (ed.), *Second Homes: Curse or Blessing?* Oxford: Pergamon Press.

Countryside Agency (2000), *State of the Countryside 2000*, Cheltenham: Countryside Agency.

Countryside Agency (2003), *State of the Countryside 2003*, Cheltenham: Countryside Agency.

Cribier, F. (1966), '300,000 résidences secondaires', *Urbanisme* 96–7, pp. 97–101.

Cribier, F. (1969), *La Grande Migration d'Été des Citadins en France*, Paris, Centre National de Recherche Scientifique.

Crofts, R.S. (1977), 'Self-catering Holiday Accommodation: The role of Substitution', in Coppock J.T., (ed.), *Second Homes: Curse or Blessing?* Oxford: Pergamon Press.

Crook, A., Curry, J., Jackson, A., Monk, S., Rowley, S., Smith, K. and Whitehead, C. (2002), *The Provision of Affordable Housing Through the Planning System*, Department of Land Economy: University of Cambridge.

Crouch, D. (Ed) (1999), *Leisure/Tourism Geographies: Practices and Geographical Knowledge*, London: Routledge.

Crouch, D. (1999), 'The intimacy and expansion of space' in Crouch, D. (ed), *Leisure / Tourism Geographies*, London: Routledge.

Crouchley, R. (1976), *Towards a Model of the Spatial Distribution of Second Homes in the UK*, University of Wales, Cardiff, Unpublished MSc Thesis.

Cymdeithas Yr Iaith Gymraeg (1971), *Tai Haf*, Caerdydd, Cwmni Gwasg Rydd.

Cymdeithas Yr Iaith Gymraeg (1989), *Homes, Migration, Prices: Community Control of the Property Market*, Aberystwyth: The Welsh Language Society.

Cymdeithas Yr Iaith Gymraeg (1999), *Property Act Handbook Working Paper 2: The Right to a Home, Community and Language – The Responsibility of Cynulliad Cenedlaethol Cymru*, Aberystwyth: Welsh Language Society.

Dartington Amenity Research Trust (1971), *The Gower Coast* Totnes: DART.

Dartington Amenity Research Trust (1977), *Second Homes in Scotland: a report to Countryside Commission for Scotland, Scottish Tourist Board, Highlands and Island Development Board, Scottish Development Department*, Totnes: DART Publication No. 22.

Davies, R.B. & O'Farrell, P. (1981), *An Intra-Regional Locational Analysis of Second Home Ownership*, Cardiff: Department of Town Planning, University of Wales.

Dawes, R.M. (1972), *Fundamentals of Attitude Measurement*, New York: John Wiley & Sons.

Dawe, N. & Ryan, K. (2003), 'The faulty three-legged-stool model of sustainable development', *Conservation Biology*, 17, 5, pp. 1458–1460.

Department of the Environment (1981), *Proposed Modifications to the Cumbria and Lake District Joint Structure Plan*, London: DoE.

Department of the Environment (1984), *Circular 15/84: Land for Housing*, London: HMSO.

Department of the Environment (1991), *Circular 7/91: Planning and Affordable Housing*, London: HMSO.

Department of the Environment (1992), *Planning Policy Guidance Note 3: Housing*, London: HMSO.

Department of the Environment/Welsh Office (1992), *Planning Policy Guidance Note 7: The Countryside and the Rural Economy*, London: HMSO.

Department of the Environment (1996), *Circular 13/96: Planning and Affordable Housing*, London: HMSO.

Department of the Environment (1997), *Circular 1/97: Planning Obligations*, London: HMSO.

Department of the Environment, Transport and the Regions (1998), *Circular 6/98: Planning and Affordable Housing*, London: The Stationery Office.

Department of the Environment, Transport and the Regions (1999), *Housing in England 1997/1998*, London: The Stationery Office.

Department of the Environment, Transport and the Regions (2000), *Our Countryside: The Future – A Fair Deal for Rural England* (Cm 4909), London: The Stationery Office.

Department of the Environment, Transport and the Regions (2000), *Planning Policy Guidance Note 3: Housing*, London: The Stationery Office.

Department of Transport, Local Government and the Regions (2001a), *Council Tax: A consultation paper on proposed changes for second homes and long term empty homes*, London: DTLR.

Department of Transport, Local Government and the Regions (2001b), *Housing in England: Results of the Survey of English Housing 1999/00*, London: DTLR.

Department of Transport, Local Government and the Regions (2001c), *Planning Obligations: Delivering a Fundamental Change*, London: DTLR.

Department of Transport, Local Government and the Regions (2001d) *Planning: Delivering a Fundamental Change*, London: DTLR.

de Vane, R. (1975), *Second Home Ownership: a Case Study*, Bangor: Occasional Papers in Economics, No. 6, University of Wales Press.

Dourlens, C. & Vidal-Naquet, P. (1978), *Résidences Secondaires, Tourisme Rurale et Enjeaux Locaux*, Aix en Provence: Centre d'Etude du Tourisme.

Dower, M. (1965a), 'The fourth wave', *Architects Journal*, 20 January, 1965, pp. 123–190.

Dower, M. (1965b), *The Fourth Wave: The Challenge of Leisure*, London: Civic Trust.

Dower, M. (1977), 'Planning Aspects of Second Homes', in Coppock, J.T., (ed.), *Second Homes: Curse or Blessing?*, Oxford: Pergamon Press.

Downing, P. & Dower, M. (1973), *Second Homes in England and Wales*, London: Countryside Commission, HMSO.

Drabble, M. (1990), *Safe as Houses: An Examination of Home Ownership and Mortgage Tax Relief*, London: Chatto & Windus.

Dunn, M., Rawson, M. & Rogers, A. (1981), *Rural Housing: Competition and Choice*, London: George Allen & Unwin.

Early, C. (2004), 'Housing study warns of social apartheid threat', *Planning 1564*, 9th April 2004, p. 4.

Edwards, A.L. (1957), *Techniques of Attitude Scale Construction*, Appleton-Century-Crofts, Inc.

Edwards, B., Goodwin, M., & Woods, M. (2003) 'Citizenship, community and participation in small towns: a case study of regeneration partnerships', in Imrie, R. & Raco, M (eds), *Urban Policy: Community, Citizenship and Rights*, Bristol: Policy Press, pp. 181–204.

Edwards, R. (1991), *Fit for the Future? Report of the National Parks Review Panel* (The Edwards Report), Cheltenham: The Countryside Commission.

Emmett, I. (1964), *A North Wales Village*, London: Routledge and Kegan Paul.

Emmett, I. (1982), 'Blaenau Ffestiniog', in Cohen, P. (Ed.) *Belonging*, Manchester University Press: Manchester.

European Union (1993), *Tourism 1993 Annual Statistics*, Luxembourg: Office for the Official Publications of the European Communities.

European Union (1996), *Social Portrait of Europe*, Luxembourg: Office for the Official Publications of the European Communities.

European Union (1997), *Rural Change*, Strasbourg: European Union.

European Union (1998), *Social Portrait of Europe*, Strasbourg: Statistical Office for the European Communities.

Eurostat (1994), *Facts through figures: a statistical portrait of the European Union*, Luxembourg: Office for the Official Publications of the European Communities.

FDP Savill (2004), *Are first time buyers being forced out of the market by investors?* Press Release, 14th April 2004, London: FDP Savill.

Finnerty, J., Guerin, D. & O Connell, C. (2003), 'Ireland', in Gallent, N., Shucksmith, M. & Tewdwr-Jones, M, (Eds), *Housing in the European Countryside: Rural Pressure and Policy in Western Europe*, London: Routledge, pp. 129–145.

Folkesdotter, G. (2003), 'Sweden', in Gallent, N., Shucksmith, M. & Tewdwr-Jones, M, (2003), *Housing in the European Countryside: Rural Pressure and Policy in Western Europe*, London: Routledge, pp. 44–59.

Fraser, R. (1991), *Working Together in the 1990s: A Guide for Local Authorities and Housing Associations*, Coventry: Chartered Institute of Housing.

Gallent, N. (1997a), 'Improvement grants, second homes and planning control in England and Wales', *Planning Practice and Research*, 12, 4, pp. 401–10.

Gallent, N. (1997b), 'Planning for affordable rural housing in England and Wales', *Housing Studies* 12, 1, pp. 145–155.

Gallent, N. (2000), 'Planning for affordable housing: from old values to New Labour', *Town Planning Review*, 71, 2, pp. 123–147.

Gallent, N., Tewdwr-Jones, M. & Higgs, G. (1998), 'Planning for residential tourism in rural Wales', *Contemporary Wales*, 10, pp. 102–126.

Gallent, N. & Allen, C. (2003), 'Housing Pressure and Policy in Europe: A Power Regime Perspective', in Gallent, N., Shucksmith, M. & Tewdwr-Jones, M, (Eds), *Housing in the European Countryside: Rural Pressure and Policy in Western Europe*, London: Routledge, pp. 208–225.

Gallent, N. & Bell, P. (2000), 'Planning exceptions in Rural England – past, present and future', *Planning Practice and Research*, 15, 4, pp. 375–384.

Gallent, N., Mace, A. & Tewdwr-Jones, M. (2002), *Second homes in rural areas of England*, Countryside Agency: Cheltenham.

Gallent, N., Mace, A. & Tewdwr-Jones, M. (2003a), 'Dispelling a myth: Second homes in rural Wales', *Area*, 35, 3, pp. 271–284.

Gallent, N., Mace, A. and Tewdwr-Jones, M. (2003b), 'Second homes: a plan of action?' in *Town and Country Planning*, January 2003, pp. 23–24.

Gallent, N., Mace, A. & Tewdwr-Jones, M. (2003c), 'Delivering affordable housing through planning: explaining variable policy usage across rural England and Wales', *Planning Practice and Research* 17, 4, pp. 465–483.

Gallent, N., Shucksmith, M. & Tewdwr-Jones, M, (2003), *Housing in the European Countryside: Rural Pressure and Policy in Western Europe*, London: Routledge.

Gallent, N. & Tewdwr-Jones, M. (2000a), *Second Homes in Europe: Examining Housing Supply and Planning Control*, Ashgate: Aldershot.

Gallent, N. & Tewdwr-Jones, M. (2000b), 'Seconds out?', *Town and Country Planning*, 69, 1, pp. 13–14.

Gallent, N. & Tewdwr-Jones, M. (2001), 'Second homes and the UK Planning System', *Planning Practice and Research*, 16, 1, pp. 59–70.

Gardavský, V. (1977), 'Second Homes in Czechoslovakia', in Coppock, J.T., (ed.), *Second Homes: Curse or Blessing?*, Oxford: Pergamon Press.

Getimis, P. & Kafkalas, G. (1992), 'Local development and forms of regulation: fragmentation and hierarchy of spatial policies in Greece', *Geoforum*, 23, pp. 73–83.

Gilbert, J. (2001), *Second Homes: A Market Report*, London: Council of Mortgage Lenders.

Gilliatt M. (1973), *A House in the Country: the second home from cottages to castles*, London: Hutchins.

Godfrey, K.B. (1998), 'Attitudes towards 'sustainable tourism' in the UK: a view from local government', in *Tourism Management*, 19, 3, pp. 213–224.

Goodlad, R. (1993), *The Housing Authority as Enabler*, Coventry: Chartered Institute of Housing and Longman.

Häbermas, J. (1987), *The Theory of Communicative Action: Vol 1, Reason and Rationalisation of Society*, translated by Thomas McCarthy, Cambridge: Polity Press.

Häbermas, J. (1991), *The Theory of Communicative Action: Vol 2, Lifeworld and System: a critique of functionalist reason*, translated by Thomas McCarthy, Cambridge: Polity Press.

Halifax (2003), *Welsh House Price Index Fourth Quarter 2003*, 16th January 2004, http://www.hbosplc.com/economy/includes/walesq42003.doc (accessed 05 April 2004).

Hall, J. (1973), 'Europe's seaside: landscape for leisure', *Built Environment*, 2, pp. 173–175.

Hansard (1985), *Housing surplus in England and Wales*, Written Answer, Col. 16, London: HMSO.

Hansard (1997), *National Minimum Wage Bill, Column 186*, Tuesday 16th December 1997, www.parliament.the-stationery-office.co.uk/pa/cm199798/cmhansrd/vo971216/deb text/71216–22.htm (accessed 05 April 2004).

Heins, S. (2003), 'The Netherlands', in Gallent, N., Shucksmith, M. & Tewdwr-Jones, M, (Eds), *Housing in the European Countryside: Rural Pressure and Policy in Western Europe*, London: Routledge, pp. 60–70.

Hetherington, P. (2000), 'Young lose out in housing boom', *The Guardian*, 17 March.

Henshall, J.D. (1977), 'Second homes in the Caribbean', in Coppock, J.T., (ed.), *Second Homes: Curse or Blessing?* Oxford: Pergamon Press.

HM Government (1985), *Housing Act 1985*, London: HMSO.

HM Government (1996), *Housing and Construction Statistics No. 63 (September Quarter 1995)*, London: HMSO.

HM Government (2003), *Planning and Compulsory Purchase Bill*, London: TSO.

Hoggart, K. (2003), 'England', in Gallent, N., Shucksmith, M. & Tewdwr-Jones, M, (Eds), *Housing in the European Countryside: Rural Pressure and Policy in Western Europe*, London: Routledge, pp. 153–167.

Hoggart, K. & Buller, H. (1995), 'British home owners and housing change in rural France', *Housing Studies*, 10, 2, pp. 179–198.

Hoggart, K., Buller, H., & Black, R. (1995), *Rural Europe: Identity and Change*, London: Arnold.

Hoggart, K. & Paniagua, A. (2001), 'The restructuring of rural Spain?', *Journal of Rural Studies*, 17, 1, pp. 63–80.

Housing Corporation (1998), *F2–28/98 The Replacement of the Tenants' Incentive Scheme and Do-it-yourself Shared Ownership with Homebuy*, London: Housing Corporation.

Housing Corporation (2004) *How Homebuy Works* (http://www.housingcorp.gov.uk/yourhome/homebuy.htm#intro: accessed 08 April 2004).

Hughes, G. (1995), 'The cultural construction of sustainable tourism', *Tourism Management*, 16, 1, pp. 49–59.

Hughes, R.E. (1973), *The Planning Implications of Second Homes* Unpublished MSc thesis, Edinburgh: Department of Town and Country Planning, Edinburgh College of Art/Heriot-Watt University.

Hunter, C. (1997), 'Sustainable tourism as an adaptive paradigm', *Annals of Tourism Research*, 24, 4, pp. 850–867.

Hutton, R.H. (1991), 'Local needs policy initiatives in rural areas: missing the target?' *Journal of Environment and Planning Law*, April 1991, pp. 303–311.

Instituto Nacional de Estadistica (1983), *Censo de viviendas, 1981, tomo IV: resultadas a nivel municipal* (Madrid), p. 9.

Ireland, M. (1987), 'Planning policy and holiday homes in Cornwall', in Bouquet, M. & Winter, M. (eds.), *Who From Their Labours Rest? Conflict and Practice in Rural Tourism*, Aldershot: Avebury.

Jackson, A., Monk, S., Royce, C. and Dunn, J. (1994), *The relationship between land supply and housing production*, York: Joseph Rowntree Foundation.

Jacobs, C.A.J. (1972), *Second Homes in Denbighshire*, Ruthin: County of Denbigh Tourism and Recreation Report No. 3.

James, C. & Williams, C. (1997), 'Language and planning in Scotland and Wales', in Macdonald, R. & Thomas, H. (eds.), *Nationality and Planning in Scotland and Wales*, Cardiff: University of Wales Press.

Jansson, B. (1994) Borta bra men hemma Bäst: svenskars turistresor under sommaren. *Gerum* 22, Geografiska Institutionen, Umeå.

Jenkin, N.M. (1985), *Towards a Policy Package for Second Homes in Anglesey*, Unpublished Diploma thesis, Cardiff: University of Wales Cardiff.

Jersey States Assembly (2004), *Draft Housing (Amendment No. 11) (Jersey) Law 200-*, St Helier: States of Jersey.

Joseph Rowntree Foundation (1994), *Inquiry into Planning for Housing*, York: Joseph Rowntree Foundation.

Joseph Rowntree Foundation (1995), *Evaluating Rural Housing Enablers*: Housing Research 141, York: JRFJurdao Arrones, F. (1979), *Espana en Venta*, Madrid: Editorial Ayuso Madrid.

Kalbro, T. & Mattsson, H. (1995), *Urban Land and Property Markets in Sweden*, London, UCL Press.

Kemeny, J. (1992), *Housing and Social Theory*, London: Routledge.

Kemeny, J. (1995), *From Public Housing to the Social Market: Rental policy strategies in comparative perspective*, London: Routledge.

Lake District Special Planning Board (1977), *Draft National Park Plan*, Kendal: LDSPB.

Lake District Special Planning Board (1978), *26ᵗʰ Annual Report 1977–78*, Kendal: LDSPB.

Lake District Special Planning Board (1980), *Cumbria and Lake District Joint Structure Plan, written statement*, Kendal: LDSPB / Carlisle: Cumbria County Council.

Larsson, G. (1969), *Undersökningar rörande fritidsbebyggelse* Institutionen för fastighetsteknik, sekt. Lantmäteri, Tekniska högskolan, Stockholm, Bulletin No. 6, Part 4.

Le Roux, P. (1968), 'Les residences secondaires de Français en Juin 1967', *Etudes et Conjoncture*, Supplement 5, 1968.

Lewes, F. (1970), *The Holiday Industry of Devon and Cornwall*, London: HMSO.

Ljungdahl, S. (1938), 'Sommarstockholm', in *Ymer*, 38.

Llywelyn, E. (1976), *Adfer a'r Fro Gymraeg*, Pontypridd: Modern Cymreig Cyf.

Loughlin, M. (1984), *Local needs policies and development control strategies. An examination of the role of occupancy restrictions in development control*, SAUS Working Paper No. 42, Bristol: University of Bristol.

Lowe, P. & Ward, N. (2002), 'Virus-crisis-institutional change: the foot and mouth actor network and the governance of rural affairs in the UK', *Sociologia Ruralis*, 42, 3, pp. 201–214.

Martin, I. (1972), 'The second home dream', *New Society*, 18th May 1972.

Martin, I. (1978), 'The impact of second homes: some comments on the experience in Wales', in Talbot, M. & Vickerman, R.W. (eds.), *Leisure Studies Association Conference Paper No. 8*, London.

Massey, D. (1993), 'Power, geometry and a progressive sense of place', in Bird, J., Curtis, B., Putman, T., Robertson, G. & Tickner, L. (eds.), *Mapping the Futures: Local Cultures, Global Change*, Routledge: London.

Mayle, P. (1989), *A Year in Provence*, London: Hamish Hamilton.

Mayle, P. (1990), *Toujours Provence*, London: Hamish Hamilton.

Meacher, M. (1999), Speech to Labour conference fringe meeting, Bournemouth, September 1999 (see http://news.bbc.co.uk/hi/english/uk_politics/newsid_462000 /462354.stm).

Messenger, J.C. (1969), *Inis Beag: Isle of Ireland*, New York: Holt, Rinehart & Winston.

Mitchell, L.J. v The Secretary of State for the Environment and The Royal Borough of Kensington and Chelsea (1993), Court of Appeal Judgement CO-834–92.

Monbiot, G. (1999), *Hidden extras: homelessness and second homes*, in Urban 75 (on-line magazine): see http://www.urban75.org/archive/news072.html.

Montero, P.L. (1998), 'Components of the Spanish supply of tourist accommodation: special reference to dwellings renting for tourist purposes'. Paper presented at the *Fourth International Forum on Tourist Statistics*, Copenhagen, June 1998.

Morris, A.S. (1985), 'Tourism and planning in Spain with particular reference to the Costa Brava', in *Proceedings of the First Joint Conference of Hispanists in Polytechnics and other Colleges and the Iberian Social Studies Association*, Newton, M.T. (ed.), p. 112, Newcastle upon Tyne Polytechnic.

Müller, D. (1999), *German Second Home Owners in the Swedish Countryside: On the Internationalisation of the Leisure Space*, Umeå: Department of Social and Economic Geography, Umeå University and Östersund, European Tourism Research Institute, Mid Sweden University.

National Assembly for Wales (1999), *Mapping Social Exclusion in Wales*, Statistical Briefing Unit, National Assembly for Wales: Cardiff.

National Assembly for Wales (2001), *Population figures supplied by the Statistics Division*, December 2001, National Assembly for Wales: Cardiff.

National Federation of Housing Associations (1988a), *Building Your Future; Self-Build Housing Initiatives for the unemployed*, London: NFHA.

National Federation of Housing Associations (1988b), *Self-Build*, London: NFHA.

National Federation of Housing Associations (1994), *Working households: affordable housing and economic needs*, London: NFHA.

Newby, H. (1980a), *Green and Pleasant Land?* Middlesex: Harmondsworth, Penguin.

Newby, H. (1980b), 'A one-eyed look at the country', *New Society*, 14 August 1980.

O'Connor, P. (1962), *Living in Croesor*, London: Hutchinson.

Offices of Population Censuses & Surveys (1992), *1991 Census: Definitions Great Britain*, London: HMSO.

Office of Population Censuses & Surveys (1993), *1991 Census: Housing and Availability of Cars*, London: HMSO.

Official Journal of the European Communities (1995), 'Opinion on the proposal of a Council Directive [in OJ/95/c236/06] on the collection of statistical information in the field of tourism', *Official Journal 95/c236/20*.

Office of the Deputy Prime Minister (2002), *Fiscal Policy Options to Promote Affordable Housing*, London: ODPM.

Office of the Deputy Prime Minister (2003a), *Sustainable Communities: Building for the Future*, London: ODPM.

Office of the Deputy Prime Minister (2003b) *Review of the Use Classes Order and Part 4 of the GPDO (Temporary Uses)*, London: ODPM.

Office of the Deputy Prime Minister (2004), *Planning Policy Statement 1: Creating Sustainable Communities (Consultation Draft)*, London: ODPM.

Oppenheim, A.N. (1966), *Questionnaire Design and Attitude Measurement*, London: Heinemann.

Osgood, C.E., Tannenbaum, P.M. & Suci, G.J. (1958), *The Measurement of Meaning*, Illinois: University of Illinois Press.

Ouren, T. (1969), 'Fritig og feriemilj', *Norwegian Geographical Studies*, 8.

Padovani, L. & Vettoretto, L. (2003), 'Italy', in Gallent, N., Shucksmith, M. & Tewdwr-Jones, M, (Eds), *Housing in the European Countryside: Rural Pressure and Policy in Western Europe*, London: Routledge, pp. 91–115.

Pahl, R. (1966), 'The social objectives of village planning', *Official Architecture and Planning*, 29, pp. 1146–1450.

Pahl, R. (1970), *Whose City? And Further Essays on Urban Society*, London: Longman.

Palatin, G. (1969), 'Le dévelopment des résidences citadines dans la région Grenobloise', *Revue de Géographie Alpine*, 57, pp. 747–757.

Pardoe, A.R. (1973), Personal communication about survey of second homes in the Aberystwyth Rural District to J.T. Coppock.

Pardoe, A.R. (1974), '*Social Implications of Second Home Development in Mid-Wales*', Paper presented to the IBG Conference, Norwich.

Pembrokeshire Coast National Park (2002), *Occupancy Study*, Haverford West: Pembrokeshire Coast National Park Authority.

Pembrokeshire County Council and Pembrokeshire Coast National Park Authority (2002) *Joint Unitary Development Plan Deposit (2000 – 2016)*, Haverford West: Pembrokeshire Coast National Park Authority.

Petersson, R. (1999), 'Foreign second home purchases – the case of Northern Sweden 1990–1996', Working Paper No. 14, Centre for Regional Science, Umeå University, Umeå.

Phillips, D. and Thomas, C. (2001) *The Effects of Tourism on the Welsh Language in North-West Wales*, Centre for Advanced Welsh and Celtic Studies: Aberystwyth.

Pilkington, E. (1990), 'Burning Issue', *Roof*, 15, 2, pp. 18–19.

Psychogios, T.E. (1980), *Second Homes in the Greater Area of Athens*, Unpublished MSc Thesis, Cardiff: University of Wales.

Pyne, C.B. (1973), *Second Homes*, Caernarvonshire County Planning Department.

Ragatz, R.L. (1970), 'Vacation homes in the North-Eastern United States: seasonality in population distribution', *Annals of the Association of American Geographers*, 60, pp. 447–455.

Ragatz, R.L. (1977), 'Vacation Homes in Rural Areas: Towards a Model for Predicting their Distribution and Occupancy Patterns', in Coppock, J.T., (ed.), *Second Homes: Curse or Blessing?* Oxford: Pergamon Press.

Reader's Digest (1970), *Survey of Europe Today*, Reader's Digest.

Robbins, L. (1930), 'The elasticity of demand for income in terms of effort', *Economica*, June 1930, pp. 123–129.

Robertson, R.W. (1977), 'Second Home Decisions: The Australian Context', in Coppock, J.T., (ed.), *Second Homes: Curse or Blessing?*, Oxford: Pergamon Press.

Rogers, A.W. (1971), 'Changing land-use patterns in the Dutch polders', *Journal of the Royal Town Planning Institute*, 57, 6, pp. 274–277.

Rogers, A.W. (1977), 'Second Homes in England and Wales: A Spatial View', in Coppock, J.T., (ed.), *Second Homes: Curse or Blessing?* Oxford: Pergamon Press.

Ross and Cromarty County Planning Department (1972), *Holiday Homes: Progress Report*, Dingwall.

Rural Development Commission (1995), *Section 106 Agreements and private finance for rural housing schemes*, Salisbury: RDC.

Salletmaier, C. (1993), 'The development and superimposition of tourism – Second homes and recreation within the rural fringe of an urban center', *Mitteilungen der Osterreichischen Geographischen Gesellschaft*, 135, pp. 215–242.

Saunders, P. (1984), 'Beyond housing classes: the sociological significance of private property rights in the means of consumption', *International Journal of Urban and Regional Research*, 8, pp. 202–227.

Saunders, P. (1986), *Social Theory and the Urban Question*, London: Hutchinson.

Savage, M. (1989), 'Spatial difference in modern Britain', in Hamnet, C., McDowell, L., & Sarre, P. (eds.), *Restructuring Britain: The Changing Social Structure*, London: SAGE.

Savage, M., Warde, A., & Ward, K. (2003) *Urban Sociology, Capitalism and Modernity* (second edition), Basingstoke: Palgrave.

Scottish Executive (1999), *Skye Bridge: Socio Economic Impact Evaluation*, Edinburgh: Scottish Executive (see also www.scotland.gov.uk/library2/doc16/sbse-01.asp).

Shucksmith, M. (1981), *No Homes for Locals?* Farnborough: Gower Publishing.

Shucksmith, M. (1983), 'Second homes: a framework for policy', *Town Planning Review*, 54, 2, pp.174–193.

Shucksmith, M. (1985), 'Public intervention in rural housing markets', *Planning Outlook*, 28, 2, pp.70–73.

Shucksmith, M. (1990a), *Housebuilding in Britain's Countryside*, USA & Canada: Routledge.

Shucksmith, M. (1990b), 'A theoretical perspective on rural housing: housing classes in rural Britain' *Sociologia Ruralis*, 30, 2, pp.210–229.

Shucksmith, M., Tewdwr-Jones, M. and Gallent, N. (2000), *International Experience of Pressured Rural Areas*; Report Commissioned by Scottish Homes, University of Aberdeen: Department of Land Economy.

Simms, A., Oram, J., MacGillivray, A., and Drury, J. (2002), *Ghost Town Britain: The Threat from Economic Globalisation to Livelihoods, Liberty and Local Economic Freedom*, London: New Economics Foundation.

Soley, C. (1990), 'Seconds out', *Roof*, 15, 2, pp.38–39.

South West Economic Planning Council (1975), *Survey of Second Homes in the South West*, London: HMSO.

Statens Offentliga Utredningar (1964), *Friluftsliver i Sverige*, Part I: Utgångsläde och utvecklingtstendenser.

Stewart, J., (2002), *Building a Crisis – Housing under-supply in England*, http://www.audacity.org/Building%20a%20crisis%2004.htm (accessed 05 April 2004).

Stoker, G. (1999), *The New Management of British Local Governance*, Basingstoke: Macmillan.

Tewdwr-Jones, M. (1995), 'Development control and the legitimacy of planning decisions', *Town Planning Review*, 66, 2, pp.163–81.

Tewdwr-Jones, M. (1997), 'Land use planning in Wales: the conflict between state centrality and territorial nationalism', in Macdonald, R. & Thomas, H. (eds.), *Nationality and Planning in Scotland and Wales*, Cardiff: University of Wales Press.

Tewdwr-Jones, M. & Gallent, N. (2002), *The Socio-economic Impacts of Local Needs Housing in the National Park* (Report for Pembrokeshire Coast National Park Authority), London: Bartlett School of Planning.

Tewdwr-Jones, M., Gallent, N., Fisk, M. & Essex, S. (1998), 'Developing corporate working approaches for the provision of affordable housing in Wales', *Regional Studies*, 32, 1, pp.85–91.

Tewdwr-Jones, M., Gallent, N. & Mace, A. (2002) *Second and Holiday Homes and the Land Use Planning System Research Report*, Cardiff: Welsh Assembly Government.

The Guardian (1995), 'Housing: filling the empties', *The Guardian*, 26 July 1995.

The Independent (1995), 'For sale: country pad for city slicker', *The Independent*, 17 August 1995.

The Independent (2004), 'Focus: country strife – are second homes killing rural Britain?', *The Independent*, 11 April 2004.

The Observer (1994), 'Welsh shed few tears as English beat a retreat', *The Observer*, 14 April 1994.

Thompson, P. (1977), *An Investigation of Second Home Social Research Methodology*, Cardiff: University of Wales, Unpublished Diploma Thesis in Town Planning.

Thornhill, J. (2002), 'Capital gains tax and your second home', *This is Money*, 22nd April 2002.

Triandis, M.C. (1970), 'Attitudes and attitude change', Summers, G.F., (ed.), *Attitude Measurement*, New York: Rand McNally.

Tuck, C.J. (1973), *Second Homes*, Merioneth Structure Plan, Subject Report No. 17, Merioneth County Council.

Urban Task Force (1999) *Towards an Urban Renaissance*, London, Spon Press.

Valenzuala, M. (2000), 'Spain', in Shucksmith, M., Tewdwr-Jones, M. & Gallent, N. *International Experience of Pressured Rural Areas*; Report Commissioned by Scottish Homes, University of Aberdeen: Department of Land Economy.

Valenzuala, M. (2003), 'Spain', in Gallent, N., Shucksmith, M. & Tewdwr-Jones, M, (Eds), *Housing in the European Countryside: Rural Pressure and Policy in Western Europe*, London: Routledge, pp.116–128.

Wall, G. (1997), 'Is ecotourism sustainable?' *Environmental Management*, 21, 4, pp.483–491.

Weatherley, R.D. (1982), 'Domestic tourism and second homes as motors of rural development in the Sierra Morena, Spain', *Iberian Studies*, 11, pp.40–46.

Welsh Assembly Government (2002), *Objections to the Joint Pembrokeshire Unitary Development Plan (to 2016)*, Cardiff: Welsh Assembly Government.

Welsh Office (1982), *Response to the Memorandum submitted by Gwynedd County Council making proposals for action designed to limit the growth of second homes*, Cardiff, February 1982. The debate referred to was held on 11 December 1981.

Welsh Office (1986), *Circular 30/86: Housing for Senior Management*, Cardiff: Welsh Office.

Welsh Office (1988), *Circular 53/88: The Welsh Language: Development Plans and Planning Control*, Cardiff: Welsh Office.

Welsh Office (1991), *Circular 31/91: Planning and Affordable Housing* in Wales, Cardiff: Welsh Office.

Welsh Office (1992), *Planning Policy Guidance Note 3 (Wales): Housing*, Cardiff: Welsh Office.

Welsh Office (1993), *Welsh Housing Statistics No. 13*, Cardiff: Welsh Office.

Welsh Office (1996a), *A Working Countryside for Wales: Rural White Paper*, Cardiff: Welsh Office.

Welsh Office (1996b), *Planning Policy Guidance Wales*, Cardiff: Welsh Office.

Welsh Republican Comment (2003), *No Room for Welsh at the Cymru Hilton: Wales – Home of the Wealthy*, http://groups.msn.com/welshrepublicancomment/poemgwennalt.msnw (accessed 05 April 2004).

Whitehead, C. (2002), The provision of affordable housing through the planning system, Paper presented at *ERES Conference*, Glasgow, June 2002.

Whitehead, C. & Kleinman, M. (1991), *A review of housing needs assessment*, London: Housing Corporation.

Wilcox, S. (1990), *The need for social rented housing in England in the 1990s*, Coventry: Chartered Institute of Housing.

Williams, H. (1974), *Second Homes*, Cardiff: University of Wales, Unpublished Diploma Thesis.

Williams R. (1973), *The Country and The City*, London: Hogarth Press.

Williams, N.J. & Twine, F.E. (1994), 'Locals, incomers and second homes – the role of resold public sector dwellings in rural Scotland', *Scandinavian Housing and Planning Research*, 11, 4, pp.193–209.

Wilson, A.G. (1974), *Urban and Regional Models in Geography and Planning*, London: Wiley & Sons.

Wolfe, R.I. (1977), 'Summer Cottages in Ontario: Purpose-built for an Inessential Purpose' in Coppock, J.T., (ed.), *Second Homes: Curse or Blessing?* Oxford: Pergamon Press.

Index

Note: Bold page numbers refer to tables/figures; numbers in brackets preceded by *n* indicate note numbers.